ALSO BY ROB NETO

Beyond the Grate

Into the Darkness Beyond

Beyond Hope

Beyond the End of the Line

Other Adventure series

Beneath the Jungle of Cozumel: Connecting the Crowns

Non-fiction

Recreational Sidemount Diving The Not So *Comprehensive Guide*

Sidemount Diving The Almost *Comprehensive Guide 3rd edition*
Available in English, Dutch, German, and Spanish

THE HIDDEN RIVERS OF FLORIDA

DISCOVERIES

ROB NETO

Published by Chipola Publishing, LLC,
Greenwood, Florida 32443, U.S.A.
www.chipolapublishing.com

Cover photography by Laurent Miroult; Artwork & design by Rob Neto

Author photography by Jen Neto

Printed in the United States of America

PUBLISHER'S NOTE

This book is a memoir. The accounts in it reflect the author's recollection of experiences over time. Be aware that the author's recollection is not always the best. All persons within this work are actual individuals. There are no composite characters. Some names have been abbreviated to protect the privacy of those individuals. Some events have been compressed, and some dialogue has been recreated.

ISBN: 978-1-961612-18-1

DEDICATION

This book is dedicated to the preservation of the springs that continue to allow us access to the hidden rivers of Florida.

TABLE OF CONTENTS

ROB NETO

ACKNOWLEDGMENTS

I'd like to thank all of my readers, especially those who have taken the time out of their busy lives to leave reviews for my books. While I really appreciate the good reviews, I also appreciate the constructive criticism. I take the bad with the good. Although, I haven't seen all that much bad, thankfully. I do read every review and use the comments to improve my writing.

A huge amount of gratitude goes to Patrick Taylor for inspiring me to put my adventures to paper (or eBook). I first came across Pat in 2024 on Facebook and we became fast friends. We keep in touch virtually, supporting each other and bouncing ideas back and forth. Neither of us view the other as competition even though we write in the same genre. That's because we know that many of our readers are the same and they aren't going to not read one of our books just because they've read the other. They will typically read both. So, once you're done reading this book, take a moment to visit the Recommended Reads page on my website and check out Pat's books. Click on Taylor and it will bring you to the listings. You won't be sorry.

Finally, I would like to thank my wife for her support throughout the writing of all of my books. She has been there for me every step of the way. She's a sounding board for ideas. She offers suggestions to improve my stories and my writing. She also endures my constant talk about my stories and adventures. Jen has become an integral part of the process of my writing. My books wouldn't be what they are without her input. That's not to say that any errors you may find can be attributed to her. I do the final edit for each of my books and anything that's been missed is completely my responsibility. Jen does more than her share of catching errors and typos as well as giving me ideas to include in my books. I am eternally grateful.

FOREWORD

The idea for *The Hidden Rivers of Florida* series came to me while I was writing *Connecting the Crowns*, the first book in my *Beneath the Jungle of Cozumel* series. I started with that series because I've devoted so much time and effort toward the exploration of the caves of Cozumel and it seemed like the perfect place to begin my journey into writing adventure books. As I was writing *Connecting the Crowns*, I reflected back on my exploration projects in Florida and decided a series about them was also worthy of my time. After all, Florida is where it all began.

This first book isn't so much about exploring previously unexplored cave passages as it is about my journey becoming a cave diver and learning the skills necessary to safely go into these hidden rivers. It's about exploring places that I had never been to before. If you're a cave diver, you aren't the intended reader for this book, although the stories told here may cause you to reflect on your own journeys into the hidden rivers of Florida. If you're a recreational open water diver, you aren't the intended reader, either. However, the stories may inspire you to pursue training as overhead divers, at least at the cavern diver level. The intended readers of this book are those who are interested in adventures of any kind, and those who would like to experience the wonders of the hidden rivers of Florida without having to actually enter them. This book is also intended to provide readers with a glimpse into the amount of training required to dive underwater caves safely. Whether you seek your own adventures or simply live vicariously through others', this book should resonate with you.

This first book includes tales of my early ventures into the underwater caves, or rather, the Hidden Rivers of Florida. It's more than that, though. It's about how someone who was born and raised in New Jersey and lived in Arizona became interested in cave diving. It's about the things that motivated me to drive across the country from Arizona to Florida to learn how to dive inside of the springs. It's about the good times and the bad times that my wife, Jen, and I had on this journey. It's about my love for the caves and how it pushed me to become the best cave diver I could be, and eventually the best cave explorer I could be. I hope you enjoy my story.

* * *

And now for the legal mumbo jumbo...

In no way is this book or any of the stories included intended to disparage the reputation of any living or dead person. The account is written as I remembered the events and the events are written from my own perspective. My interpretations of the things I observed involving other parties might not be correct. They are simply my opinions and not meant to be presented as factual information.

Finally, while I do explain some of the techniques and skills we incorporate when we cave dive, this is in no way meant to substitute for actual instruction and training in cave diving. If you are interested in learning how to cave dive, please find a qualified cave diving instructor and learn how to do it properly. Your life will depend on it.

It is not the mountain we conquer, but ourselves.

– Sir Edmund Hillary, 7/20/1919 – 1/11/2008

1

New beginnings

It was the final dive of our cavern diving course. My wife, Jen, and I were hovering just inches above the gravel covered limestone floor holding onto the protrusions jutting up to provide us with makeshift handholds. Normally, we wouldn't touch the cave. It was frowned upon. But this was the Devil's Spring Cave System located on the Santa Fe River in High Springs, Florida. Many divers equate the force of the current coming out of that cave to a firehose. The current would have blown us back into the Ear and up to the surface at an unsafe ascent rate if we weren't holding on. We could easily get the bends, or worse, pop a lung, if we weren't careful. So we held on for dear life.

The Ear is what the main opening of Devil's Spring is called. It was given that name because when looked at from a bird's eye view directly overhead along with the other opening, appropriately named the Eye, the two voids resembled the hollowed features of an ear and an eye. The opening named the Eye, which is located in the spring run, is oval, and the Ear, located at the confluence of the spring run with the river, is an oblong slit. Both lead to the same main tunnel of the cave, known as the Gallery. Both appear menacing when first seen. The Ear can be especially evil looking when the reddish-brown tannins in the river bleed over to mix with the clear water rushing out, giving it a blood-like appearance.

Our instructor brought us into Devil's Spring cave through the Ear for the fourth dive of our cavern diving class to give us one final test.

He also wanted to provide us with a glimpse into a different cave. He wanted us to look into the darkness beyond so we could decide whether we wanted to continue with our cave diving training. It wasn't so much to provide us with enough information to make an informed decision as it was dangling a carrot in front of us, tempting us so we would schedule the next level of training before returning to our home in Arizona. It worked.

The test was to look into two passages from just inside of the Ear and choose the one we thought would lead us out of the cave to the Eye. This was not something we would ever do. The rule was to always exit the way we entered because that was the confirmed route. That was part of the lesson. Our instructor hoped one of us would choose incorrectly. That would reinforce the rule. It was no easy task. We entered the Ear with the Eye to our right and went straight in, so it remained to the right. The options we were presented with were a tunnel straight ahead and one to our left. Jen chose the tunnel straight ahead. I chose the other one.

Seconds after we had arrived and gotten ourselves situated, I saw lights piercing through the darkness toward us. The lights were much brighter than the ones Jen and I had bought for our cavern diving class. Our lights were small, hand-held dive lights that barely illuminated the floor in front of us. They cost less than fifty dollars each. We didn't know any better at the time. I had read about the more powerful dive lights, but with that power also came a hefty price tag. We were just taking the cavern diving class to improve our scuba diving skills. We had no intention of venturing beyond the daylight zone of the cavern and into the cave.

I looked at the bright lights in awe as they moved toward us. It wasn't the current that was moving the divers behind those lights. It was the large dive propulsion vehicles (DPVs) that were pulling them along at a much faster pace than they could swim. The DPVs were significantly larger than the Seadoo scooters Jen and I had back home in Arizona. They looked like something you would expect to only see Navy SEALS using - big black tubes at least three feet long and about eight or nine inches in diameter.

When the divers piloting the DPVs were directly above us, I finally got a better look at them. Their lights were no longer blinding us with their incredible brightness. The divers were carrying multiple scuba tanks. Each diver not only had two tanks connected with a manifold on his back, but they also had two additional tanks hanging from their sides. I later learned these were called stage tanks because they are often left staged in the cave along their route rather than carried by the divers throughout the entire dive.

I saw these divers with four scuba tanks each and large DPVs that were moving them close to one hundred and fifty feet per minute through the cave, following behind the illumination of bright high intensity discharge (HID) lights that not only penetrated the darkness, but practically eliminated it. I saw these divers and the only thought that went through my mind was *I WANT TO GO WHERE THOSE DIVERS JUST CAME FROM!* It was at that moment that I was hooked. It was then that I knew I had to become a cave diver so I could explore the dark recesses of the Hidden Rivers of Florida.

It was probably also at that moment that I became obsessed with lighting up the darkness. I didn't make that realization until I wrote this book. As I sit here typing, I think of the lights I have all around our property. I can move almost anywhere around the house and barn and motion sensor lights will pop on so I'm never in the dark. I'm not afraid of the dark. Quite the contrary. As you know if you've read my other adventure book, *Beneath the Jungle of Cozumel: Connecting the Crowns*, the dark is very relaxing for me. Hovering in a cave with no lights on brings me peace, but it's the beauty of the caves that keeps me going back.

* * *

Before I continue, let's step back to before Jen and I decided to take a cave diving class. I need to tell you what made me decide to become a scuba diver despite being terrified of the ocean as a child. That's no exaggeration. The ocean gave me nightmares.

When I was young - very young - I was given a Portuguese swimming lesson. Some other cultures may claim this to be their own, but I'm sticking with what I call it. I was at the beach with my parents. We spent several days every summer down the shore (as we say in New Jersey) and usually rented a house for a week. During those visits, I spent much of the day playing in the wet sand, building sandcastles, and creating moats around them that would fill as the surf came in and empty as it went out. I loved playing in the shallow water.

One day, my father walked up behind me, grabbed me in his arms, and carried me into the ocean. The big, dark, terrifying ocean. The ocean with rough waves that threatened to drown me. I didn't like being in water where I couldn't reach the bottom while keeping my head above the surface. Keeping my waist above the surface was even better. I had only ever played in the very shallow area of the surf.

As my father carried me away from the safety of the sandy beach, I cried and screamed to be brought back to dry land. My father ignored my pleas and continued walking deeper and deeper until the water was up to his chest. This meant it would be above my head if he let go of me. I was four or five years old at the time and barely came up to his waist. Before I knew it, my father let go of me and stepped far enough away that I couldn't reach him. It was time for me to sink or swim.

I don't remember how I got out of the water and back to the safety of my mother's arms. My mind has chosen to hide that memory in some tiny dark recess. I know it wasn't my mother that saved me. At least not physically. She was just as scared of the water as I had become after that incident. She wouldn't venture any farther than knee deep. Even that was sometimes too far for her. I suppose she must have had a Portuguese swimming lesson at an early age as well.

Somehow, I made it back to shore alive. My father probably grabbed me and carried me back in response to my mother's screams. I'm sure he was disappointed in me. I didn't care. After that day, I remained on high alert when playing near the water, especially when my father was around. Fortunately, his presence became less frequent.

I still enjoyed the water after that incident, but I preferred the clear blue water in swimming pools. I could see what was in a pool. I could stay in the shallow end, and if I wanted to venture into the deeper end, I could hold onto the sides. The ocean didn't have any of these attributes. At least the ocean off of the Jersey shore didn't. After that day, whenever we went down the shore, I preferred to play in the swimming pool rather than the beach. The ocean was too scary.

The fear diminished as I grew older. Because I enjoyed swimming pools, I eventually learned how to swim. I wasn't a good swimmer. I certainly wasn't going to win any Olympic medals, but I could stay afloat. The ocean wasn't so scary knowing I had the ability to remain on the surface. One of my favorite activities became riding the waves on a boogie board. That was only after my father was out of the picture, though. I never trusted him after that day.

When I was in the Army and stationed in southern Arizona, I visited Patagonia Lake, not far from the base. Several of the guys in my platoon decided to head to the lake for a day of swimming and drinking beer. Like most Arizona lakes, Patagonia is a dark, murky brown body of water. It was so muddy that we couldn't see the bottom when standing in three-foot-deep water. We relaxed in the roped off swimming area for a while. Then my barracks roommate challenged me to a race across the lake to the bank opposite the swimming area. We were in a narrow section of the lake, so it wasn't very far. It was probably four hundred feet across. Being a young, macho Army soldier, I wasn't about to refuse the challenge.

My roommate was a much stronger swimmer and beat me across. I made it to the opposite shore, but it took me a while and there were a few moments when I wasn't sure I would make it. I had to rest and catch my breath while treading water. I finally made it and looked back to where we had begun the stupid race. There was only one way to get back. We had to swim. Walking around the lake wasn't an option. It would have been a very long walk, and there was no trail. My shoes were back on the other side. So, we swam. I chastised myself for giving in to peer pressure. I should never have accepted the challenge.

Fast forward a few years to the late 1990s. I had a patient who was a scuba diving instructor. He was a disabled veteran and lived part of the year in Mexico on the coast of the Sea of Cortez where he had a boat docked. We talked about scuba diving, and he made it sound very intriguing. I knew what scuba diving was, but I had never considered learning to do it. I left New Jersey when I was nineteen and Arizona wasn't exactly the mecca of scuba diving.

This guy invited me to visit him in Mexico and learn how to scuba dive. I was ready to give it a try. I went home that day and suggested it to my fiancée. She shot the idea down. She claimed she was too claustrophobic to scuba dive. I didn't understand, but I knew there was no arguing with her. We didn't last as a couple much longer. There were other issues, not just her refusal to learn how to scuba dive.

I was still intrigued about scuba diving, but there was no dive shop in the small southern Arizona town where I lived. I knew I could drive south to Mexico, but I wasn't sure where I would even look to get certified. I had lost touch with the scuba diving instructor that had gotten me interested in it in the first place. This was also before the internet was the vast resource that it is now. I couldn't pull up google and search dive shops in San Carlos, Mexico. That wasn't a thing in the nineties.

I dated a woman for about a year after my fiancée and I broke things off. The idea of scuba diving was still on my mind, and I mentioned it to her. There was a problem I hadn't thought about. She was allergic to latex rubber. Anaphylactic allergic. Airway closure with no breathing allergic. There is a lot of latex rubber in scuba diving. The wetsuits contain it. The masks contained it (there were very few silicone masks at that time). The hoses that we use to get air from the scuba tanks to the regulators are made of latex rubber. Scuba diving would kill her before she even entered the water. Once again, it was placed on the back burner. That relationship also ended.

Then I met Jen. It was the year 2003. Jen and I had just gotten married. We ran away to Las Vegas on a whim one evening after she returned from visiting her grandmother in Texas. Jen was gone for four days, but it seemed like four weeks. I picked her up from the airport and drove her to her apartment. It was then that I decided I didn't want to be apart from her if I could help it. I wanted to spend the rest of my life with her. We arrived at the apartment, and I asked her to marry me. It wasn't just a proposal to get married *someday*. I asked her if she wanted to go to Vegas to get married that night. She said yes.

Jen quickly swapped the clothes in her suitcase with clean ones. We left, stopped by my house about ten minutes away so I could throw some clothes into a bag, and headed to the Tucson International Airport, arriving five minutes before nine. We ran inside and got to the check-in desk with two minutes to spare. They were just about to close. We purchased two tickets on the last Vegas flight of the day. It was scheduled to depart thirty minutes later. Fortunately, Tucson airport was small and rarely busy. We were also the last passengers to go through security. We ran to the gate and boarded, finding a couple of seats together a few rows back. Fifteen minutes later, we took off and were on our way to Las Vegas.

Shortly after takeoff, I got nervous. I looked at Jen sitting next to me and thought, *What the hell am I doing?* (This is a question that has become common for me since then, but not in regard to Jen.) Jen and I had been dating for only two weeks. We had worked with each other for more than a year but only knew each other casually. I was one of her supervisors in the emergency room (ER) where we both worked. We talked on occasion whenever the patient census in the ER dropped. That was the extent of our friendship. We hadn't seen each other outside of the hospital until our first date.

We had both been involved with other people during most of that year of friendship. The friendship was just that. There were no indiscretions. There was no underlying flirting. We had common interests and talked about them. Our friendship may have caused us to see that something was missing from the relationships we were in because we both ended those relationships at about the same time. A few weeks after the breakups, Jen and I went out with each other for the first time. Two weeks after that we flew to Vegas and got married.

Sitting there on that airplane, flying to Vegas, I questioned myself. What would possess me to do such a thing? Just weeks earlier I had resigned myself to being a bachelor for the rest of my life. I had purchased a house on five acres in the foothills of the Rincon Mountains in Tucson. I told myself I was done with relationships. The new place overlooking the city of Tucson would make a great bachelor pad. Yet, there I was, running away to Vegas to get married. It all came down to the fact that I was in love, and I wanted to spend the rest of my life with this woman.

The cold feet only lasted a few minutes. At one point, Jen turned to me and asked me if I was sure I wanted to do this. I looked into her eyes and immediately knew the answer. I told her yes, I was sure. Less than an hour after we took off, we landed in Las Vegas at what was then called the McCarren International Airport. We secured a rental car and drove toward the Vegas Strip to look for a hotel room. I drove while Jen called various hotels on the Strip searching for a room for the next two nights. None of them had vacancies.

We continued driving up and down the Strip, noting the names of the hotels. We started to think we might have gone through a space time continuum and landed in Asia. Ninety percent of the people we saw walking along the sidewalks and around the resorts were of Asian descent. One of the receptionists that Jen spoke with finally clued us in. It was the week of the electronics convention. All of the Asian high-tech companies had sent representatives to the city. There wasn't a single vacant room on the Strip.

We began searching off the Strip and finally managed to find a vacancy at an Extended Stay America hotel. Even back then, a room off the Strip during the electronics convention cost almost one hundred and fifty dollars a night. That was in addition to the four hundred dollars we had spent on airfare, and one hundred dollars for a rental car. It was still less than the cost for most weddings. We drove to the hotel to drop off our luggage. Then we were off to find a chapel where we could get married. It was one in the morning.

Keep in mind that this was 2003. Smartphones weren't popular at that time, and we certainly didn't have any. Our phones were capable of making calls and sending and receiving short text messages. Looking for hotels and twenty-four-hour chapels wasn't as easy as it is today. We couldn't pull up the information online and make reservations, at least not while driving around in a car. We had to rely on talking to receptionists and looking through the yellow pages.

Yellow pages were business listings provided in the second half of phone books, for those of you that may not be familiar with them. Oh, and phone books were things that landline phone companies printed and mailed to customers every year. The first half contained the white pages, or listings of residents and businesses in the coverage area. Fortunately, there was a phone book in the hotel room. We grabbed it on the way out of the door.

We also didn't have Google maps. We had to navigate with paper maps. While I drove, Jen assumed the role of navigator. Once we were on the Las Vegas Strip, it was easy, but getting there from the Extended Stay wasn't so easy. We managed and we didn't get lost. Sometimes I think back to those days and wonder how we got things done.

We decided to go to the Little White Wedding Chapel located on the north end of the Las Vegas Strip. It was one of the few chapels open twenty-four hours a day according to the yellow pages listing. It was brightly lit and easy to find. The marquis proudly displayed that Michael Jordan and Britney Spears were married there (although not to each other). We parked in front of the chapel and walked inside to inquire about the process. The Little White Wedding Chapel had a variety of packages we could choose from. They offered a simple ceremony, an Elvis package (not the real one, although that would have been interesting), or a drive-thru ceremony, to name a few. We asked about wedding rings. They had rings, but they weren't precious metals. They were fake alloys that would turn green within minutes of being put on our fingers. We decided to hold off on those.

They asked us if we had gotten our marriage license. Our hearts sank. We hadn't thought about that. Not only was it two in the morning, but it was Friday night, or rather early Saturday morning. Had we traveled to Vegas to get married only to be turned away empty handed? We were flying back Sunday morning. This is what happens when you don't have the internet to research things.

Surprisingly, not only could we get a marriage license on a weekend, but we could get one at night. At the time, the marriage license bureau of the Las Vegas courthouse was open twenty-four hours a day, seven days a week. The person at the chapel told us to drive north on the Strip for six blocks, turn left on Clark Avenue, then drive two blocks until we saw the courthouse on the right. We ran to the car and sped away.

We found the courthouse brightly lit with several cars parked in front. We weren't the only ones with this idea. We parked and ran inside. We were the fourth couple in line. More couples arrived after us. We heard the couple in front of us talking. They were getting married to each other for the second time. I doubted that one would last. But who was I to judge? I was getting married to someone I had been dating for only two weeks.

We filled out the marriage license application as we waited. About twenty minutes later, we stepped up to the window and handed the woman the form along with the fee. The clerk entered the information into the computer and printed the license. That was it! The only question we were asked was if we had been in previous marriages and if those were dissolved. The woman never asked for identification. She didn't ask for proof of dissolution. She didn't ask anything else. Apparently, no official paperwork was required. We could have been there to play a practical joke on a couple of our friends. Even funnier would have been to marry a couple of friends who couldn't stand each other. Funny to us, anyway.

We left the courthouse and tried to find a place to buy wedding rings. Nothing was open but touristy souvenir shops and pawn shops. We tried one of the pawn shops on the Strip that claimed it was open twenty-four hours a day. It was locked with a sign on the door directing us to ring the bell for service. We rang it, someone appeared at the door, and we asked about wedding rings. He told us they only made purchases in the middle of the night. We would have to return at nine if we wanted to buy something. We thanked him and walked away laughing. They were taking advantage of desperate gamblers. We weren't overly disappointed. We preferred new rings, anyway. We would find something later that day.

We drove back to the Little White Wedding Chapel and opted for the drive-thru package. We pulled in behind another rental car and waited as they went through their ceremony. We started naming people we could get marriage licenses for and get them married as a joke. It was crazy that identification wasn't required. I'm sure someone has already played that practical joke. I hear identification is now required.

The drive-thru was covered for most of its length in what the chapel called the Tunnel of Love. Cars entered the property and followed the drive about one hundred feet before turning right into the tunnel which extended back to the road. Painted on the ceiling of the tunnel were several cherubs lying on clouds. The words *I love you! I need you! I can't live without you!* were painted among the cherubs from one end of the Tunnel of Love to the other.

A little history on this wedding chapel might be appropriate, although this wasn't why we chose this particular location to get married. The drive-thru wedding at the Little White Wedding Chapel was the original drive-thru wedding in Las Vegas. The concept was created in 1996 after the owner saw a disabled couple having trouble walking into the chapel. The idea stuck and both disabled and non-disabled people have used it ever since. We chose the chapel simply because it looked like the ideal spot for us.

11

About ten minutes after we arrived at the Tunnel of Love, we eased up to the window and were greeted by a kid. To be fair, he was probably a legal adult, but he looked like he could have been in high school. However old he was, he was the officiant. He was the one that was going to perform our ceremony and make it legal. We handed him our newly acquired marriage license, paid the fee, and the ceremony began.

Jen and I tried to contain our laughter as the kid went through his script telling us the secret to a long happy marriage together. We were in our early thirties and both of us had been in practice marriages. I wasn't sure if the kid had lost his virginity yet. He finally got to the end of his spiel and pronounced us husband and wife. We kissed, were given our official paperwork and told the marriage certificate would be mailed to us within six weeks. We were a married couple.

Jen and I drove back toward the Strip. Along the way, we saw a Denny's near the Stratosphere and stopped for our *reception*. We recognized the car that had been in front of us in the Tunnel of Love already parked in the Denny's parking lot.

Jen and I were starving. Neither of us had eaten since long before we took off for Vegas from Tucson. We ordered our entrees and devoured the food. The waitress offered us a free dessert to celebrate our new union. I guess it was obvious. We shared a slice of chocolate lava cake. I almost licked the plate clean. With our reception complete, we headed back to the hotel, and I carried Jen across the threshold.

The next morning we woke up and drove to the Strip to find coffee and breakfast. Afterwards, we looked for a jewelry shop and found one in Caesar's Palace. We picked out a set of plain gold rings with rounded edges and paid for them. From there, we went to the Venetian, paid for a private gondola ride, and exchanged rings in *Venice* as we were being serenaded by a gondola driver. About an hour later, I called my family to give them the news. My mother called us *fucking idiots*. I don't think she knew I was dating anyone at the time. I don't blame her for her reaction, but more than twenty-two years later, we're happier than ever.

What does all of this have to do with cave diving?

2

Happy life with a happy wife

If it hadn't been for Jen, I wouldn't have become a cave diver. I don't know if I would have become a scuba diver. I could have gone by myself to get trained, but before I moved to Tucson, I lived in Arizona in a town that didn't have a dive shop. It wasn't something that would have been easily done. I also wasn't one to go on a vacation by myself. If I was in a relationship, I vacationed with the person I was dating. Scheduling several days for a dive course wasn't likely to happen.

It wasn't long after we got married that I discovered Jen was interested in learning how to scuba dive. The subject came up over a National Geographic issue, which we still have. Jen found this issue with a photograph on the cover by the well-known underwater cave diving photographer, Wes Skiles, who the Florida state park in Luraville has since been named after. Wes took this photograph of himself inside Diepolder II, a cave system near Tampa. There are four divers in the image. Wes is all four divers. He took a long exposure and moved around the room to illuminate it and create this image.

Jen showed me the photograph and mentioned that she would like to dive there someday. I looked at it and told her I doubted we could ever do something like that. I didn't know it was the same diver in four different positions at the time and told her those were scientific divers. They had a lot of training. It would be a big commitment and a lot of expense to get to that level of diving. I wasn't wrong. There was a big commitment and a lot of time and money invested. It wasn't an impossible goal, though. Unfortunately, we never got to dive in Diepolder II before access to dive it was no longer permitted.

A few weeks after seeing the photograph, Jen and I signed up for an open water scuba diving class. I had purchased an Entertainment coupon book for the Tucson area that year. Entertainment coupon books were the Groupon of the print world. They cost about twenty dollars and were filled with hundreds of coupons for local businesses. I found a coupon offered by one of the local dive shops for a buy one get one free ninety-nine-dollar class. There were two dive shops in Tucson (three if you counted the one that seemed more of a hobby than a business), and we visited all of them. The one with the coupon was the better fit for us.

Of course, the class didn't cost only ninety-nine dollars. There were additional charges. We had to purchase a student manual, masks, snorkels, fins, and dive boots. That ended up adding about five hundred and sixty dollars. Then there was the additional five hundred dollars for the open water check-out dives in Mexico. It would have been more if we had to rent scuba equipment for those dives. We had fallen in love with scuba diving during class and purchased our own gear before we did our check-out dives. I won't mention how much that set us back!

Scuba diving quickly became a passion, and one I could share with the love of my life. Life couldn't get any better. Then, something terrible happened. Jen wasn't able to pass one of the required skills. She wasn't able to remove her mask underwater without bolting for the surface.

Jen had issues with the water going up her nose when she removed her mask, and it caused her to get anxious. No matter how hard she tried, she couldn't stay underwater once that mask came off of her face. She tried pinching her nose as soon as the mask came off, but then she couldn't let go to put the mask back on. Things were looking grim. We left the dive shop with our shoulders slumped.

Back home, I told Jen it was fine. We didn't have to finish the class. We could try to return all of the dive equipment we had just purchased, or we could sell it to someone else. We should be able to get most of our money back. I was ready and willing to do that, but secretly, I was hoping it would piss Jen off enough that she would dig down deep inside of herself and figure out how to get through the skill.

Jen figured things out. Part of it was that she did not want to return the dive equipment. My attempt at reverse psychology worked. I was a little surprised but very happy. Jen practiced the skill repeatedly until she was able to do it. She figured out that she could slowly exhale through her nose and keep the water out while she had the mask off. She took quick breaths as needed. She passed the confined water portion of the class.

Two months later, we headed to Mexico to do our first open water dives in the Sea of Cortez with our brand-new scuba diving equipment. We set up our tent on the beach and passed out after the long drive. We were up early Saturday morning ready to do our first dives. We couldn't wait to experience the amazing underwater world of the Sea of Cortez, the place Jacques Cousteau called the *aquarium of the world*.

Later that afternoon, after we had completed three dives, we sat on the beach watching the other divers head into the water. Our instructor told us about the different specialties we could do and pushed us to work toward getting our Master Scuba Diver certifications. It required five specialties and fifty dives. At the time, I thought we would do well to complete ten dives a year. If we were lucky, we might do fifteen or twenty. Fifty dives seemed like a very long-term goal.

Six months later, we completed our fiftieth dive in an Arizona lake. Soon after getting our certifications, we discovered the lakes and began traveling around the state to explore as many as we could. Not all of them were worth it. We looked anyway. We also planned and did dives when visiting family, including several dives in Dutch Springs, Pennsylvania, only an hour from where I grew up. We were hooked.

A couple of months later, we signed up for a divemaster class and spent a month learning how to supervise and lead scuba divers underwater. The class involved more underwater mask removal. Jen had no issues this time. She had not only overcome her difficulty with removing her mask underwater, she had mastered the skill.

Less than a year after getting our certifications, we visited Florida to go wreck diving and snorkel with the manatees. The weather caused less than optimal diving conditions along the eastern coast of Florida, so we headed inland, choosing to go to the Florida springs as a consolation. We did our first cavern dive in Blue Spring, Orange City.

We fought the current to get as deep as we could. At sixty feet of depth, I felt dizzy. I thought it was the current that was throwing off my equilibrium. I later realized it was nitrogen narcosis, or the Martini Effect. The combination of the depth and the current caused me to feel out of sorts. I didn't know that was what was happening and kept going deeper. I wanted to see as much of the cavern as possible. On the way up, I squeezed myself into the small nooks along the wall. Only the scuba tank on my back kept me from going farther into them.

Our one hundredth dive happened in Blue Spring with a gentleman we met in the parking lot. Solo diving isn't allowed in Florida state parks, so Chuck approached us and asked if he could sign into the park to dive with us. We had met a lot of great folks while scuba diving over the previous year and had no problem helping him out.

We pulled into the park and found a parking space. I checked out the gear and van that belonged to Chuck. He was what we call a vintage diver. Picture Mike Nelson of Sea Hunt. He had a double hose regulator and a J-valve on his scuba tank. He also had a small compressor in the back of his van that he used to fill his tank between dives. I watched as he stuffed a dive light down the front of his wetsuit right before we headed toward the spring. Dive lights weren't allowed in the spring unless you were certified as a cavern diver. Apparently, Chuck wasn't.

A few weeks later, while on one of the internet forums, I discovered that Chuck was well known in the scuba world and particularly in Florida. It was rumored that he would douse his scuba compressor filter with whisky for a little added taste in his breathing air. I don't know if that was true, but it made for a good story. I was glad that we had enough scuba tanks with us, and I was able to decline his offer to fill our tanks with that compressor!

From Blue Spring State Park, we headed to Rainbow River, in Dunedin, Florida and did three short dives. It was an amazing experience. Not only was Rainbow River not overgrown with weeds as it is now, but we were able to see our first Florida Gar, as well as dive another cavern. It was a very small cavern in which only two of us could fit. We weren't going to do any laps, but we had a great time.

We headed to Crystal River the next day to have our first manatee experience. It was absolutely fantastic. The manatees came to us seeking back and belly rubs. We had a mom and baby approach us and roll over, exposing their bellies. They followed us for a while as we snorkeled around the spring. These gentle giants were adorable and amazing. If that was all we got to do during that trip, we would have been happy. Manatees are absolutely remarkable creatures.

After snorkeling with the manatees, the dive operator took us to King's Cavern, located in the middle of Crystal River. This was the only location in Crystal River where diving was allowed. It was a guided tour, but there were enough of us that I was able to get away on my own for a short while and explore the cavern. This probably wasn't the best idea. I squeezed myself into every crack I could find. I discovered areas where I couldn't see daylight streaming in from the opening. I continued into them anyway. One of the rules of cavern diving is that daylight must always be visible. I wasn't trained yet, so I didn't know. I'm not sure it would have stopped me from doing what I did.

This first trip to Florida ended with us completing our first four cavern dives. It also convinced me to seek out a cavern diving instructor. I had no desire to become a cave diver. I didn't think I could travel to Florida enough to justify it. The cavern diving class would help us improve our scuba diving skills. I was more interested in diving shipwrecks, and I knew the skills learned during a cavern diving class were invaluable. When we returned to Arizona, I researched our options and found an instructor. We scheduled our cavern diving class for seven months later.

3

Fight or flight

The months dragged by. I kept a mental countdown of the days as our next trip to Florida approached. I was anxious to return so Jen and I could learn how to safely dive the caverns. There would be no more haphazard penetrations hoping we would survive. Or rather, too ignorant to even recognize the risks we were taking. My focus was still on diving shipwrecks. I hoped the skills we learned could be applied to the metal caves found at the bottom of the sea.

We completed a wreck diver class at Dutch Spring in Pennsylvania during a previous family visit. A small boat that was intentionally sunk as an attraction was used for the wreck. We didn't go to any offshore sites. The class focused on maintaining horizontal trim in the water, doing frog kicks (a finning technique that minimizes silt disturbance), and simple penetration inside of a small boat that had been stripped of most hazards. It was a good primer, but it only scratched the surface.

The day came for us to begin our drive across the country. I was beyond excited. I couldn't wait to dive in Florida and learn new skills. Three days later, we arrived and settled in. The next day, we met our instructor at Ginnie Springs. It was a hot day, and I was ready to get into the water to cool off. That would have to wait. We spent the morning in a classroom at Ginnie Springs Outdoors. The air conditioner was old and loud and barely cooled the room. It clattered in the background, struggling to fight the heat of late spring. We spent three hours learning everything there was to know about safely diving caverns. I pushed through the distraction of the hot and humid air and focused on the curriculum. I was eager to absorb as much knowledge as I could.

We broke for lunch. I was ready to finally get in the water. Unfortunately, it wasn't time for that. Instead, we spent the afternoon looking over our scuba equipment and doing drills along cave line that our instructor strung up waist high among the trees next to the Ginnie Springs basin. I kept glancing at the cool seventy-two-degree water wanting to dive into it as sweat poured off of me. I forced myself to focus on the lesson.

When cave divers first discover underwater caves, they reel out a thin, braided nylon line in the passages. The line extends from just outside of the opening into the depths of the cave. It remains there until it breaks or deteriorates from years of exposure to harsh conditions. When that occurs, it's replaced. The line is a lifeline for cave divers. It provides us with a safe exit from the cave. It serves as a *breadcrumb* trail when the visibility is clear, but more importantly, it serves to guide us out when the visibility becomes diminished or completely eliminated. During the cavern diving class, we were taught how to follow the line with no visibility and to trust it to get us back to the surface. We were taught how to survive.

The first part of the lesson was completed on dry land. Standing there next to the spring basin, we formed circles around the line with our thumbs and forefingers. We closed our eyes and followed the line, allowing it to pass through the circle, the feel of it keeping us on course. When the line was wrapped around a tree and changed directions, we navigated past it using a procedure we were taught that ensured we remained on the same line and didn't unexpectedly end up on a different line that didn't lead out to the surface. This exercise didn't substitute for the drills we would be doing underwater. It gave us the opportunity to practice the skills and ask any questions we might have while we could still communicate with words rather than hand signals.

As we were doing our line drills, I repeatedly glanced at the time,

19

hoping to finish class early enough to dive that afternoon. I wasn't bored or distracted. I just wanted to get in the water. I had been thinking about it all day. The temperature was rising as the day progressed. The heat of the sun on our backs was almost unbearable as we walked along the line. The glistening water in the basin less than fifty feet away teased us. Every now and then, a snorkeler would enter the water, causing ripples to travel across the basin. The sun would reflect off of the ripples onto our faces, into our eyes, reminding us that it was there. Teasing us as we suffered the hot Florida sun.

We finally finished our drills shortly after four. The first dive of the class wouldn't happen until the next day. I was disappointed. We spent the previous three days driving across the country and that entire day in class. I was anxious to get wet. We probably should have gone back to our rental house to rest. Instead, after our instructor left, we unloaded our equipment from the truck so we could do one dive before returning to the house to collapse.

We had our drysuits with us, diving suits that were designed to keep us warmer by preventing the cold water from coming into contact with our bodies. In a drysuit, the only parts exposed are the head and the hands. The rest of the body remains dry. Hopefully. Most dry suits are better described as damp suits. Warmth is added with the use of undergarments. Air is injected into the suits to relieve the squeeze of the pressure that builds as we descend. The air also acts as a layer of insulation to keep us warm.

The air temperature was eighty-five degrees Fahrenheit. In Arizona that would have been tolerable. We weren't in Arizona. We were in Florida where you step out of your vehicle and your sunglasses instantly fog. The humidity was almost unbearable. I had been sweating during the line drills. My shirt was sticking to my back. It looked like I had already been in the spring basin. I couldn't bear the thought of putting on my undergarments and drysuit. Instead, we put on our three-millimeter-thick wetsuits. They were a little chilly in the seventy-two-degree water, but the adrenaline from the excitement of what we were about to do helped us tolerate the cool temperature.

Jen and I spent thirty-five minutes in the Ginnie Springs cavern practicing our buoyancy skills and the line drills we had learned earlier that afternoon. My buoyancy and trim felt off and I was having doubts about whether I was ready for a cavern diving class. This wasn't a class in which we were simply paying for a certification card. We had to earn the card.

The last several dives we did in Arizona were great. We had no issues, and I felt ready to start the cavern class. That afternoon I was ready to cancel the next day of diving. I wasn't going to learn anything if I was struggling with my buoyancy and trim. I felt like a brand-new diver fresh out of my initial open water class. I couldn't figure out why things were so different.

Jen and I signaled each other to end the dive and ascended to the surface. We tried to figure out what was wrong and realized we had inadvertently swapped diving equipment. I was wearing Jen's rig, and she was wearing mine. The rigs were almost identical. The only difference was the backplates. Jen's was heavier than mine. We should have returned to the house to rest instead of doing a dive. Clearly, we were not in the proper state of mind to be diving if we could make such a simple mistake. We still didn't call it a day. We swapped rigs and dropped below the surface a second time.

Things returned to normal. Our buoyancy and trim had improved from only moments earlier. I couldn't believe how much being in Jen's rig had thrown off my buoyancy and trim so easily. It was one of my early lessons that I would eventually incorporate into the sidemount diving classes I taught. Scuba equipment had to be tuned to the diver.

There was a lot planned for the next day. We began early and did two dives in the morning, broke for lunch, then two dives in the afternoon. These weren't short twenty-minute recreational dives. The first dive lasted more than an hour. The next three dives lasted forty-five minutes each. We did drill after drill. We deployed the line from our primary reel. We did the line drills we had learned the previous afternoon. We ventured into the cavern and did more drills. We shared air a lot. I was happy that Jen and I had done a dive the day before and had a chance to explore the cavern because there was no time for that during class. We weren't there to tour the cave. We were there to learn to survive.

The last dive of the class was the one described at the beginning of this book. That was the dive that changed my life. During that dive, shipwrecks dropped a few notches. They were no longer my primary interest. I wanted to dive them, but caves had my heart. Caves were where I wanted to be. They were where I had to be.

There was one issue. Jen didn't pass the class. She didn't receive her cavern diver certification. She was devastated. So was I. I had fallen in love with the caves. While I was fairly confident Jen would support me if I wanted to continue the training without her, I didn't feel right doing so. We began the adventure together. We were scuba divers because of that old National Geographic issue she came across. We were in it together. I wanted to pursue these adventures with Jen. I wanted to share the experiences with her.

Jen wasn't prepared to give up. The only thing keeping her from earning her cavern diver certification was the ability to remove her mask, breathe from her regulator for several seconds with it removed, and then replace it. We were both surprised by this. Jen had worked hard to overcome that issue a year earlier during our initial scuba class. We couldn't understand why she was having issues with it again.

It didn't take long to figure out the problem. When the cold water hit Jen's face, the temperature difference shocked her. The cold water stimulated her vagus nerve and initiated a fight or flight response. Jen was choosing flight. She had the immediate urge to bolt to the surface. There was no surface inside of the cavern. She couldn't bolt to the surface if her mask was knocked off of her face.

We stood in the shallows of the Ginnie Springs basin and practiced the skill. I suggested to Jen that she submerge her face in the cold water while we were standing there to see how it felt. She was able to do that.

It was something about the warmth of the air in the mask from exhaling through her nose and the sudden change in temperature when the cold water hit her face that was problematic.

After dunking her face in the water several times and practicing the skill, Jen was finally able to complete it. That wasn't enough for our instructor to feel confident about issuing her a cavern diver certification. He wanted to see her do it again the next time we were in Florida. That was fair. We understood his hesitancy. He needed to see that Jen could complete the skill repeatedly. It could be a matter of life and death.

We scheduled our next class confident that Jen would do fine. She overcame it during our initial scuba diving class. She would do it again. We would return to Florida seven months later to complete the introductory cave diving class. Jen would be ready. We were so confident that we also scheduled a decompression diving class to immediately follow the cave diving class.

We remained in Florida for another four days after we completed the cavern diving course. Even though Jen wasn't technically certified as a cavern diver, we did a mini tour of the caverns in the central part of the state. None of them required a certification. We went to Blue Grotto, Paradise Springs, Alexander Springs, and returned to Blue Spring, Orange City. We did nine cavern dives that week. Jen practiced removing her mask underwater during every dive. We wished we could have met with our instructor one more day, but we were confident she would earn her cavern diver card at the beginning of the next trip.

I thought back to the past year of diving. I recalled that moment on the beach in Mexico when I told Jen it would take us forever to do fifty dives. We hadn't been diving for a year yet and we had celebrated our one hundredth dive. We were that obsessed with scuba diving. It consumed our lives.

We were divemasters when we began our cavern diving class and already working on becoming scuba diving instructors. It was a quick transition, but we knew we loved it that much. We didn't want to just

23

experience it. We wanted to share it with others. The best way to do that was to teach them how to scuba dive.

We hadn't yet ventured into the world of diving with two scuba tanks. We were still in recreational single tank configuration, even in the wreck and cavern diving classes. In order to take the introductory cave and decompression diving classes, we needed to use manifolded scuba tanks. We needed to buy two sets of double tanks and begin practicing as soon as possible. We only had seven months to become proficient in them.

I found a good deal on double tanks at Tech Diving Limited, a dive shop in Lake Havasu City, Arizona that was located about a four-and-a-half-hour drive from us. This shop belongs to Joel Silverstein, one of the pioneers of diving with Nitrox, a breathing gas that contains more oxygen than we find in air. Joel and another expert, Dr. Bill Hamilton, co-authored a book on the subject. I purchased the tanks and arranged to stop in and pick them up on the way to Las Vegas for a long weekend getaway. No late-night mad rush to the airport this time. It was only eight hours from Tucson. Besides, driving would allow us to visit new dive sites in Lake Mohave and Lake Mead on the way to and from Vegas.

We stopped at Scuba Training and Technology, the home of Tech Diving Limited, and met Joel for the first time. Joel was a very nice guy and very thorough. He took time to make sure we had everything we needed. It wasn't a sales pitch. Joel was just a natural teacher. When he learned that neither of us had been diving in a set of double tanks, he brought us into his workshop to teach us the basics of the manifold, make sure the bands were adjusted to our back plates, and that we weren't about to get ourselves killed taking those scuba tanks into the water for the first time. We spent a couple of hours in the shop that day.

I had put together a couple of sets of regulators based on things I read online. They would have worked, but they were far from optimal. Joel gave us advice on how to improve the set up. We purchased two new sets of regulators to dedicate to the doubled tanks. I didn't want to have to reconfigure our regulators every time we switched from double tanks to single tanks. I absorbed every bit of information Joel gave us. Jen was right beside me learning, as well. She made an observation during our session with Joel which she communicated to me once we were back on the road. She sensed that Joel was more than a little concerned for our safety. She felt that he was genuinely worried that we might end up getting ourselves killed in our new tanks. I thought about what she said. I saw it as well.

Who wouldn't be? We were two newish divers arriving at his shop to pick up technical diving equipment. We planned to take this equipment into an Arizona lake with no supervision. Sure, we were divemasters and cavern divers. We were working on our instructor ratings. None of that qualified us to dive with double tanks. None of that qualified us as technical scuba divers. We were new divers with only one hundred and seventy dives each. We thought that was quite a lot, especially considering we had only been diving for a year and a half.

For someone like Joel, who had thousands of scuba dives, many on the Andrea Doria and USS Monitor shipwrecks, his concern was understandable. I was thankful that Joel took the time out of his day to share his knowledge. I felt I was a better and safer diver because of Joel. I would eventually talk to Joel about it, and he would confirm Jen's observation. I've learned a lot from Joel over the years since that day. His lessons have made me a better diver.

Partly thanks to Joel, we didn't die during our first double tank dives in Lake Mohave. The dives were fun, and we felt extremely comfortable in our new equipment. We did four dives in Lake Mohave that day, three with our new scuba tanks. There wasn't anywhere nearby to fill the tanks after the third dive, so we grabbed a couple of our single tanks so we could continue to explore the cove. While we were at Lake Mohave, we also acquired a new cat.

When we arrived, we parked and began setting up our dive equipment. As we were testing our new scuba equipment, Jen heard a mewing sound. She mentioned hearing a kitten, which we both thought strange. We were miles from any residential area. Then I heard it as well. We searched for the source of the mewing and found a small black kitten hiding beneath a bush about twenty feet away. I reached in, picked it up, brought it to the van, and set out a bowl of water.

We continued setting up our equipment and went diving. Eight hours later, the kitten was still under the van. At the end of the day, we set our new double tanks into the back of the van with the backplates still attached to them. The kitten jumped into the van and curled up in the middle of my backplate. We were claimed.

We secured the rest of our equipment and got in the van to continue to Las Vegas. We were concerned that the kitten wouldn't survive if we left it there. It would either starve or become some untamed creature's snack. Jen was allergic to cats, so she drove while I held the kitten. The plan was to leave it with someone at the entrance to the park. As it turned out, the gate shack was closed for the day, and no one was there to take the kitten. Jen continued driving toward Las Vegas while I held it. When we arrived in Vegas, we found a Walmart and went inside to buy supplies.

With a litter box, litter, and food in hand, we checked in at the resort. We didn't have any intention of keeping the kitten, but we had to do something until we could find a new home for it. We snuck the kitten into the room, set up the litter box and food in a cardboard box we had found, and placed a towel inside to form a makeshift bed. We showered and changed and headed out to the Strip with kitten in tow. I emptied a small duffel bag and put the kitten inside of it so it could tag along. I carried the bag at my side and kept one hand inside, petting the kitten, and trying to keep it calm. It didn't work. It kept sticking its head out of the bag and when I shoved it back in, it just meowed loudly. We turned around and walked back to our room. There was no way we could wander around the resorts and casinos with the kitten trying to crawl all over me. We locked it in the bathroom with its supplies and headed back out for a night on the town.

A few hours later, we returned to the room, found the bathroom door open, and the kitten wandering around the room. Either it had jumped up, grabbed the doorknob, and twisted it open, or someone had entered our room and let the cat out. We leaned toward the latter theory. We found evidence to support it. There was a sheet of paper in the room with information about the resort that had the bottom right corner torn off. We didn't remember it being that way earlier but didn't think much of it. A bit later we found the missing corner. On it in bold black print were the words *No pets!* Whoever entered our room must have seen the kitten and had a soft spot for it. The corner of the paper was torn off and inadvertently dropped.

We were there for three nights and left the kitten roaming the room whenever we left to explore the city. There was no more evidence of anyone entering the room when we were out. The kitten grew accustomed to its surroundings and began to explore. One night we returned to find it hanging from the window curtain! Thankfully, no one mentioned the kitten when we checked out.

We had our scuba tanks filled at a dive shop in Boulder City, just outside of Lake Mead, on our drive back home.. We stopped at Lake Mohave for another two dives in the new tanks. Jen discovered that kittens didn't develop dander until they were about twelve weeks old. Mohave didn't have anything on him for her to be allergic to. We had a new member of the family. He would eventually be referred to as Mr. Kitty.

We completed six dives using our new double tanks during that trip and lived to tell about it. They felt comfortable. We had more dives to do before we could feel proficient in them. We needed to build to that proficiency before returning to Florida for our introductory cave and decompression diving classes. We continued diving the Arizona lakes regularly over the next few months, stepping it up the last couple of months before returning to Florida. We were ready to see the inside of the caves away from the daylight zone for the first time.

4

Into the Earth

The time finally arrived to return to Florida. We faced another long haul across the country. It was more convenient than flying because of all of the dive equipment we had, especially since we had our own sets of double tanks. The drive was considerable, though, even with a two-night stop in Texas while visiting family. Having more room in the new van we purchased made it tolerable.

While we were at Ginnie Springs for our cavern diving class, I noticed several cargo vans lined up in the parking lot. As I walked along behind them, I admired the shelves and straps used to organize scuba equipment in the rear cargo area. I decided I needed my own scuba van. We purchased one about two weeks after returning home from that trip. Back at Ginnie, I felt like an imposter parking my cargo van among those belonging to the already trained and certified cave divers. One day I would be legitimate.

We drove the last leg of the trip at night to avoid traffic and so we could spend part of the day touring the area. We were already considering moving to Florida and wanted to familiarize ourselves with the towns around the caves. That's right! After the cavern diving class, we were ready to uproot our lives and move to Florida.

As the sun appeared on the horizon ahead of us, I began to feel sleepy. Jen was also tired. We were just outside of Marianna, Florida and decided to park at the truck stop south of the second Marianna exit to get a few hours of sleep in the back of the van. We had opted for an extended cargo van that had plenty of room to hold an inflatable mattress in the back, even with all of the dive equipment. We wouldn't have wanted to stay in it long-term, but it was comfortable enough for a few hours during a road trip. We put it to use that morning.

We had heard about the caves in Marianna before stopping there for a nap but didn't know much about them. Information was scarce back then. We placed sunshades across the windshield and hung towels over the door windows to darken the interior of the van before losing ourselves in sleep. I fell asleep thinking about the caves, wondering what they looked like and how passable the roads leading to them were. I imagined them to be remote and difficult to get to. Little did we know that only a year and a half later, we would move to the area.

About three hours later, we woke up, went into the truck stop to splash some water on our faces, and topped off our travel mugs with coffee before continuing to High Springs. We took a detour through Lake City to scope out the two hospitals that might become future employers. As a nurse, moving and transitioning to a new state was quite easy. We just needed to find a house. We set a timeline of five years for the big move.

With our tour of Lake City done, we headed to the rental house. We were exhausted and ready to sleep in a real bed. We had a couple of days before our class was scheduled and planned to use them to recuperate from the travel and get some practice dives done.

The day finally arrived. Jen and I were about to do our first real cave dive. We were going beyond the cavern zone into a location that had never seen the light of day. We met our instructor at Ginnie Springs and spent the morning doing line drills. After a brief lunch break, we headed to Devil's Spring Cave. We were about to go where those two divers had been coming from during the final dive of our cavern diving class. I was about to see what they had seen. I was about to go into the darkness beyond.

We had purchased new, brighter dive lights and were ready to light up the cave with them. We descended into the Ear and pulled our way toward an area named the Lips. Many of the passages and formations were given names by the original explorers based on their attributes. The Lips is one of the landmarks in the cave located about four hundred feet from the opening. On approach, they resemble a slightly open mouth ready to swallow you up…or spit you out.

We fought against the current coming from the depths of the cave. There was no swimming against it. Each fin stroke resulted in a couple of feet forward. Before the next fin stroke could happen, the current pushed us three feet back. If we were lucky. The only way we would make any forward progress was by pulling ourselves into the cave.

We followed our instructor closely and tried to mimic his moves. He made it look simple and easy. Jen and I struggled with every foot of forward movement. We pulled ourselves through the tunnel, scraping our fingertips against the hard, rough surface of the cave. We only made it two hundred feet from the opening, barely halfway to the Lips. Jen had reached her turn pressure and signaled us to turn around.

We surfaced and debriefed the dive. I was ready to get out so we could refill our tanks. That wasn't the plan. We were doing the second dive with nothing more than the remaining air in our tanks. I doubted we would make it to the beginning of the gold-colored guideline that began less than one hundred feet from the opening. The rule of air management in introductory cave diving dictates that we use one sixth of the pressure in our tanks before we turn around to exit. That leaves one sixth for the exit and the remaining two thirds for emergencies. This gave us plenty of room for error. It gave us plenty of air to work through issues and make it back to the surface alive.

We hadn't made it to the Lips using one sixth of full tanks. What kind of dive would we have starting with less air? Would there even be time to do any drills on the way out? I didn't understand why we weren't refilling our tanks. Our instructor insisted it would be fine. I trusted him. He had been doing this for a long time. Besides, I had no choice.

As it turned out, we made it to the Lips during the second dive. Our instructor gave us some tips on how to get through the Gallery, the tunnel between the opening and the Lips. The primary line from open water to the permanent guideline in the cave was already in place, saving us time. In addition to that, we hadn't used one sixth of our air to exit. The current in the cave pushed us out rather quickly. While we could use six hundred psi to penetrate the cave, the current got us out while breathing only four hundred psi, leaving us with twenty-seven hundred psi for the second dive.

Jen also turned this dive. I was confused. This was highly unusual. I was typically the one turning our dives. Jen had much smaller lungs that required less air to fill them. She had what we affectionately called *girly lungs*. This is something every scuba diver wants, even the toughest of the toughest deep technical divers. Having girly lungs meant breathing less air from our tanks. Breathing less air meant staying in the water longer. We all wanted that!

Jen and I finally penetrated beyond the cavern zone and into a part of the cave that didn't have natural light streaming into it. We went where those two divers had come from. I was even more hooked. I had no doubt that I wanted to be a cave diver. We debriefed the dives, talked about areas to improve, and made plans to meet at Peacock Springs State Park the next morning. We were going to see new caves!

The next morning we met at the Peacock Springs State Park parking area. This was our first time there. I was excited to get in the water and see a new cave. I was excited to experience a low flow cave for the first time. I was even more excited to be diving in the cave that was the subject of Sheck Exley's *Taming of the Slough*.

Sheck was one of the early pioneers of cave diving. He had become obsessed with the statistics of cave diving fatalities, a natural tendency as a math major and high school math teacher. Cave diving fatalities were common back then. The state was threatening to restrict access to many caves. Sheck studied the fatalities and developed the guidelines of cave diving based on his findings. This led to the creation of the first cave diving training course in Florida. It led to safer cave diving. Sheck wrote several books, and I devoured them between trips.

I thought about Sheck as we began the first dive into Peacock I, the main opening to the Peacock Springs cave system. The dive did not go very well. I had difficulty with my buoyancy control and Jen signaled to turn around only one hundred and fifty feet from the opening. It seemed neither of us was having a good day. I couldn't figure out what was going on with Jen's breathing rate.

Peacock Springs is much shallower than Devil's and has minimal water flow. We should have made it a lot farther. We barely left the cavern zone. Jen shouldn't have signaled us to turn around so soon, but there we were facing the opening. We did some drills in the cavern zone and surfaced. Once again, tank refills weren't happening between dives.

This time we swam into the Peanut Restriction tunnel. The Peacock Springs opening leads to a large cavern that has two tunnels branching off of it. The tunnel to the right is called the Olsen line and the one to the left is called the Peanut line. There are two permanent gold-colored guidelines that begin in the cavern only a few feet from the basin.

We entered the cavern and began our swim into the left side tunnel. I hoped to make it more than one hundred and fifty feet this time. We swam six hundred feet! We made it just beyond the first restriction (not the Peanut Restriction) before Jen signaled to turn the dive. I was ecstatic! It was our farthest penetration. We had done a real cave dive.

Jen's reason for turning around this time was because we encountered other divers swimming out. We gave the exiting divers the right-of-way, as is the rule in cave diving, and turned around to follow and complete more drills. As we swam out, I questioned why we were penetrating so much farther with less air in our tanks? It made no sense.

My buoyancy was much better during the second dive. Things were falling into place. We finished our dive with all of our drills completed. We were officially cave divers. Introductory cave divers, but cave divers, nonetheless. The limitations for that level of cave diving were to penetrate no more than one sixth of our starting air pressure, go no deeper than one hundred feet, remain on the main line of the cave, and be able to pass through tunnels without having to remove any of our scuba equipment. They were simple to learn and easy to follow.

We finished early enough in the day that Jen and I had time to do a couple of dives on our own. We drove down the street to get our tanks filled at one of the dive shops located nearby and returned to dive Orange Grove Sink, located near the entrance to the park. Peacock and Orange Grove are part of the same cave system, connected through an underground river. It meant almost a mile of swimming, but it was possible to enter one opening and exit through the other. We would need a lot more training before we could do that.

It took us a while to find the correct opening to the cave. Orange Grove is an offset sinkhole with a wall on one side that contained three openings leading to tunnels that led to independent areas. When we descended, we went too deep to find the opening that connects to the Peacock Springs opening. It took us nearly twenty minutes to find the current opening where the Debra Reeves plaque was located.

Debra Reeves was a cave diver that breathed her scuba tanks empty of air and drowned while on a dive that she and her boyfriend began in Orange Grove Sink. Debra's story is a tragic one. It was probably the single most significant fatality in the history of cave diving. I've included it in several of my books, both my thrillers and my adventure series. I'll repeat it here for anyone who hasn't read my other books yet.

Gold line made its first appearance in underwater caves in 1989 after Debra's death. As I stated, Debra and her boyfriend were diving in Peacock Springs cave starting from the Orange Grove sinkhole. It is the first sinkhole you encounter when you enter the park. In 1988, Debra entered the Orange Grove cave opening with her boyfriend. They were planning to swim along the main guideline until they reached turn pressure. In cave diving, this is typically one third of the starting air pressure in the scuba tanks. When they breathed one third, Debra and her boyfriend would turn around and begin their swim out of the cave. About thirty minutes into the dive, Debra had a primary light failure. Her boyfriend, who was leading the way, noticed he no longer saw a light coming from behind him. He stopped, turned around, and found

Debra with a nonfunctioning primary light retrieving a backup light from her pocket. He faced Debra and provided light for her while she got situated. During this time, both divers inadvertently ascended to the ceiling of the cave.

Once Debra deployed her backup light, they signaled to each other that the dive was over. When there's an equipment failure, cave divers turn and exit. We have redundancy, but that's meant to help get us out of the cave after a failure, not to continue the dive. Debra and her boyfriend descended back to the guideline with Debra leading the way out. A few minutes later, Debra's boyfriend signaled to get her attention. She turned around and he communicated to her using hand signals that they were going in the wrong direction and should turn around. He didn't recognize the tunnel they were in and believed they had somehow followed the wrong guideline. Debra didn't believe him. After a couple of moments arguing using hand signals, Debra turned around and continued to swim the way she had been going. Her boyfriend, knowing that was not the right direction, turned and headed back from where they had come. That had to be one of the toughest decisions he ever made. I don't know if I could do the same thing as Debra's boyfriend under similar circumstances. That decision saved his life, though.

One thing that's drilled into the heads of cave diving students is that one fatality is better than two. You do what you can to save your dive buddy, but if things become critical, save yourself. It's a tough situation and one I've faced myself. Fortunately, in my case, it didn't result in a fatality for anyone. My dive buddy and good friend made it out of the cave unscathed. It was miscommunication and misunderstanding rather than confusion that led to him swimming off. That incident was the inspiration for my thriller, *Beyond Hope*.

A few minutes after Debra's boyfriend turned to go the opposite direction, he came to the end of the guideline he was following. About fifteen feet away from it, against the wall on the opposite side of the tunnel he was in, there was another guideline. He recognized this area as the location of Debra's light failure. He was at an intersection of tunnels. He swam across to the other line and followed it to the left and out of the cave. He removed his equipment and raced up the street to the dive shop a couple of miles away to call for help. This was before mobile cell phones were commonly used. The shop wasn't far, though, and he held onto the hope that there was still time to save Debra. Unfortunately, there wasn't. Debra was found lifeless in the cave in the tunnel where they had argued about which way to go. Her scuba tanks were empty. She had drowned.

A couple of weeks later, members of the board of directors for two of the cave diving training organizations met to discuss Debra's death, analyze the details, and come up with a way to prevent a similar fatality from happening. Accident analysis was something that was still being done at that time. It was concluded that if the guideline in the main tunnel had been distinguishable from the guideline in the offshoot tunnel, Debra would have known without a doubt that she was going the wrong way and wouldn't have swum down that tunnel. The board members had a cause and came up with a solution to prevent any further deaths from happening as a result of that cause.

The decision was made to replace the guidelines in the main tunnels of all popular Florida caves with a thicker, different color line. Calls were made, and a supplier happened to have an overstock of gold-colored line that would withstand the harsh environment found in underwater caves. The supplier agreed to sell what he had at cost. Two weeks later, the guidelines in the main tunnels of Peacock Springs cave system, more than forty-five hundred feet, were replaced. It took another couple of months to replace the main guidelines in the other popular Florida caves. A plaque now sits at the opening in the Orange Grove sinkhole to commemorate Debra's memory and her unwitting sacrifice to cave diving.

We didn't know Debra's story at that time. We hadn't heard about Debra before seeing the plaque that was placed at the entrance to the cave in honor of her memory. All we knew was that she had most likely died in the cave. It was a reminder of the unforgiving environment we were about to enter. We stopped to reflect on what we were about to do on this first unsupervised cave dive. It was a harsh reminder of the risks and dangers involved in cave diving.

After a moment of reflection, we wrapped our guideline around the plaque and swam past it into the cave. We made it to a sign located one hundred feet from the opening. A sign that warned untrained divers not to go beyond it. I thought it was placed too far in. We couldn't see daylight from that location.

We turned around, swam back to the plaque, and left our primary line secured to it for the next dive. We ascended and took a ten-minute surface interval to debrief the dive, talk about the plaque, and calculate our turn pressure for our final dive of the day. We descended and followed our line to the opening and into the cave. This time we penetrated the cave about two hundred feet. It wasn't much farther, but we saw more cave passage.

We exited the overhead environment and spent about ten minutes swimming around the sinkhole and exploring it. It was a good day. We did four dives and experienced two new caves. More importantly, we lived through our first two unsupervised cave dives. We were ready to get our tanks refilled in preparation for the next day. It was another day of training. We were about to begin our Advanced Nitrox and Decompression Procedures course.

5

A new focus

We were ready to continue farther into the caves. We wanted to see what was around each of the next corners. We wanted to see what the tunnels that intersected the main passage looked like. We visited various caves and did a few dozen cave dives at the introductory cave diving level. I was ready to explore more. I tried to convince Jen to push the limits. Just a little bit. I wanted to use one fourth of our starting air pressure. She wouldn't do it. She was a stickler for the rules. She kept me in line.

We had to continue our training if we were going to penetrate farther into the caves. Farther penetration meant longer dives, which in turn meant decompression obligations. We would no longer be able to ascend to the surface directly or with a three-minute safety stop once we left the overhead. We had to stop at twenty feet of depth and allow the tissues in our bodies to off-gas the nitrogen they had absorbed while we were in the caves.

Before we could do dives that required decompression stops, we had to learn how to plan and execute those dives. A practice that originated in the days before breathing air with a higher percentage of oxygen and pure oxygen on scuba was to learn decompression diving during the cave diving class. There were no separate classes for decompression diving. Part of the reason for this was because decompression was much simpler in those days. It wasn't necessarily safer.

In the early days, cave divers breathed air throughout the entire dive, including during decompression. Decompression obligations were calculated using dive tables, and divers continued to breathe the air they had been breathing during the dives. There was no accelerated decompression outside of military diving. Decompression practices were taught as part of the cave diving class. This practice continued after accelerated decompression diving was introduced into the non-military diving world. The cave diving training organizations hadn't updated their standards to require decompression dive training as a prerequisite for the cave diving class.

Cave diving instructors began teaching their students to use oxygen during decompression stops as part of the class. However, they weren't adding any days to the class schedule, and they weren't covering decompression dive theory as thoroughly as they should have been. Cave divers were using oxygen during decompression stops without having the appropriate knowledge or training to do so.

We didn't know that the decompression diving class was not required. We were simply taking it because it seemed like the next logical step in our training. Not that it would have mattered. We wanted the knowledge and training. We wanted to be able to do decompression diving outside of the caves as well. As far as we knew, before we could cave dive and end up with decompression obligations, we had to take classes that would provide us with the knowledge and skills to do so.

We arrived at Ginnie Springs the day after completing our introductory cave diving class. We spent the morning in the classroom with the loud, rattling air conditioner blowing lukewarm air onto us while we learned about the theory of Advanced Nitrox and Decompression Procedures. Nitrox is an oxygen enriched breathing gas that contains a higher percentage of oxygen than the usual twenty-one percent found in air. It allows divers to remain at depth longer either without incurring a decompression obligation or incurring less of a decompression obligation.

We were already Nitrox certified, which allowed us to breathe up to forty percent oxygen on dives. The Advanced Nitrox portion of the class would increase that to one hundred percent. The Decompression Procedures portion would teach us how to use the higher percentage mixtures during decompression stops to accelerate our decompression and surface sooner.

We spent three and a half hours learning the theory and how to apply it to our dives. After lunch, we met at Devil's Spring to do our first dive. We swam to the Lips and drifted back out, noting our starting and ending tank pressures. This provided us with the information we needed to calculate our breathing rates so we could properly plan our dives. We had to know how long our dives would be to plan decompression stops. The only way to know that was by knowing how long it would take to breathe the air we had in our scuba tanks.

Having been in the Devil's Ear a couple of times, we knew what we had to do to be able to make it to the Lips, and fortunately, we made it. We had improved in only two days. When I reached the Lips, I looked longingly through them, wanting to continue beyond to see what was around the next corner. That wasn't the plan. I had to turn around.

The dive to the Lips was the only cave dive we did that day, but not the only dive. After a ten-minute surface interval, our instructor ran the cave line from his primary reel through the spring run between the Devil's Cave openings and the Little Devil's opening. Little Devil's Spring is a narrow slit in the bottom of the spring run, located on the opposite end from Devil's Spring. It's possibly connected to Devil's Spring, but the passage is too small for a person to fit through. The cave isn't even large enough for sidemounted tanks.

We worked on drills for the next hour and fifteen minutes in the eight-foot-deep spring run. We swam along the line back and forth and practiced handling our decompression tanks and doing out of air drills. Jen and I would have gone for another dive after class, but we were exhausted. Three days of training and diving was catching up with us. We decided it was more prudent to relax for the rest of the evening and be refreshed the next day.

We met at Forty Fathom Grotto the next morning. This is a sinkhole that was owned by the late Hal Watts, a deep air diver who created a training agency that offered deep air diving classes. A sinkhole that was forty fathom deep, or two hundred and forty feet deep, was the perfect location for such training. It was also ideal for decompression dive training.

There are a couple of areas in the sinkhole that are considered caves. These are places where divers can find themselves in an overhead environment. The problem was that the visibility was usually horrible, and you didn't necessarily know when you were in the overhead. At one time, the sinkhole had decent visibility, but this was not the case when we were there. The water was brown. We had seen much better visibility in the Arizona lakes. We could only see a couple of feet in front of us. If it wasn't for the permanent guidelines that were placed in Forty Fathom Grotto, we would have most certainly gotten lost. We might have even inadvertently wandered into one of the caves.

We planned a simulated decompression dive in the Grotto, establishing time limits at various depths, both while descending and ascending. We followed the plan, following the guideline until we reached our maximum depth. We began our ascent and surfaced only a minute behind schedule, the poor visibility causing us to move slower. The other two students in the class got lost. At the surface, our instructor directed us to remain in place while he searched for them. Fortunately, their exhalation marked their location.

Our instructor decided that another dive in those conditions was not in anyone's best interest. We wholeheartedly agreed and called it a day. We considered heading to Ginnie or Peacock for another dive or two, but we headed to the rental house to relax for the rest of the evening instead. We took the next day off to recuperate. We had just completed our fifth day in a row of diving. A break was much needed.

Feeling refreshed and somewhat rejuvenated after a day away from the water, we returned to Ginnie Springs. We were done with our training and free to be tourist divers. We went back to dive Devil's Spring Cave and decided to enter through the Eye as we had yet to see that passage. The Eye led to the same location as the Ear, but the route was a bit longer. We descended into the oval opening and pulled our way to the bottom. The floor was covered in gravel from that point on, and we fought against the current with little to hold onto, finally making it to the beginning of the permanent guideline. We looked to the right and saw the daylight streaming in from the Ear. It was already time to turn around and head out.

We returned to Devil's Spring after lunch for two more dives. This time we not only made it to the Lips, but we swam through them. I was finally going to see what was around the next corner. We ventured farther into the hidden river below the Santa Fe River. It was amazing how much better we performed when we weren't being watched by an instructor. We were more relaxed, and our breathing rates reflected it.

We pulled ourselves into the cave and turned around just before the next landmark, named the Keyhole because its shape required us to turn our bodies just so to make it through to the other side. I poked my head in to see what was beyond the small opening but did not venture through it. Jen had already signaled me to turn the dive and I was pushing it just by looking.

During the second dive of the afternoon we headed to the Catacombs, a series of small tunnels to the left of the Gallery. The Catacombs has a few outlets back to the Gallery along the way before the final exit point before the Lips. We were diving with Jack, one of the other students from our Decompression Procedures class, and he led the way as he let line out from his primary reel. Unlike most other passages that have been explored in underwater caves, the Catacombs didn't have a permanent guideline. It remained unlined so it could be used in training.

There isn't much current flowing through the Catacombs. The area is located to the side of the Gallery where the majority of water flows. Because of this, the Catacombs have a carpet of sediment covering the limestone floor. Unfortunately, Jack kicked it up as he swam in and I experienced my first silt out in a cave. I didn't lose visibility completely, but it was significantly diminished. I couldn't see the guideline and had to make contact with it.

We learned in class that sometimes you can wait for the silt to settle and the visibility to be restored. I waited to see if this was one of those times, but it wasn't. The sediment hung in the water, making the visibility worse than in Forty Fathom Grotto. I looked back and signaled Jen to turn around. I tapped Jack's leg and alerted him to the diminished visibility. We swam out to clear water and waited for Jack to emerge from the silt cloud. This is no judgment on Jack. I can't say I wouldn't have silted the passage myself if I had been running the line. We were all new to cave diving and still learning.

We took a break from the high current of Devil's Spring and returned to Peacock Springs State Park the next day. We planned a dive in Orange Grove where we could relax in a low flow cave. We found the opening and the plaque quickly and began running our line into the cave. We tied our line to the permanent gold line and continued past the warning sign. The floor beyond the sign was covered in sediment and visions (or the lack of) of our dive in the Catacombs the day before flashed through my mind. Fortunately, this passage was larger, so we were able to get through it without affecting the visibility, but it was a test of our buoyancy control and finning technique. Jen even pulled a muscle during this dive from straining to stay in trim and off of the floor.

When we surfaced, we floated for about half an hour to see if her muscle cramp would pass. Unfortunately, it did not. Jen was done diving for the day. Our reel was still inside of the cave and had to be retrieved. Jen descended a few feet to keep an eye on me while I went to get it. Solo diving isn't allowed in Peacock Springs State Park, so she had to be in the water with me. Besides, we were new cave divers, and she wouldn't allow me to be completely solo.

I swam past the plaque with my reel in hand and as we ascended, I found another opening in the wall of the sinkhole. It was a horizontal slit in the wall about twenty feet below the surface. I signaled Jen to wait and poked my head into the wide and low passage. Jen hovered in the water just outside of the opening while I swam farther in. I penetrated the cave about twenty-five feet when I became jammed in between the floor and ceiling. The tanks on my back were too big to allow me to continue and pushed me into the floor. Silt immediately rose into the passage, and I found myself in zero visibility. I couldn't see the beam from my dive light.

I was in my second silt-out in two days. This was also my first time getting stuck inside of a cave. It was a good thing I couldn't see because things weren't looking good for me. I wiggled around until I was able to break free and back out. Fortunately, I hadn't penetrated into the crack very far and managed to be able to exit with minimal issues other than a rat's nest of line in my hand. I didn't do a great job of reeling the line back up. It wasn't as easy while backing up as it was swimming forward.

The next day we returned to Devil's Spring. We approached the Devil's Ear, but the tannic water of the river was encroaching on the entrance enough that we couldn't see the crack. This often happens when it rains and the river level rises. It makes for a really cool effect as you look up from inside of the Ear to the surface. It appears as if blood is seeping into the cave.

While it was fascinating to see, it made Jen uncomfortable, so we headed to the Eye instead. We made it to the Keyhole again. This was impressive because entry through the Eye was close to one hundred feet longer than through the Ear. We were penetrating just a little farther with every subsequent dive. Either our technique or our breathing rates were improving. Maybe both. One thing that wasn't improving was the abrasions on our fingertips from pulling ourselves along the cave to get to the Lips.

There's a technique in cave diving called pull and glide that is sometimes used when cave diving high current caves. It's a misnomer. There's a lot of pulling and very little gliding, especially in the caves with really strong current. Most of the gliding is backwards. We hadn't quite

43

mastered the technique and were scraping our fingertips as we pulled ourselves into the cave. This had the same effect as rubbing our fingertips over sandpaper. It was very painful.

Jen and I bought a tube of liquid skin to protect our wounds. If you've never tried liquid skin, I suggest you do not place it over an open wound, even abrasions. As we dropped the vile concoction onto our fingertips, the devil emerged from his spring to laugh at us. The liquid fire burned through to our cores. Some colorful words came out of both of our mouths during those extreme moments of pain. Fortunately, we were in a rental house on ten acres and not in a hotel room when this occurred, otherwise someone would have called local law enforcement to report a disturbance. We may have invented new profanities during this tirade of obscenities. When the pain began to subside, we laughed at each other and our stupidity. All while continuing to cuss at the pain we were still experiencing.

Our trip to High Springs came to a close. It was time to go home. We completed eighteen dives over eight days and received our introductory cave and advanced nitrox diver certifications. We still had to do another dive to complete the Decompression Procedures class. The poor visibility in Forty Fathom Grotto had interfered. We would complete that dive when we returned to Florida five months later.

We weren't quite done with the dives for the trip. I did some research and was able to finally dig up information about the caves in Marianna. It happened to be on our way to Arizona, so we decided to stop in Marianna to do a couple of dives in one of the caves. That cave was Jackson Blue Spring, the headspring of Merritt's Mill Pond.

At the time, divers had to sign in at the sheriff's office to get the gate key allowing access to the spring basin. It was quite different than what we had experienced in High Springs and Luraville. We exited the interstate and drove through town. We were definitely getting the small-town vibes of Marianna, Florida. It looked like a sleepy southern town. We continued along the main street until we found the sheriff's office outside of the city limits on the opposite end of the town.

We signed in, paid our fee, and received one of the keys. We were also given directions to the park where we would be able to access the cave. It was a simple process. We drove back across town. There was very little traffic for a weekday. We liked it. We also liked the fact that there were many old houses that had been there for more than a century. Hurricanes were one of our concerns regarding a move to Florida. Marianna was more than sixty miles from the coast. That provided a good buffer. It might not be a bad place to settle down.

We turned off the main road and continued to follow the directions we had received, eventually turning onto Blue Spring Road. My preconception of the caves in Marianna appeared to be true. We were heading to a remote location. A few minutes later, we arrived at the park without having to leave paved road. That was one preconception that proved false. We let ourselves in the gate and drove down to the parking area. What we saw in front of us was not what I had expected. There were a couple of pavilions, a diving platform over the cave opening, and restrooms. There was even electricity. I didn't hear any banjos in the distance.

We began our dive, easily finding the beginning of the permanent guideline one hundred and ten feet from the opening against the wall on the right. Jackson Blue had a strong current but not quite as strong as Devil's Spring. Our fingers were safe. We continued farther into the cave. About two hundred and fifty feet from the opening, we arrived at the top of a large fissure crack in the floor. Jen and I descended into it, arriving at the bottom. We had just dropped from forty-five feet to eighty-five feet of depth. We hovered there looking into one of the largest rooms we had seen in a cave up until that point. This room could easily hold two semi-trucks with trailers side by side with plenty of room to swim around them.

Not far into the room, about three hundred feet from the entrance, we turned and swam out to the spring basin. We were back inside the cave after a twelve-minute surface interval. This time, we swam an additional one hundred feet to the end of the room. We were still penetrating farther into the cave on the second dive with less air in our tanks than we were during the first dive. I couldn't quite figure out how that was happening, but it was.

I was overwhelmed by this dive in Jackson Blue. Not in a bad way. There was so much to look at. There were so many options in the first four hundred feet of the cave. I found a line leading to an offshoot tunnel on the floor to the right side of the large room as well as another one on the ceiling to the left. My head whipped back and forth as if on a swivel trying to take it all in. I was so distracted that I lost reference to the gold line a couple of times. It was information overload. It was so easy to get drawn away from the guideline.

Those were our final dives of the trip. We were sad to be leaving Florida, but we were happy to have found a new place to dive. Jackson Blue was amazing. Something about it drew me in much more than the caves we had been diving in High Springs and Luraville. We felt at home in Jackson County. We were so drawn to it that we picked up a real estate magazine and began looking at the listings to see what was available. We also drove by the hospital to check it out for possible future employment. High Springs was no longer on our radar. We wanted to move to the Marianna area. We wanted to buy a place in Jackson County. And that's exactly what we did during our next trip five months later.

6

A secret revealed

I discovered a secret that Jen was keeping from me during our previous trip to Florida. If you recall, I mentioned that she was the one that signaled the turn of every dive we did during class. This was highly unusual. Her girly lungs were so much more efficient than mine, and I couldn't figure out why this wasn't the case in the caves. I finally learned the reason. Our instructor stressed the air planning rules during our training. He didn't just mention it. He spoke about it several times. He was sure to impart upon us just how important it was that we never violate that rule. He went so far as to tell us that if he ever found out someone he was diving with did not turn when turn pressure was reached, he would never dive with that person again.

There was sound logic to what he told us. It wasn't about being safe for yourself but being safe for your dive buddy. The rule of thirds reserves one third of the air in the scuba tanks for emergencies. Following the rule gives us time to deal with just about anything that can happen during a cave dive. There's more to it. That reserve air is there in case your dive buddy has an issue that results in the loss of air. That reserve air is not just for you. It's also for your dive buddy.

If your buddy has an issue during the dive that requires air sharing, it's your duty to supply him or her with that air. It's your duty to have one third of the air you begin with ready to give to your dive buddy. If you penetrate the cave without turning around when you've breathed one third of the air in your scuba tanks, you're dipping into that reserve air and that is supposed to be saved for your buddy. You're breathing your dive buddy's emergency air.

While I was willing to push the limits during our dives in between training sessions, I did follow the rule during training dives. I never pushed the limits at all because Jen wouldn't allow it. Our instructor's stress on this matter had the appropriate effect on Jen. It concerned her. It scared her. She was afraid of accidentally breathing her tank pressure beyond the turn pressure. She was afraid of being told by our instructor that he would no longer dive with her. Because of this, she always turned the dive one to two hundred psi before we reached turn pressure. She was doing this even though we were planning dives using the introductory cave diving rule of sixths.

Starting with thirty-six hundred psi meant we could penetrate the cave using six hundred psi before turning to exit. Jen didn't want to leave anything to chance. She was turning after breathing only four hundred psi! We could have stayed in the cave longer had she allowed herself to use the full amount of air planned for the penetration. We could have gone farther into the cave.

I was certain that our instructor meant if one of his dive buddies *intentionally* breathed more than a third of the starting pressure to penetrate the cave. Unintentionally breathing a little beyond it wouldn't cause him to ban someone as a buddy or a student. Besides, how would he have known if she had missed it by fifty psi? He wasn't omniscient. Or was he? You'd be surprised by what cave diving instructors know.

In Devil's Spring Cave, the current pushed us out faster. We were surfacing with a lot more than two thirds of our starting air. In Peacock Springs, we might surface with less, but we were doing drills during the exit. Our breathing rates were faster because of that. There was no way to know. That didn't matter to Jen. If only I had known she was turning sooner I would have brought it up in front of our instructor and asked him about it. We might have reached the Lips and even gone beyond the Keyhole on every single dive!

* * *

We returned to Florida and stopped in Marianna for a few days before continuing to High Springs. Our plans included doing some dives as well as shopping for a house. We were going to drive around Jackson County to look at houses and check out the towns and neighborhoods they were in. We knew nothing about Jackson County other than it had a very beautiful cave within its boundaries.

Upon arrival, we took a couple of days to recuperate and learn the area. We explored in and around Marianna and drove by houses we found online. Our tour of Jackson County allowed us to eliminate several options and narrow our list to two houses. We met with an agent, and after he showed us additional listings, we headed out to look at four houses in Jackson County.

We liked one of the houses we looked at and submitted an offer, which was accepted immediately. We began the process to purchase our new house. Things were getting real. We were setting down roots during our third trip to Florida, our second trip to Jackson County. We weren't ready to move to Florida yet, but we were visiting often enough that having a house in the state was going to make our trips easier. We could leave clothing and dive equipment and have our own bed to sleep in. We could also bring our dogs with us rather than leaving them in Arizona with a sitter. To help cover the property taxes and utilities, we would rent the house to other cave divers in between trips.

We were hyped from finding a house and being back for more cave diving and didn't want to wait until the next day to get in the water. After a quick dinner, we signed in at the sheriff's office, got the key, and headed to Jackson Blue for a couple of dives. It was long overdue.

It was evident that we had been away for five months. We had done lots of diving in Arizona and practiced our skills repeatedly, but it wasn't the same as being in a cave. The first penetration into Jackson Blue was average at best. I stumbled through running the line from my primary reel into the cave and to the beginning of the gold line. Once there, we pulled ourselves against the strong current to the top of the chimney fissure and descended to the large room below. We turned around and began our exit. It was a short dive.

After a twelve-minute surface interval, we headed back into the cave. The second dive went much better! Granted, we left the line in the cave, but we moved against the current much more easily. Even starting with less air in our tanks, we made it farther in. We finally saw the area on the map known as the first breakdown, making it beyond the six-hundred-foot line marker. That was the farthest we had made it in Jackson Blue. It was the farthest we had been in any cave.

Most popular caves in Florida have line markers shaped like arrows that are positioned every one hundred feet on the gold line. This lets divers know how many feet they have penetrated. It makes it easier to plan dives and calculate decompression obligations. It helps with planning dives. The markers are not necessary. They are a convenience.

The next day we decided to rent a boat so we could head to Twin Cave, a cave located in Merritt's Mill Pond that wasn't accessible by land. We headed north on the pond, amazed at all of the cypress trees growing out of the water. We passed a small dock located in front of Hole in the Wall cave and continued toward Twin. We found the old wooden dock near Twin cave. Neither dock touched land. They were both nestled among cypress trees, which served as their posts.

The Twin Cave opening is not readily apparent to the casual observer. Even to those searching for it, it's easy to miss. It was located about fifty feet from the dock in the bottom of the pond. It's a hole in the floor that drops about eight feet and has an opening into the cave on one of the walls. We somehow found it on our first try. At the time, the gold line in Twin Cave began two hundred feet from the opening, not at the opening like it is now. I extended the gold line in 2009 for a cave diving convention, and it has remained like that ever since.

Jen followed me into the head-and-shoulders-shaped opening as I spooled out the line from our primary reel. We had to get very close to the silty bottom to make sure our backmounted tanks cleared the arch of the entryway. The opening was almost too small for Jen's comfort level. I convinced her to try it. Once she stuck her head through and saw that the cavern was a decent size, she followed me in. The cavern floor was covered with a thick layer of sediment. One errant fin kick and the room would black out from the silt. We moved slowly and carefully, not wanting to disturb the visibility.

At the far end of the cavern, we found a stop sign warning untrained divers to stay out. It was shaped like a stop sign, but it was yellow rather than red. It would have been better placed closer to the opening, maybe even outside of it. No one without cave training should enter that cave. I know fully trained cave divers that consider the entrance and cavern as advanced level. Several years later, an open water diver ventured into the Twin cavern and immediately silted out the entire room. She found the large air pocket in the ceiling and only survived by remaining there until help arrived. She was lucky to have survived.

Directly in front of the stop sign was a large hole in the floor of the cavern that led to a silty floor about eight feet deeper. Other than the shape, it was very similar to the hole in the floor of the pond into which we had descended to enter the cave. The main opening of the cave was round while this one was oblong. What was more intriguing was that Twin Cave had multiple levels.

We descended into the hole and continued to follow the tunnel. At this point, we were in a long, tall room with a sediment covered floor that had been named the Subway Tunnel according to the map. About seventy feet later, we found the beginning of the gold line secured to the wall on our right. This was the farthest back that we had encountered the beginning of a gold line. The other gold lines we had seen were no more than one hundred and ten feet from the surface.

We secured our line to the gold line and followed it through the Subway Tunnel, quickly realizing why it was so named. It was a long, straight, arch-shaped tunnel that continued for hundreds of feet. I definitely got New York City subway vibes. About two hundred and fifty feet after the beginning of the gold line, the floor sloped down and

51

the wall on the right opened to a low passage. I descended until I was in front of the opening so I could peek inside. It appeared to get smaller. According to the map, this was the offshoot to Skiles' Passage, named after Wes Skiles, the cave explorer who first went into the passage. This tunnel is small, low, and narrow and eventually loops back to another passage, reconnecting to the main passage.

Soon after the Skiles' Passage offshoot, we passed a couple of other divers that were on the way out of the cave. We made way for them to pass. We waved at each other and continued in our respective directions. Jen signaled me to turn around when we were at the eight-hundred-foot marker. This was our farthest penetration as cave divers. It doesn't seem like much of a penetration now, but back then it was a big deal. We were new intro cave divers with minimal experience. We were thrilled that we made it so far. Little did we know that we had turned about two hundred feet short of one of the most amazing sights in a cave. We exited the cave an hour after we had entered it. I think Jen finally allowed herself to continue until the pressure in her tanks was actually at turn pressure.

After our dive, we dropped off the boat and met with the agent to sign the real estate contract. We returned to the hotel and prepared to leave the next morning. Our Marianna portion of the trip was over. We would stop at Peacock Springs State Park and dive Peacock I before continuing south for a week of diving in the Bahamas.

At Peacock the next morning, we opted to go to the tunnel on the right and head toward Olsen Sinkhole fourteen hundred feet away. We didn't make it that far. We didn't even make it six hundred feet. We stopped at Pothole Sink, located about four hundred and fifty feet from the opening, and looked for daylight streaming into the passage. We couldn't see any of the sun's rays, so I ascended about ten feet along the line on the wall until I finally saw a sliver of light peeking through the ceiling. It wasn't a large opening. We were told that Pothole Sink could be used as an emergency exit, but I didn't see how. It didn't look big enough for someone to fit in. I didn't rise to the surface to find out.

We turned around and headed back to the opening where we recalculated our turn pressures and rerouted the primary reel line to the Peanut Tunnel guideline. That was the nice thing about having the lines practically below the surface. We didn't have to actually exit the cave. With our newly calculated turn pressures, we headed into the other tunnel and made it just beyond the seven-hundred-foot marker. Jen was back to turning the dive before reaching turn pressure. This time she had a valid excuse, though. She had to pee! We were wearing drysuits and peeing inside of them wasn't advisable. We could do it, but it would be most unpleasant, especially when taking them off after the dive. The dive lasted almost one hundred minutes, so it was understandable that her bladder had finally decided to let its presence be known.

Cave diving was done for a couple of weeks. We were off to the Bahamas followed by a week of diving in south Florida. We did some shore diving and wreck diving before returning to cave country. Back in High Springs, we did a drift dive from Devil's spring run to the Ginnie spring run through the Santa Fe River. This was my first river dive, and it was definitely interesting.

The visibility was diminished, and the current was strong. Transitioning from the clear water in the spring run to the tannic water of the river was spooky. Visibility was limited. Gators were in the back of my mind. As we drifted, I was afraid we would miss the turn into the Ginnie spring run and continue down the river. Fortunately, we saw and felt the clear, cool spring water entering the river from our left. We swam toward it and completed the dive with a cavern dive at Ginnie Springs, our first since being trained cave divers.

The next day, Jen and I returned to Ginnie Springs to enjoy one last day of practice before meeting our instructor to continue our training. We had five days scheduled. Five more days of cave diving before we had to head back to reality and be responsible adults. We hoped to schedule the closing on our house before we left Florida, but we hadn't heard anything from the real estate agent. We were counting down the days to being fully certified cave divers and Florida homeowners.

7

Guidelines and drills

Jen and I arrived at Ginnie Springs early the next morning with plans to do three dives in preparation for our upcoming cave diving class. Our main focus was to work on reeling our guideline in and out of the cave. We could simulate it in the Arizona lakes, but it wasn't the same. We both needed practice, so we took turns deploying the line into the cave. We secured our line to the gold line and continued through the Gallery, making it to the Lips on one occasion and beyond the Keyhole on the other. We were getting better at deploying the line, reading the cave, and avoiding the current. Our fingertips still suffered. We hadn't figured out how to avoid scraping them as we pulled ourselves into the cave against the current. We didn't dare use liquid skin on them again. One time was once too many.

During two of the dives, we recalculated turn pressure once back at the beginning of the gold line and ventured into the Catacombs for more line deployment practice. We also practiced our finning technique in the smaller, siltier passage. Unlike the first time, we exited with clear visibility. At least we had that going for us.

We decided this would be the last time we went diving at Ginnie Springs on a weekend. It was filled with people, and not just cave divers. There were a lot of non-divers floating on innertubes and inflatable rafts hanging out on the surface getting drunk. Couples were doing things that should only be done behind closed doors. It was a free-for-all. We had to step through the crowds to get to the water. The steps that

Ginnie Springs designated for use by divers were also being used by non-divers. They either didn't care about the signs or didn't know how to read. I suspected it was a little of both.

The cave divers weren't much better. During one of our dives, while we were reeling the line back out, a diver climbed over us as he pulled his way into the cave. He grabbed our tank valves and used them to pull himself past us. There didn't seem to be any consideration or etiquette among the people there that weekend. Our weekday experiences had been much better.

When we returned to Ginnie Springs after lunch, we decided to dive in our wetsuits. It was hot and humid, and we couldn't bear the thought of putting our drysuits back on. We had to cool off. While it was nice in the water, we were miserable on the surface. The water temperature was seventy-two degrees Fahrenheit/twenty-two degrees Celsius. We could tolerate that in our seven-millimeter wetsuits.

We continued diving in our wetsuits over the next four days. It was a nice change. It not only kept us cool, but it allowed us to pee during the hour and a half long dives we were doing. They say there are two types of divers – those who pee in their wetsuits and those who lie about peeing in their wetsuits. I'm one of the first type. I pee in my wetsuits, and I proudly admit it. There's no shame in it. I stay well hydrated, and when I have to go, I have to go!

We were excited about the first day of class. Not only were we ready to see more of the caves, but we were looking forward to swimming off of the main guideline for the first time and seeing some of the offshoot passages. We couldn't wait to venture into these new areas and see new things. We studied the map with our instructor and planned a dive to a room called the Bone Room, so named because bones were found there when it was discovered. To get to the Bone Room, we would go beyond the Keyhole restriction, to the Park Bench, a rock formation resembling one of those curved benches placed around large trees in parks. Just in case we didn't recognize the formation, we also knew that we had to stop at the first set of double arrows that we came across.

There's a system that's used in underwater caves to assist divers with navigation. Line arrows are placed on the guidelines to indicate offshoot passages. Typically, in Florida, if there are two line arrows placed about three inches apart, they indicate a more popular offshoot passage that's large enough to accommodate more than one team of divers. If there is only one line arrow, and it's not one of the hundred-foot distance markers, that indicates a less popular offshoot passage. It may also mean that the offshoot passage is only large enough for one team at a time. There are also unmarked offshoot passages that you just have to know where they are located.

We arrived at the Park Bench. I knew we were there before I saw the double line arrows. The formation was appropriately named. It was unmistakable. I even thought about taking a seat on it. I didn't. We try to avoid making contact with the cave. I secured the line from one of my jump spools between the line arrows and swam around the Park Bench toward the white line behind it. This line would lead us to the Bone Room. When I secured the other end of the line on my jump spool to the permanent white line, I placed one of my personalized non-directional markers onto the line from my spool.

Cave divers use both directional line markers, or line arrows, and non-directional line markers, or line cookies. The arrows are used whenever we transition from one line to another where there isn't a permanent system marker already in place. The cookies are used to indicate that we are still in the cave as well as to tell us which way we came from when more than one navigational option exists. In this case, it was letting others know I placed the jump spool line there and I was still in the cave, so the jump spool should not be removed.

Why not permanently connect the white line in the cave to the gold line? Why should we have to carry spools of line with us to bridge these intentional gaps? Most popular caves do not have line intersections during the first several hundred feet, sometimes thousands of feet, in the main passage. We do this out of courtesy. Introductory cave divers cannot make navigational decisions and are limited to following the main guideline in and out of the cave. A line intersection creates a navigational decision. If there were intersections in the first several hundred feet of the caves, introductory cave divers would have to turn around when they encountered one. In some caves, that would mean stopping and turning around only a few hundred feet from the opening.

Fully trained cave divers are taught to deal with the gaps between lines. We carry Delrin or stainless-steel spools that hold between fifty to one hundred feet of line. We use the line on those spools to close the gaps. This provides us with a continuous guideline to the opening of the cave. If the passage gets silted and we have to make contact with the line, we can follow it all the way out to the surface using the arrows and cookies to direct us.

The number one rule in cave diving is to always have a continuous guideline from your location to the surface. The lines in the caves aren't there to follow in, although they are used for that purpose. The more important reason for the lines is having something we can follow out of the cave regardless of whether or not we have good visibility. If we have good visibility, we simply follow the lines out, referencing our line markers. The arrows and cookies are more important at the intersections than anywhere else. They indicate the way out of the cave.

If the visibility is not good, we make a circle around the line with our thumbs and forefingers and use it to guide ourselves out. If we encounter an intersection, we feel which way the arrows are pointing. They are always pointing to the closest opening. We also place cookies on the exit side of the intersections because they provide confirmation that we came from that direction and are heading the right way.

In good visibility, the guidelines should only be a reference. We must learn the cave by sight. Cave divers should become familiar enough with the caves they dive that the guidelines are only there in the event that we lose visibility. It should be no different than driving through your own neighborhood. You don't need a map program to drive from your house to the supermarket. You shouldn't need guidelines to swim into and out of a cave as long as you have good visibility. They are there because visibility is never guaranteed.

Once I secured the line from my jump spool to the permanent guideline, I signaled Jen and Jack that they could follow me. Jack had joined us for this class as well. We swam through a smaller tunnel and followed the new line. We passed more line arrows and saw other lines to our left leading off to unknown places. Several minutes later, we arrived in the Bone Room and turned the dive. I didn't get to see the bones. I was too focused on the training.

That was when the games began. At this level of cave diving training, we were doing drills during most of the exit from the cave. We did out of air drills, lost line drills, lost diver drills, and more. We spent an hour and a half in the cave on this dive, including a nine-minute decompression stop in the Devil's Ear holding onto the log that had fallen into the opening and wedged itself conveniently at twenty feet of depth, the depth where most decompression stops were done. We held onto that log for dear life against the current ripping past us from inside of the cave. We felt like flags in the wind. We completed our decompression obligation and used the walls of the opening to slowly ease our way to the surface.

We returned to Devil's Ear after lunch for our second dive. We had to bring three spools because we were planning on completing three jumps. This is what we call the gaps between the guidelines. The first jump was from the main guideline to a white line in an offshoot passage. The other two were at gaps between white guidelines. These were the lines I had seen during the morning dive.

We didn't even make it to the first jump. I blamed it on our tanks being short-filled. It was more likely a higher breathing rate due to the anticipation of what was to come once we turned around and began our exit. During our morning dive, we had gotten a taste of what the exits were going to be like during this final class of our cave diving training. That resulted in increased anxiety levels. I swam through the cave dreading what was to come once we turned around. Each time I saw the turn pressure on my gauge, or Jen signaled to turn around, I felt my heart begin to race.

The anticipation was well justified. We turned the dive and the drills began immediately. As soon as we turned, our instructor took off into a rabbit hole and disappeared. I hadn't noticed the hole in the wall during our penetration into the cave. Our instructor was part of the team for this dive, so we had to search for him while figuring out how much of that one third of emergency air we could use. It wasn't all available for the search. We had to save some for other issues.

As we searched for our instructor, the sneaky bastard appeared behind us. The small tunnel he had disappeared into brought him through a loop that came out of another hole that was located behind us. We turned and Jen tried to lead him back to the guideline. He took off again. I dropped the safety reel I had deployed and swam in the direction they had gone. When I found them, he took off a third time! At that point, we should have left him in the cave and exited on our own. It would have been a much less stressful exit. We didn't. We were gluttons for punishment.

Eventually, our instructor returned. The lost diver drill was over. However, the training wasn't. He signaled out of air, and I donated my regulator to him. We exited through the Lips while sharing air. This was no easy task. The Lips do not have much clearance, especially for divers in backmounted tank configurations. Add to that the increase in the intensity of the current because of the smaller passage. It was challenging to remain together during our exit. We made it through the Lips, the drill ended, and it was time for a lost line drill.

I was given a blacked-out mask, moved off of the guideline, and tasked with finding it again. Sounds simple, but it wasn't. The current was not my friend. The last opening to the catacombs was nearby. I ended up swimming into the Catacombs. This drill taught me that I should never lose reference to the guideline. I should also never get so far from it that I would have difficulty returning to it should I lose visibility. That was the point of the lesson. We finally surfaced, exhausted. We passed out in bed by nine that evening.

We returned to Peacock Springs State Park the next morning, thankful we wouldn't have the strong current of Devil's Spring to contend with. We swam into the Olsen Tunnel of Peacock I for our first dive, making it to the eight-hundred-foot marker where we installed a jump line to the left and continued until reaching turn pressure. On the way out, our instructor showed us a piece of paper with the words "You lost a fin, remove one fin and swim out."

We had not practiced this! I didn't know if I could swim with only one fin. How would it be possible? I envisioned us moving around the cave in circles. At least the room we were in was large enough for that. We each removed one fin and slowly began swimming. Surprisingly, we were able to swim in a straight line and made decent progress. It wasn't quite as difficult as I expected it to be. It was a good lesson, and one that would come back to me several years later during a dive in one of the Cozumel caves. I didn't lose a fin, not permanently anyway. I did lose the spring strap that held the fin onto my foot. Fortunately, I didn't have to go very far on that dive because I came up with a solution for the missing strap that allowed me to use the fin again.

About one hundred feet later, we were told to replace our fins and continue our exit. A short time afterwards, my instructor pulled me into an alcove and signaled me to cover my light and hold my position. After a few seconds, Jen and Jack eventually noticed that I was missing and began the procedure for a lost diver drill.

This was one of the best times during training for me. I enjoyed hiding and watching them search. I enjoyed the sneakiness of what I was doing. This may have been the moment I started to consider becoming a cave diving instructor. I wanted to play hide and seek with my students. Jen and Jack found me and another drill began almost immediately. We did an out of air drill followed by a simulated zero visibility exit. Our instructor turned our lights off and we swam in the darkness while sharing air. I was beginning to think all of our cave exits were going to be in zero visibility.

After lunch, we went to the Orange Grove sinkhole for what was mostly a leisure dive. We swam to the midpoint arrows located nine hundred feet from the opening, putting us equidistant from the Orange Grove sinkhole and Challenge Sink, another sinkhole in the Peacock Springs cave system. Challenge was so named because it is not easy to get into or out of. It can be done, but it is a challenge to do because of its steep bank.

As we swam along, I noticed Jen's position in the water placed her feet much lower than her head. One of the things we had to do was remain horizontal in the water. We had to keep our feet up so that we didn't disturb the sediment on the floor. Jen wasn't disturbing the sediment, but I knew our instructor was a stickler for proper positioning. He had already spoken to Jen about it during our previous class. She had improved but seemed to be having a relapse. I wasn't sure if she was aware of her position, so I swam ahead to signal her to pick up her feet. Jen gave me the universal one finger salute. Apparently, she was aware and was having trouble keeping her feet up. I backed off. I knew when to stay quiet. I later found out that our instructor had witnessed the interaction and found it quite amusing.

We continued beyond the opposing arrows after placing cookies on our exit side to mark the direction we had come from. Even though we knew the way out, in moments of duress it was easy to get confused. In zero visibility, it would be even easier. A short distance later, we arrived at a set of double arrows, set a jump line to the white line in the offshoot tunnel, and swam along it until it was time to turn around. That was when I tensed up in anticipation of more drills. We didn't do any. Instead, we had a leisurely swim out. I felt like our instructor was trying to get us to lower our guard. It wasn't going to work.

We were officially done with the first half of the cave diving course. We were only four dives from being certified as full-fledged cave divers. Jen and I also received news that evening that we could close on our new house. That was exciting! We would have the keys before leaving Florida. We extended our stay for one day so we could spend our first night in the house before heading back to Arizona!

8

WWF takes the show underwater

We met at Ginnie Springs the next day, and the first dive was a major clusterfuck. There's no other way to put it. We planned to do three jumps during that dive. We barely made it to the first jump before turning around. It wasn't Jen that was turning the dives early this time. Jack hadn't developed his girly lungs yet. When we turned, Jen and I were directed to share air. Our dive lights were turned off and we began to exit in the dark once again. We made it to the Keyhole restriction but not through it. We were single file but still having difficulty finding the correct position so that we would fit.

Things got worse. There was confusion over the line and the restriction. This area was much smaller than the opposite side of the Keyhole. There were four of us squeezed into a closet-sized space, in the dark, trying to figure out what was going on. We weren't making forward progress, and our air was quickly dwindling away. The situation felt more urgent than ever.

Jen finally had enough and turned on her light. It was taking far too long for her liking, and she was over it. She didn't care what the instructor thought. She was ready to see again and to figure out how to get out of the situation we were in. With visibility restored, we made it through the Keyhole and another diver appeared behind us trying to exit. This only added to the confusion we were already having. I tried to get out of the way. Jen, who was in front of me, misinterpreted my signal and started coming back toward me, cutting the diver off. Jack never saw the diver and blocked his way out.

Did I mention this dive was a clusterfuck?

We finally got out of the diver's way and let him pass. Our instructor cut the drill. He might have tried to cut it sooner, but we hadn't noticed. We were too busy being idiots. We started swimming toward the exit expecting more drills through the Gallery. They never came. When we surfaced, our instructor didn't debrief the dive. He swam to the steps, exited the water, and headed to his van. He was pissed. We had fucked up. If our instructor hadn't been there with us, there could have been multiple fatalities. This was when we realized just how serious cave diving was. It was a wakeup call.

We looked at each other, embarrassed and ashamed. We knew we had performed poorly. I wondered whether we would be allowed to continue the class or if that was it. Had we performed so badly that our instructor was done with us? Was he going to tell us we had failed and that we should pursue less demanding activities? We didn't know. He was nowhere to be found. Fortunately, his van hadn't moved.

After lunch, our instructor was finally calm enough to talk to us. He spoke in a hushed tone, forcing us to get closer to hear him. He explained what we had done wrong. We all nodded our heads. We weren't going to argue or make excuses. We knew we had screwed up. The important thing was that we had learned something from that dive and would not repeat the same potentially deadly mistakes.

After our come to Jesus talk, we quietly entered the water for another dive, this time through the Devil's Eye. This dive went much better...kind of. We swam to the Park Bench and deployed a jump spool line to the Bone Room guideline. We turned the dive shortly after that. Jack had an instructor-caused light failure and deployed one of his backup lights. He left his jump spool behind, which our instructor promptly retrieved. It wasn't a failing point, but we later learned that a light failure was not severe enough to require leaving spools and reels inside of the cave. It only meant we needed to end the dive and turn around.

As we continued our exit, our instructor began acting disoriented and confused. This is where the fun really began. Jen took the spool he was holding away from him while I grabbed his other arm and pulled him toward the guideline. He dropped his primary dive light. Fortunately, in those days, we used lights with separate light heads and battery canisters and a cable connecting the two. The light head didn't hit the floor. It dangled below him. I grabbed his arm again, and he pulled away. He resisted. I had flashbacks to shifts in the ER during which I had to struggle with combative patients.

I tried to think of a way to get the situation under control and had an idea. I took the regulator out of my mouth and signaled that I was out of air. It worked! My instructor gave me his regulator to breathe from. However, instead of grabbing his backup regulator and breathing from it, he grabbed my backup regulator and put it in his mouth. This was the regulator that was connected to my scuba tank with a short hose and hanging from a bungee necklace around my neck. The hose was very short. We were face to face, inches from each other, and unable to move farther apart because of it. I had flashbacks to the previous dive debriefing with his face inches from mine. There was no way we would be able to turn and get side by side to swim out of the cave. I gave up and handed him his regulator. My plan had been foiled.

Our instructor continued to behave disoriented and confused and started to swim *into* the cave. Jen and I had both worked many years in emergency departments and had wrestled many disoriented patients and restrained them to gurneys. We each took an arm and directed our instructor to the floor of the cave just in front of the Lips. Fortunately, the floor in this area was composed of hard limestone and small pieces of gravel and didn't have a silty layer. Small sediment that could disturb and affect the visibility was absent. There was nothing to damage.

We pinned our instructor to the floor, one of us on each side, as he fought to get free. Jack hovered above us watching the fun. I glanced up, expecting him to descend next to us so he could slap the floor with his open palm. After a countdown to ten, Jen and I would be declared winners of this cave diving wrestling match. I was disappointed that Jack didn't descend and count off. He remained above us watching the fun.

Our instructor finally managed to raise his hand above his head and make a cutting motion with his index and middle fingers. He was ending the drill. I was suspicious of his true intentions. I wasn't sure if he was really cutting the drill or if we were in for more hijinks. Apparently, he had learned his lesson. The drill was really over. Jen and I had proven that we would do almost anything to save our dive buddy.

When we surfaced, our instructor asked us why we tried so hard to get him under control. He told us we put our lives at risk by not letting him go. We should have exited the cave and left him behind. One fatality was always preferrable to two or three. We told him that we knew we were only four hundred feet from the opening, and we had plenty of air in our scuba tanks. We had checked our pressure gauges several times and were nowhere near being at risk. If the situation continued, we would have left him to his own devices. But as long as we had air to spare, we were going to do everything we could to get him out of the cave. He acquiesced. I think he learned more of a lesson than we did that time. Don't fuck with ER nurses.

The next day we returned to Peacock Springs State Park to dive Peacock III. The water flowed into the cave at Peacock III rather than out of it, making it a siphon. The current wasn't strong, but it did require us to adjust our turn pressure to account for it. We subtracted two hundred psi from penetration allowance to make up for the siphon.

Jack set the primary reel into the cave and had difficulty finding the gold line. To give him credit, it wasn't easy to find. Peacock III was a dark, spooky-looking cave. The visibility was hazy, the walls were dark, and the gold line was stained dark brown. Light beams seemed to get sucked into a void. When Jack finally found the guideline and secured the primary reel line to it, we continued into the hazy black cave. We made it to the first jump and all three of us practiced deploying our jump spools. During our practice session, Jen was directed to signal me that she was out of air. I dropped my jump spool and donated my regulator. We began to share air, and our lights were turned off once again, forcing us to exit with no visibility. The drill didn't last long, and I retrieved my jump spool before starting our swim out.

When we reached the beginning of the gold line, the primary reel was gone. It was missing. Nowhere to be found. We no longer had a continuous guideline to the surface. The worst part was that we also couldn't see any daylight. I had no idea how our instructor had relocated the primary reel line. I could have sworn he was with us the entire time.

Jen saved the day and grabbed one of her safety spools. She secured it to the gold line and swam away looking for daylight. She found it a minute later. We only had to swim about fifty feet before the opening appeared before us. Somehow the primary reel reappeared when the drill was cut. Again, I had missed our instructor retrieving it from wherever he had hidden it. There was some ninja sorcery happening.

We packed up and drove to Little River cave in Branford for our final dive of the class. The good news was that we were about to see another new cave! The bad news was that this cave had a strong current. The plan was to enter the cave, pull ourselves to the first set of double arrows, jump to the Mud Tunnel line, and continue through the Mud Tunnel. I didn't like the sound of it. Why would someone name a tunnel after mud?

The dive went as planned. We must have been getting better. Either that, or our instructor was adapting the plans to our level. Probably the latter. The Mud Tunnel was a small, low passage with a thick layer of sediment on the floor. It would be easy to stir up the sediment and destroy the visibility. We didn't do that though. Our skills were improving. My primary light was turned off immediately after turning around. I deployed my backup light and took the first position on exit. Then Jen's light went out. We got back to the jump where Jen and I crossed to the main guideline to wait for Jack to retrieve the jump spool. As we were waiting for him to finish, we were surprised with a big silt

66

cloud moving through the passage toward us. I looked down at the sandy floor below me. There was no disturbance. I wondered if we had disturbed the sediment in the Mud Tunnel, after all.

It turned out our instructor had waved his hand just above the sandy floor to show us what it would look like to be in a real silt out. There was no damage to the floor, and the diminished visibility didn't last long. The current in the cave carried the silt out and restored the visibility in less than a minute. Little did our instructor know that we had already experienced a silt-out in the Catacombs during our previous trip. I had also experienced a silt-out in that shallow horizontal crack in Orange Grove Sink. Neither of those had cleared up so quickly. We exited the cave as fully certified cave divers. The long journey was finally over. Well, sort of.

The next day we returned to Peacock Springs State Park to complete our Decompression Procedures course. We had one more dive and that class would be complete. We were diving Lower Orange Grove cave, the third and deepest opening in Orange Grove Sink. It was surrounded by several fallen boulders and well hidden, making it rather difficult to find. Fortunately, our instructor knew the way. It was a single file entry shaped like a corkscrew. At the other end was a dark, hazy cave about one hundred and thirty feet deep.

Our instructor ran the primary line as we followed him into the cave. We penetrated about thirty feet before Jack signaled us to turn. He was feeling the effects of nitrogen narcosis. Jen and I also felt it, but not enough to turn around. We had both done a dive to one hundred and forty feet of depth in the famous Belize Blue Hole. Conditions in the Blue Hole were similar to the conditions we were experiencing, minus the corkscrew entrance. We exited without any issues and were done with training.

We finished early enough to do another dive that day, but Jen and I were exhausted. It had been a long week, and we needed a long surface interval to recuperate. We also had to get back to Marianna to sign the closing contract on the purchase of our new house.

9

A hole in the wall

We arrived in Marianna the next day and finalized the house purchase. We had an inflatable mattress in our van and decided to extend our stay for two nights. We not only wanted to become familiar with the house, but we also wanted to do a couple of dives in the caves of Jackson County. The next day we headed to Hole in the Wall to do our first dive there and our first dive as certified cave divers.

The opening to Hole in the Wall is on the east bank of Merritt's Mill Pond. At the time, there was a very small dock that had been built by cave divers many years earlier. It was just big enough for three people to stand on, if the three knew each other well. It was a tight squeeze for two people to gear up. It was shaped like a pizza slice with the wide end measuring about three feet across. The dock has since been rebuilt and made much larger.

Hole in the Wall is a somewhat unique cave with two major branches. There is another cave in Jackson County with similar attributes. That's a story for a later book in this series where I tell you about that exploration project. When standing on the dock in front of the cave, a small opening is visible on the wall above the surface. Directly below that is a much larger opening that leads into the hidden river. I had to check out the dry opening before we began our dive.

We nudged up to the bank in the pontoon and I hopped onto the steep slope, careful not to slide into the water only a few feet below. Just as my feet hit the dirt, a bat came flying out. I ducked and waited for more bats to exit. None did. I climbed the bank until I was on the small ledge in front of the opening. It was just an alcove. It couldn't even be called a cave. It extended about three feet in and a foot or two on each side. I was disappointed that it didn't lead anywhere.

I returned to the boat, and we tied it to the dock. We geared up and began our dive. The first room in Hole in the Wall is the smallest underwater cavern of the three main caves on the Mill Pond. The back wall is about twenty feet in and the side walls are about thirty-five feet apart. At the bottom of the back wall, about twenty feet deep, is a restriction leading to a narrow tunnel that extends forty feet beyond the cavern. At the end of the tunnel is a room where the floor drops away into a large oval-shaped chimney. We were about forty feet deep and looking down into a dark abyss. The visibility was a bit hazy and sucked our light beams into a void, so we couldn't see the floor of the chimney. We swam beyond the edge and began our descent.

We arrived at the bottom of the chimney, forty-five feet deeper, and saw a dark opening in the left rear corner. There was another dark opening almost directly across from that to our right rear. I had studied a map of the cave and knew there were two tunnels. According to the map, the passage in front of us led to the downstream tunnel and the one behind us to the upstream tunnel. I turned and went toward the upstream opening.

I slowly swam into the tunnel while looking for the permanent guideline. When I was about ten feet in, I saw a rear wall twenty feet away. I continued searching for an opening but found none. No opening and no guideline. I was in another alcove, one that wasn't depicted on the map. I turned around and backtracked to the chimney where Jen was waiting. Looking at its relation to the other opening, it looked like it had been created by the water flowing out of the downstream side. At one point, the current must have been much stronger.

We noticed the current as we swam through the small tunnel at the top of the chimney, but it seemed nonexistent once we were above the chimney. The current was there, but the room was large enough that it wasn't significant. Even the current in the small tunnel was nothing like Jackson Blue or Devil's Spring. It was just enough to be noticeable. While I was looking in the alcove, Jen found the beginning of one of the gold lines on the opposite wall, the one that was in front of us when we arrived at the floor. I followed her, secured our guideline to it, and we continued into the downstream passage.

The current in Hole in the Wall actually springs from both the upstream and downstream passages. Neither one is a siphon, so the names are misnomers. Both passages measure between fifteen to twenty-five feet from floor to ceiling and wall to wall. The water flowing out of both tunnels converges at the bottom of the chimney and out to the pond through the small forty-foot-long tunnel. The intensity of the current is not equally distributed.

While the passages are similar in size, there is a difference in the volume of water between them. The downstream side is made up of more tunnels and many of them are located beneath Merritt's Mill Pond. The upstream side contains about a mile of tunnels and less than a thousand feet of that is located beneath the pond. I believe there's also a connection on the downstream side to one of the other caves in Merritt's Mill Pond. That's also a story for another book in the series.

Knowing that the map depicted a downstream and an upstream side, I was more aware of the current and what it was doing. Just like when we went diving in Peacock III, I wanted to make appropriate adjustments to our air management plan if we were swimming into a siphon. Because we were going into the downstream passage first, an adjustment was necessary, so I signaled to Jen that we would shorten our penetration by two hundred psi.

We swam along the gold line, and I noted that the water flow was siphoning after all, although it wasn't a strong siphon. About three hundred feet in, things changed. The current was no longer heading into the cave. It felt like it was springing out. I stopped and held my position. The direction of the flow had reversed. Again, it wasn't a strong current, but it was definitely moving against us rather than with us. Both passages are springs with the water flowing out. However, because the passages converge at the chimney and only have a small tunnel to continue out to the pond, one side overpowers the other. That explained the designations of upstream and downstream. The upstream flow overpowered the downstream flow, and near the chimney it felt like the downstream side was siphoning.

I signaled to Jen, asking if she also detected the change in direction of the current. We decided to stick with our original turn pressure. We would have only added back one hundred psi anyway. We continued our swim into the cave, in awe of the beauty surrounding us. Diving in Hole in the Wall cave reaffirmed our decision to purchase a house in Jackson County. It was absolutely amazing.

Jen and I turned around sixteen hundred feet in and began to exit. We swam slowly, taking in as much as we could. There was so much to see that it was overwhelming. We only noticed the most obvious formations, such as the Big E located seven hundred feet from the opening. The limestone had three arms stretching out from the wall resembling the letter E. This formation was about five feet tall and four feet wide and couldn't be missed. At the time, the gold line was wrapped around the middle arm of the E. The formation was also noted on the map, so I was looking for it.

The seven hundred feet of passage between the chimney and the Big E was made up of several chambers about forty to fifty feet in diameter, separated by large arches. Another notable formation we noticed only existed on the ceiling of three of the chambers between the two hundred- and four-hundred-foot distance markers. There were large, dark brown formations that extended down from the ceiling and spread out with the appearance of exotic mushrooms. I ascended to take a closer look, careful not to touch them. They were very thin and appeared fragile. I later found out that they are composed of goethite, an iron-bearing material that is the main component of rust. That made sense. The color of the formations had a close resemblance to rust.

Jen and I couldn't stop talking about the cave once we surfaced. It was so beautiful. It became our favorite cave. We looked forward to doing more dives in it when we returned to Florida. I was tempted to do our second dive of the day there, but I wanted to see Twin again, so we headed up the pond and prepared for a second dive. Jen and I swam along the Subway Tunnel until we reached turn pressure. We didn't get far. Apparently, the long month of diving was catching up with us. We were tired and breathing faster than we normally did. We barely made it beyond the eight-hundred-foot distance marker where we had turned around during a previous introductory cave dive. Yet, we had made it twice that distance just that morning in Hole in the Wall, which is about twenty feet deeper. On the swim out, I saw a cozy space on the floor near the wall on the right. It wasn't much different than any other spot in the cave, but I was so tired that I was ready to curl up and take a nap in that spot. I was worn out. We had pushed it a little too hard.

Before we made it out, we encountered our first albino salamander less than one hundred feet from the beginning of the gold line. Albino salamanders are tiny creatures, measuring between one and three centimeters in length. They are troglobites, meaning they live in complete darkness, they are a translucent white, and they are blind. Because their world is always without light, except when annoying cave divers swim through their homes, they don't need sight. The species we saw is only found in the underwater caves of Florida and Georgia. In fact, they're called the Georgia Blind Salamander. It was exciting to have seen one and was the perfect way to end the last dive of our trip.

10

Settling into house and cave

The next two months were difficult. No, they were torture! We wanted to be in Florida full time and cave diving every day. Okay, maybe every other day would have been more reasonable. We had to fund it somehow. And no one was going to pay me to cave dive. Or were they? Concentrating on daily life knowing we had a house in Jackson County only ten minutes from some of the most beautiful caves in Florida was tormenting. We longed to be diving in the hidden rivers deep inside the Earth.

We finally left Arizona and pulled into our new driveway about an hour before midnight three days later. We walked the dogs, letting them explore the new scents in their strange new world. We were anxious to head into the springs to explore our own new world. As much as we wanted to venture into the hidden rivers the next day, it wasn't happening. The effects of the long drive were taking a toll on us. The excitement of the road trip had worn off somewhere on the long stretch of highway between El Paso and Fort Worth. We opted to stay dry and get settled into the new house, but only for one day.

Somewhat recuperated and anxious to go cave diving, we left the house the following day to dive Jackson Blue. It felt good to be back in the clear water of a dark cave. This was our first post training dive in Jackson Blue. Prior to this, the dives we had done there had been as intro cave divers. Sadly, anyone who saw us that day would have thought we were intro divers. We only made it to the six-hundred-foot line marker, just a little farther than we had on the previous dive in Jackson Blue when we were diving intro cave limits. It was certainly not twice the distance that we expected, being that we could breathe twice the amount of air.

I thought back to the last dive Jen and I had done in Twin. We could blame that on being the final of fifty dives in a month of diving. I would have liked to blame the current in Jackson Blue on our lack of improvement, but it wasn't much stronger than it had been. The problem was me. I was excited and pulling and swimming faster than I should have been. Jen signaled me repeatedly to slow down because I was outpacing her. Each time, I stopped and turned around to rejoin her, slowing our progress. We would have made it a lot farther if I had paced myself better and stayed with Jen. I was still new at cave diving and the excitement had me in overdrive. I would eventually learn that going slower meant going farther.

We managed an hour and twelve-minute dive despite only penetrating six hundred feet. Fifteen minutes of that was spent in the Deco Room on a decompression stop. As I write this, I wonder what we did over that hour of swimming to only get six hundred feet into the cave and how we had accumulated such a long decompression obligation from such a short dive. That was twenty years ago. I barely remember what I did last week. I probably spent a lot of time poking around exploring the various branches of the river.

The next day, we returned to Jackson Blue for a late afternoon dive. It went much better than the previous one. We were becoming familiar with the cave, and I was learning to slow down. We made it to the first line intersection located nine hundred feet from the opening, arriving at a fork in this underground river. The tunnel split into two. We could go to the right or to the left.

The passage to the right had a low ceiling and minimal sediment on the floor. The passage to the left was much bigger, but the floors were covered by a thick layer of mud. It looked like there was plenty of room to swim high above the floor, but there didn't appear to be anywhere to pull against the current. We would have to use our legs to propel ourselves farther into the cave. Not only that, but the passage to the left also appeared darker and less inviting. It was spooky. In contrast, the right side looked brighter and more appealing. It was almost inviting us in, so we accepted. One hundred feet later, we turned around.

During the exit, I explored the main passage. We took our time and looked into every hole. We poked our heads into each nook and cranny we could find. That became our norm. We swam in at a leisurely pace, giving us time to explore the cave on the way out. We didn't linger. We had to closely monitor the air pressure in our scuba tanks so as not to dip into our reserves, but we took our time.

I noted a few jump lines leading into offshoot branches. We had yet to navigate away from the main passage. While we were trained to make navigational decisions, we believed in progressive penetration. We wanted to become familiar with the main passage before leaving it. I still do that more than twenty years later.

On our third day, we returned to Jackson Blue even later than the day before, not leaving until after dinner. We had to be a little responsible and get the house in order. We couldn't cave dive every day all day long…as much as we would have liked to. Jen and I decided we would venture out of the main passage this time. We had been too focused on penetration distance, or at least I had been. It was time to change that focus and learn the entire cave.

We explored a portion of each offshoot tunnel from the large room at the bottom of the chimney fissure. There were three of them – Young's Siphon, the Squirrel Passage, and the Horseshoe Circuit. Young's Siphon was the most obvious one, so we went there first. We set the jump line between the gold and white lines and continued into it. About fifty feet in, we saw another guideline to our left heading into a bedding plane. I noted it for future exploration. We continued along the Young's Siphon guideline and the passage started to get smaller.

The floor and ceiling sloped together, presenting us with a restriction about two-thirds of the way in where we had to slide through the sand.

Fortunately, the silt we disturbed was comprised mostly of large sand granules that quickly settled to the floor. It was a short restriction allowing Jen to see through to the other side, so she continued as well. A short distance later we arrived at the end of the line. On the map it appeared that the passage led back to the Rock Garden room, the second room in the cave where the beginning of the gold line was located. It was so named because there were huge rocks scattered all over it. By huge, I mean car size. I didn't realize it at the time, but those rocks had once been attached to the ceiling. They had fallen to the floor at some point, hopefully centuries earlier.

We returned to the main line and moved the jump spool line from the Young Siphon guideline to the Squirrel Passage guideline which was tied to the ceiling on the opposite side of the room. This earned its name because of its small size. It's also the location of an incident involving an instructor and his students that occurred a few years later.

* * *

This is the story as I heard about the incident shortly after it occurred. The instructor was from out of state and only visited Florida when he had cave diving students. He hadn't done a lot of dives in the caves of the area outside of teaching, so he wasn't very familiar with them. He took his students into Jackson Blue with the intent to dive the Horseshoe Circuit, the third offshoot from the large room.

The students weren't familiar with the cave and the instructor couldn't remember the exact location of the offshoot tunnel. The opening is tucked into a corner that can be more easily seen while swimming out, but even then, it's not obvious. They arrived in the large room and swam past the Horseshoe Circuit tunnel. The students placed a jump line from the main line to the Squirrel Passage line instead. Everyone, the instructor included, thought they were about to head into the Horseshoe Circuit.

Because the Squirrel Passage was a small tunnel, it's not one that should be used for the beginner levels of cave diving training. It requires single file penetration and gets too small to properly supervise students. The students didn't know this and pushed on with the instructor following them. The students got stuck in a restriction about halfway through the tunnel where the ceiling dipped. They had difficulty passing through it in their backmounted double scuba tanks.

They persisted and managed to squeeze through the restriction. There was a thick layer of sediment covering the floor and they burrowed into it. This allowed them to continue but also destroyed the visibility in the passage. The instructor was not able to follow them. He not only couldn't see anything, but he was diving with backmounted scuba tanks as well. He was also bigger than his students and couldn't fit through the restriction. The sediment on the floor wasn't thick enough to allow him to pass.

The instructor turned around and exited. Had he been familiar with the cave, he would have known he could have turned left at the gold line and met his students at the other end of the Squirrel Passage line just beyond the first breakdown. The tunnel looped back into the main passage just before the six-hundred-foot line marker. Unfortunately, he wasn't familiar enough with the cave and rushed out in a panic.

There happened to be another cave diver at the park getting ready to do his own dive. He quickly geared up and went into the cave to look for the lost students. He saw the jump spool leading from the gold line to the Squirrel Passage line and, being familiar with the cave, swam past that to the first breakdown and the other end of the line. He found the students crossing the main passage with their safety spools in hand. They had reached the end of the Squirrel Passage line, thought they were in the middle of a lost buddy drill, and began searching for their instructor.

One of my friends was diving Jackson Blue that day and saw the safety spools that belonged to the students laying on the floor of the cave about ten feet from the gold line with the lines on them leading back to the Squirrel Passage. The spools had been dropped by the students and left behind when they were told to exit. My friend later encountered the students and heard the story of the dive from them. The students were clueless as to what had happened in the cave. They thought they were in the middle of a drill and didn't know there was an issue until they surfaced from the dive.

The Squirrel Passage became known as the Lost Student Tunnel after this incident. I prefer to call it the Lost Instructor Tunnel because the students were never lost. They didn't know they were in the wrong place and that they had gone the wrong way. They didn't even know that their instructor had exited the cave. I used this incident in my thriller *Into the Darkness Beyond*. Sometimes reality is better than fiction.

* * *

After installing the jump spool line to the Squirrel Passage, Jen and I ventured in. We got as far as the restriction where the instructor couldn't fit. Our backmounted doubles wouldn't allow us to fit without forcing our way through. This happened several years before the incident described above, and the path hadn't been carved out at that time. Sure, we could have dug a trench in the sediment like the students, but we knew better and that wasn't our style. This isn't meant to disparage the students that did this. They didn't know any better.

We exited the Squirrel Passage and found the line leading into the Horseshoe Circuit. It was about twenty feet away from the chimney fissure, tucked behind a ceiling dip. It wasn't obvious and we wouldn't have known it was there if I hadn't studied the map and known where to look. I headed into the circuit while Jen hung back. She's a bit claustrophobic and doesn't like diving in small passages. She had enough from the previous two tunnels we explored, and this passage didn't allow her to see what was on the other side. The Horseshoe Circuit isn't that small, but it was beyond her comfort level at that point. After the first part of the tunnel, the ceiling slopes down so there's not much clearance when diving with backmounted scuba tanks. She would eventually build up the courage to venture into it.

I followed the passage for about a hundred feet before turning around. I didn't want to get too far from Jen. I could also feel the water current pushing me farther into the Horseshoe Circuit. I realized I was in a siphon. It was odd because Young's Siphon didn't feel like it was siphoning, but the Horseshoe Circuit definitely did. I wondered if the names had been swapped on the map. I turned around and faced into the current before I lost sight of Jen's dive light.

The next day we returned to Jackson Blue even later than we had the day before for our final dive of the trip. We had seen quite a bit of the offshoot tunnels in the first part of the cave and decided to stick to the main passage this time. We made it beyond the line intersection and two hundred feet later found that the gold lines rejoined. The first and second intersections formed a line circuit. We swam past the second line intersection another hundred feet before turning around. This dive went much better than the previous dives. I slowed my pace and remained close to Jen. We both felt better about our buoyancy and trim and our breathing rates were improving. We were finally relaxed. Of course, that would happen on our last dive of the trip.

We turned around and took our time on the exit, exploring as much of the cave as we could. We found more offshoot tunnels to explore during our next trip to Florida. I even found the other end of the Horseshoe Circuit line. Our dives for the trip were completed, but we already had plans in place to return four months later. We were in for a bit of a surprise on that next trip.

11

Hold my beer; I'm gonna use this redneck master key

We returned to Florida for another couple of weeks, arriving late at night on a Friday, as was our usual practice. The length of the drive meant we always pulled in around midnight. We contacted our neighbor before leaving Arizona to check on things and let her know we would be there at the end of the week. She told us she heard water running in the house and had contacted the town to turn it off. This happened less than a week before our arrival.

The water was indeed turned off when we got to the house. I went out to the main to turn it on so I could assess the issue. It was locked. The water had not only been turned off, but someone from town hall decided to place a padlock on it. The town hall didn't open until Monday, which meant we were facing a weekend with no water. We were too tired to deal with it after the long drive. We had water for the dogs to drink and for us to brush our teeth. Showers would have been nice, but they weren't happening.

We looked up the town hall website when we woke up the next morning but couldn't find an emergency contact number. The town hall was less than a mile away, so we drove to it hoping to find an off-hours number posted on the door. There was none. No number, no email, no way to contact anyone. We were left without water for the next forty-eight hours. That wasn't going to work. I had to figure out a way to turn the water on so I could fix the leak, and we could shower. We had four dogs with us and couldn't go to a hotel. Airbnb didn't exist at the time.

Jen and I drove to Lowes and bought a master key for the padlock that was on our water main valve. Some of you may know it better by its more common name – bolt cutters. I would deal with the repercussions Monday morning. We returned to the house, I cut the lock off, and we had water. The leak was simple to fix. One of the Pex connections had come loose. Another trip to Lowes to pick up plumbing supplies and within a couple of hours, we were showered and refreshed.

Two days later, we went to the town hall first thing in the morning to return their padlock. Although I was pretty sure they could no longer use it.

"We had to shut the water off," was their response.

"That doesn't mean you had to put a lock on it."

"That's what we normally do."

"Well, here's your lock. We couldn't wait until this morning to have water in our house again."

"We have to fine y'all $80 to replace the lock."

"This lock doesn't cost $80. I'm not paying the fine. You had no right to place a lock on my main. We've always paid the bill on time and have had no issues."

"Y'all should have contacted us so someone could come out with a key. I live right around the corner."

"We tried to contact you. You don't have an emergency number on the website or anywhere on this building. How am I supposed to know where you live?"

"Y'all should have asked your neighbor. She knows how to contact us."

"First, we arrived late at night. Then Saturday morning, our neighbor wasn't home. Besides, contacting a neighbor to get in touch with town hall isn't the way things should be done. Why didn't you call me to notify me when you turned off the water?"

"We did."

"What number did you call?"

They read me my mobile number. I pulled my phone out of my pocket and scrolled through my list of recent calls.

"When did you say you called me?"

"Last Monday."

I double checked. No history of a missed call.

"Well, this is the phone that you claim to have called and there's no record of a missed call. I also have voicemail on this phone, and I don't have any messages from you. You may claim you called me, but you did not, and I don't appreciate being lied to."

A look of panic flashed across their faces. I had caught them in their deceit.

"I'm not paying you $80. This lock doesn't even cost $20, which I'm also not paying. You locked my main without cause. You never contacted me. You didn't even try to. Then you lied to us about it."

They continued arguing with me. I finally had enough and turned to Jen. "I can't do this anymore. You speak southern. You talk to them."

This isn't meant to disparage southerners. Most southerners are kind and helpful. They go out of their way to help others. We've had mostly great interactions with people living in the panhandle. Unfortunately, the people of our town hall were none of the above. I was tired, frustrated, and done talking to them. They were testing my patience, and I decided to quit before I said something worse. They didn't understand that what they had done wasn't appropriate. I didn't know how to explain it any differently.

One thing that might help paint the picture better is that the town population was about six hundred people at the time. The people working in the town hall came off as if they liked to exert a bit of a power play over the residents, especially to people new to the town. We weren't going to play that game. They finally figured that out and waived the lock replacement fee that I already told them I wasn't paying. That was the one and only issue we had with those particular people. They decided it was best to leave us alone.

About a year after we moved to Florida, our neighbor confided in my wife and told her a secret. Apparently, there was a rumor going around the town, the folks at town hall included, that Jen and I were bank robbers or some other type of criminals. They came to this conclusion because we were from Tucson and there had been a rash of bank robberies in the city that year. We always arrived in the middle of the night, only stayed for about a week or so, and disappeared again for a few months. This led them to believe we were using the small town of Greenwood as a hideaway from the FBI. Quite an elaborate story!

After all that, we still live in the same town. We've had a couple of minor run-ins with different folks at the town hall over the years. This is usually after they change mayors and town clerks. Apparently, they don't keep a blacklist. Each new regime always quickly learned not to test us. They might still think we're big-time criminals hiding in plain sight in their little southern town. I'm okay with that as long as they treat me with respect.

With the town hall fiasco behind us, we turned our attention to diving. Most of the dives we had planned were focused on practice and training. We were new to cave diving and knew we had to maintain our skills. We also had Trimix dive training scheduled.

Trimix is a mixture of breathing gas that contains three gases - oxygen, nitrogen, and helium - thus the name. The deeper in the water that we go, the more affected we are by the nitrogen that's absorbed by our bodies. We begin to experience nitrogen narcosis, or what Jacques Cousteau called the Martini Effect. Every atmosphere of pressure, or thirty-three feet of depth, is the equivalent of drinking one Martini. In the South, we can equate that to one beer. Most people don't feel much different at thirty-three feet of depth. At sixty-six feet of depth, or two Martinis/beers, we experience a slowing of our reflexes and thinking processes. It's so subtle that most people don't realize it.

One of the tests I used to give my deep diving students was a simple math equation at seventy feet of depth. I used the equation twenty-five times four. Simple enough being that there are four quarters in a dollar. Every student I presented this equation with did the math long hand.

They wrote it out and carried the one, or actually the two. It took them several seconds to calculate the answer. I even had a few students that wrote the wrong number down. After the dive, I presented them with the equation again and they easily and quickly did it in their heads. They all claimed that they felt fine at depth. Had it not been for the math test, they would never have known they were affected.

By the time we get to ninety-nine feet of depth, or three Martinis/beers, many people begin to recognize the effects of nitrogen narcosis. The effect is significant enough that others can observe it. It's not severe, but it's definitely there. One hundred and thirty feet is the maximum depth allowed for recreational divers and is also the equivalent of four Martinis/beers. The effect is quite apparent at this depth. Most people shouldn't be diving that deep while breathing air. They do anyway despite judgment and response time being affected. Fortunately, time at that depth is limited because a scuba tank also doesn't hold enough air to remain there for long.

Jen and I have been affected by nitrogen narcosis. I didn't realize it was happening to me during my worst experience. Less than a year after we got certified as open water divers, we went on a trip to Ambergris Caye in Belize and had an opportunity to dive the Blue Hole. We knew that was more of a been-there-done-that dive, but the two dives scheduled for the same afternoon on the reef surrounding an uninhabited island made it well worth the three-hour boat ride each way.

We arrived at the Blue Hole and dropped into the water, prepared to descend to the small alcove located in the wall at one hundred and forty feet of depth. The dive operator actually planned the dive this way and one of the divemasters led the divers. The Blue Hole was dark with almost no sunlight penetrating the depths. By the time we were at one hundred feet, we had to turn on our dive lights. We continued deeper anyway. We arrived at the alcove, and I swam into it, following the line of divers in front of me. This was technically my first cave dive. It was also when I lost track of Jen. I didn't know where she was. I wasn't even thinking about her. All I was thinking about was being in a sea cave.

I exited the alcove and began my ascent. As I was getting shallower, I remembered I had been with Jen and began searching for her. There were so many divers in the water, it was hard to tell who was who, and I couldn't find her. There were three other boats, including a large liveaboard that had forty plus divers onboard, diving at the same time. I was surrounded by dozens of divers.

As I ascended, I wondered if Jen got such a bad case of nitrogen narcosis that she continued to descend into the dark void of the sinkhole. The bottom of the Blue Hole is more than four hundred feet deep. There was no way she could survive that. She didn't have enough air in her tank. I knew Jen was more prone to nitrogen narcosis than I was. She had experienced it at shallower depths during other dives. My concern for her safety grew. I contemplated stopping my ascent and descending to look for her. I didn't. Somehow, I knew that would be a bad idea. I knew that my chances of finding her at depth were minimal.

A strange euphoria took over. I had thoughts of surfacing with Jen nowhere to be found. I thought it would be really sad, but I wasn't panicking about it. It didn't overwhelm me. I just kept thinking about how sad I would be without her. I thought about how unhappy life without her would be.

About the time I reached eighty feet of depth, my mind cleared. I looked up and saw Jen directly above. I recognized her fins. She had been right above me the entire time. I just hadn't recognized her during my inebriated state of mind. I was diving under the influence. I was thankful I hadn't descended into the abyss to look for her. That would have been a very bad thing to do. I don't think the divemasters were keeping a close watch on the divers and no one would have stopped me. No one would have known until they did a head count on the boat.

I decided that it would always be better to dive without having that happen to me, and Trimix would make that possible. Helium prevents a large degree of narcosis. It takes up the space that would normally be occupied by nitrogen and fills it. Because narcosis is caused by nitrogen, reducing the amount of nitrogen in your scuba tank reduces the narcosis effect. If we add enough helium for it to take up thirty-five percent of the total gas in the scuba tank and we maintain the oxygen level at twenty-one percent, we're left with a forty-four percent nitrogen content. That's much better than the seventy-nine percent that's in normal breathing air. It makes a huge difference and allows us to dive much deeper without feeling that euphoric effect that almost caused me to descend back into the Blue Hole. Had I followed that instinct, I would have breathed through the air in my scuba tank and drowned.

Jen and I didn't need to dive deep caves or shipwrecks. There were plenty of shallow caves and wrecks around. However, we wanted the option available to us. There were cave passages deeper than one hundred and thirty feet that we wanted to visit. We wanted to one day be able to dive in Diepolder, the cave from the photograph that inspired us to pursue scuba diving training, and we wanted to dive these deep caves and wrecks safely and remember them.

12

The origin of the dive flag

We returned to Jackson Blue on our first day back in Florida. We practiced our skills in preparation for our upcoming Trimix diving class. It was time well spent as we needed to knock the rust off and get reacquainted with the caves. Once we completed that dive, we did a second one just to relax and enjoy the cave. The first day went much better than it had during our previous trip.

The next day we were back at Jackson Blue, this time to explore. We wanted to see the spooky looking passage to the left of the first intersection. We headed to the left at the intersection and made it about halfway to the second intersection before turning around. The passage wasn't so spooky after all. It was much larger than the one to the right and contained several large rock formations and silty mounds.

On our way out of the cave, we stopped to look at the other end of the line to the Squirrel Passage. We were still diving backmounted double tanks, so we only got as far as the restriction before we were forced to turn around. We had seen the entire length of the passage, but from opposite ends. The restriction remained unpenetrated by us.

Two days later, we returned to Peacock Springs State Park to begin our Trimix training. Peacock III, the dark cave that was a low flow siphon where we came back to a missing primary reel line, was the location of our first dive. The plan was to go to a place called Hendley's Castle, located about sixteen hundred feet from the opening. This was the deepest section of Peacock III, reaching depths greater than two hundred feet. We were going to descend to a room about one hundred and eighty feet deep and stop there. The passage beyond was small and silty and only suitable for one diver at a time. It was also deeper than the class standards allowed.

We didn't make it to one eighty. We didn't even get to the jump to Hendley's Castle. Our time away from Florida had not been good for us. Jen's leg began to cramp, and she signaled me to turn around. I was disappointed that we didn't get to experience Trimix at depth, but we did an hour-long dive and got to see some very beautiful cave. And our primary reel was where we had left it.

After lunch, we returned to Lower Orange Grove, the cave with the corkscrew opening where we had completed our final dive for our Decompression Procedures class. We breathed air during that first dive. I knew the nitrogen narcosis had affected me, but I didn't realize just how much until we visited it while breathing Trimix. This dive made it very apparent just how impaired I was on air. When we went into Lower Orange Grove while breathing air, the cave passage seemed small, narrow, and dark with hazy visibility. There were four of us in the cave, and I felt like we were crowded. We swam through the tunnel, and I felt like the walls were so close to us that we had to stay in a single file.

During our second dive in Lower Orange Grove, while breathing Trimix, the cave looked completely different. It was bigger, and the visibility was perfect. There were only three of us in the cave this time, but we had lots of space. We swam side by side with room to spare. I questioned whether we were in the same cave. I didn't think it could possibly be the same passage. We must have taken a wrong turn. Apparently, the narcosis during the previous dive had been bad.

When we turned around, our instructor signaled Jen that she was to simulate being out of air. She signaled me and I donated my regulator, switching to my back up. We proceeded to make our way out of the corkscrew opening tethered to each other by the hose from my scuba tanks to the regulator Jen was breathing from. That was quite an experience! The opening was barely large enough for us to fit individually. We had to rotate ourselves as we moved through it to keep from getting wedged between the walls. We moved in a single file through the corkscrew sharing the air in my tanks. The length of the hose prevented us from being very far apart. Jen's fins were directly in front of my face, and I had to make sure my mask didn't get kicked off. I was thankful our instructor didn't also turn off our lights to simulate zero visibility!

During the dive debriefing, Jen questioned whether we were in the same cave. Our instructor confirmed that it was indeed the same cave and the same room. Jen didn't believe him. She thought he was lying to us. I reminded her of the corkscrew entry, which we both vividly remembered as it wasn't deep enough to affect us much. We couldn't believe how much our perception had changed when almost half of the nitrogen in our scuba tanks was replaced by helium. The additional cost of having helium in our tanks was proving to be worth it.

My family arrived in Florida, and we took a few days off from diving to sightsee and get to know the area better. We didn't abstain from diving during their entire stay, though. My sister was scuba certified, so we took her on a tour of the panhandle caverns. One of the places we went to was Vortex Spring, a well-known scuba diving destination north of the town of Ponce de Leon. Many dive shops and instructors from all around the southeast bring students there for training dives. We've seen shops and instructors from as far away as Tennessee and Kentucky. It's always clear water and sixty-nine degrees, so it makes it a perfect environment to train scuba diving students.

Vortex Spring was made into a dive destination by Doc Dockery, the creator of the diver down flag, the red flag with a diagonal white stripe from the top left corner to the bottom right corner. Doc never made any money from it. He thought it better to have a standardized flag that would alert boaters that scuba divers were below than to make money from his concept. The design took off and can be seen around the world. It was even used by Van Halen for one of their album covers.

My debut novel, *Beyond the Grate*, was inspired by an incident that occurred at Vortex Spring. In the book, I renamed it Eddy Spring, but many of the attributes remained similar. In 2010, a scuba diver named Ben McDaniel was diving Vortex Spring on a regular basis, almost daily. His brother died in a rock-climbing accident a couple of years earlier, Ben had recently been divorced, and he had experienced a business failure. Ben was having a difficult time with the multiple losses. He was given the opportunity to live in the family condo in Santa Rosa Beach and moved to Florida to take a year sabbatical.

Ben was originally scuba certified as a teenager but hadn't done much diving over the years. When he arrived in Florida, he resumed the activity and was diving almost every day, mostly at Vortex Spring. He took various scuba diving classes and planned on becoming a scuba diving instructor. One of the classes Ben took was an introductory technical diving class from me. This class was held about seven weeks before Ben's disappearance. It did not involve cave diving or even technical diving despite its name. It didn't prepare Ben for diving inside of a cave.

On August 20, 2010, Ben's family hadn't heard from him for a couple of days. It was unusual for him not to call them. They contacted the Vortex Spring dive shop, and an employee noticed Ben's truck was parked on the property. Just like the family, no one had seen or heard from Ben in a couple of days. The assumption was that Ben perished inside of the cave.

I was one of the divers that was called to go into the cave to find Ben's body and bring it out to his family. I went to the back of the cave, more than fourteen hundred feet from the opening, where it gets too small for anyone to fit. There were no signs that he had been back there, but my dive buddy and I pushed into the restriction until we got stuck and couldn't go any farther. We backed out, turned around, and searched for him on the way out.

I spent two days in the intro to technical diving class with Ben. He was a couple of inches or so shorter than me, and stockier. I knew if I couldn't fit through a restriction, Ben certainly couldn't. Two other members of our team checked the only two offshoot tunnels in the cave. We never found Ben or his equipment. Several other divers searched over the next few weeks. He was not found. More than fifteen years later, we still don't know what happened to Ben McDaniel.

There were several rumors about what might have happened to Ben. Some thought he ran off to Mexico. Others thought he abandoned his truck and something happened to him. Some thought he had a disagreement with someone and was murdered. There was also a group of people who thought Ben died in the cave and his body was removed and disposed of. I fell into that last group. Ben left his dog in his family's condo in Santa Rosa Beach and several hundred dollars in his truck. He had no reason to disappear, and I didn't believe he was murdered.

There's a metal grate located about three hundred feet inside of the cave from the opening. The grate was placed there in 1991 after the state threatened to ban diving at Vortex because thirteen divers had died in the cave. Dockery came up with the solution of the metal grate to prevent divers from going into the more dangerous section. It worked...until Ben.

After Ben's disappearance, we discovered that he had been manipulating the grate and going beyond it. Law enforcement found drawings in the abandoned truck that Ben had made of the tunnels beyond the grate. Someone even admitted to seeing Ben manipulating the grate and squeezing between it and the cave ceiling to get beyond it. My belief is that Ben was beyond the grate, breathed through the air in his scuba tanks, and drowned. His body was then found beyond the grate the next day. Rather than report it to authorities, the body was removed and disposed of. One thing was forgotten though - Ben's truck.

When the family contacted the employees at Vortex Spring on the second day he was missing, one of them alerted the authorities. That's when I received a call to go search for and recover Ben's body from the cave. This incident inspired me to write my thriller, *Beyond the Grate*. This story explores one possible explanation for Ben's disappearance and why he has not been found in more than fifteen years.

* * *

The trip to Vortex Spring with my sister was my first dive there. We swam around the basin before heading down the chimney opening and through the three-hundred-foot passage to the Piano Room where the grate is located. The cave floor was covered in silt. An errant fin kick would easily destroy the visibility. Maybe the grate should have been placed at the bottom of the chimney. Maybe not. No one has died in the section before the grate.

After diving Vortex, we drove to Morrison Spring, located about twenty minutes south. Unfortunately, conditions weren't conducive to diving. The spring basin was a dark, tannic brown. Visibility was non-existent. Morrison Spring is located on the Choctawhatchee River (that's pronounced Choctaw-HATCH-ee, not chocta-WHAT-chee) and conditions are influenced by the level of the water in the river. When the river level is up, Morrison Spring is brown. Vortex is located along Blue Creek and isn't affected by the water level, so it's clear year-round. Well, except when it's crowded with divers.

Jen and I returned to Jackson Blue the following day. My family enjoyed the park while Jen and I went cave diving. It had been almost a week, and we were anxious to get back there. We set up for our first circuit dive. We would go in one way and exit another. We went to the left at the first intersection, swam to the second intersection where we placed a personalized line marker on the guideline before turning to exit. On the next dive, we would go to the right at the first intersection, and if we made it to our marker, we could continue back along the other line and complete a circuit. We were essentially going around the block. It doesn't seem like much of a dive now, but it was a big dive for us back then.

Cave divers must be detail oriented and good at planning in order to do complex dives safely. Dives should be planned knowing exactly how much air will be breathed, how long we will be underwater, and how long our decompression stops will be. We cannot leave anything to chance. We shouldn't swim into the cave simply relying on our pressure gauges to dictate when we turn around. The pressure gauges are important to have, but they are only a reference. When I plan dives, I know where in the cave I will be turning around before I place a fin in the water. I plan it that carefully. I wasn't always able to do that. I had to build my experience and learn my breathing rate. Back then, I had to look at my pressure gauge to know how much air I had in my scuba tanks. Now, I look at my pressure gauges only to confirm what I already know. That comes with years of experience.

The simple circuit we planned was one block in that experience building. There are much more complicated circuits that entail multiple navigational decisions. While I can plan those so they are executed exactly as planned, I couldn't always do that. During the early years, leaving a marker was imperative. I still plan and execute new circuits that I've never done the same way, but a circuit I've done multiple times doesn't always get that setup dive. It's no longer necessary.

Jen and I returned to Jackson Blue to complete our circuit dive the day my family left. We made it to the marker, retrieved it, and continued out along the other line. We completed our first post training dive circuit and our first circuit in Jackson Blue. I became very familiar with that dive plan and would do it many more times over the years whenever testing out new dive equipment.

The circuit dive brought our diving to an end for another trip. It was time to return to Arizona after two and a half weeks. We couldn't wait to return to Florida, though. We were planning on doing nothing but cave diving during the next trip. That was the reason we had bought the house in Florida only ten minutes from some of the most beautiful caves in the state. We already had our next trip planned four months later. Little did we know that it would be our final visit to the sunshine state.

13

Kevin had a nine-foot hose

It was our final visit to Florida. No more one-to-two-week trips. It had been a year since we purchased the house. Some major things were happening in our lives, and we wouldn't be traveling back and forth between Arizona and Florida. We didn't know it during this trip, though.

We were excited to be returning so soon after the last trip. We had a lot of diving planned. We were going to continue to explore the caves and get to know them better. We only had one day of training planned. We had to continue our Trimix training and finally make it to Hendley's Castle. The rest of the time we were going to be diving with no instructor looking over our shoulders. There wasn't going to be anyone telling us to simulate being out of air or pretend we were in a silt out.

We invited Jack to visit for a few days while we were there. He knew about the caves in Jackson County but had never been. He and his girlfriend stayed with us, and we took them to all three caves that we had been to in Merritt's Mill Pond. We took Jack on a tour of Jackson Blue the first day, showing him the main passage as well as the three offshoot branches we had already explored. His girlfriend was a cavern diver, so we did a third dive to show her the cavern zone.

The next day we headed to Hole in the Wall and Twin caves. We saw some albino crayfish that day, this time in Hole in the Wall. They were hanging out with several albino salamanders in the upstream passage. There was a haven of the albinos eight hundred feet from the opening. There were dozens of them throughout a section of the passage. Some took off swimming when they sensed us approaching. Many remained motionless on the silty floor. It was incredible to see so many in one place! There was one or more every few feet.

The salamander looked like giant sperm swimming through the water. The crayfish look like tiny white lobsters, pinchers included. They were scattered around the floor across a fifty-foot area of the passage. We slowed down and observed them in their habitat. Almost twenty years later, they continue to hang out in that same area, and I'm still amazed every time I see them. I'd love to know what it is about that area that attracts them.

We went to Twin Cave for our afternoon dive. I was diving in my wetsuit, and this was our fifth dive in two days, more than five hours in sixty-nine-degree Fahrenheit/twenty-degree Celsius water. The day before, I started to get cold during the first dive and added a three-millimeter shortie over my seven-millimeter full length wetsuit. It helped a little. About twenty minutes into the dive at Twin Cave, I felt cold again. I began shivering. The water temperature had been tolerable for a dive or two, but after five dives I was developing cumulative hypothermia. I hadn't experienced this before. In all of the diving we had done, I never got cold. We had done mostly training dives during our previous trips which meant the adrenaline was flowing. Being able to relax and enjoy the caves contributed to a mild hypothermia.

I warmed up overnight and we returned to Jackson Blue the next day to explore the Parallel Line passage. This was the other guideline we had seen during our first dive in Young's Siphon. It runs parallel to the main tunnel between Young's Siphon and the first breakdown. It's kind of like a frontage road along a highway except you can't see one from the other because of the wall between them.

We set a jump line to the Parallel line from the primary guideline and swam over large, flat boulders that appeared to have once been attached to the ceiling above us. At the end of the line, we saw the gold line about ten feet away and set another jump line to it. It wasn't much of a short-cut, but it gave us something different to see.

On the way out, Jack had a dive light failure at the first breakdown. I looked around for our instructor, expecting to see that he had snuck over to Marianna to troll us. He wasn't there. At least, not that I could see. This was a real failure, not an instructor induced, simulated one. Our training kicked in and we handled it. Jack deployed a backup light and took the lead position. A primary light failure was only a minor inconvenience. We had two backup lights each just for that possibility. It did mean that was the end of Jack's diving until he could get his primary light repaired.

Jen and I took the next day off to recover from the hypothermia. She had started to get cold, as well. We had to recover before our next dive. We were returning to Peacock Springs State Park the following day to complete our Trimix class. The adrenaline caused by the anticipation of training drills would take care of the cold. We were going to attempt another visit to Hendley's Castle in Peacock III. This time we made it and arrived at the offshoot tunnel, set a jump line, and descended into the abyss. During our descent we switched from breathing the Nitrox in our backmounted double tanks to the Trimix in our stage tanks. We continued descending with clear minds and made it to one hundred and eighty feet of depth before turning around.

It was amazing to see how deep into the Earth the cave went. We had spent most of the dive at sixty feet of depth. We were three times that depth when we turned around. It was even more amazing that we were able to go into a dark underwater cave and think clearly. This was not only the deepest we had been inside of a cave, but it was the deepest we had ever been while scuba diving. We felt no impairment. The helium in our stage tanks was doing what it was supposed to do. It was proving its value. I thought back to how I felt at the Belize Blue Hole and in Lower Orange Grove. I couldn't believe I had gone more than thirty feet deeper in Hendley's Castle without feeling any narcosis.

We ascended back to the main passage, switched to the Nitrox in our other tanks, and began the swim out. Along the way, we did drills, because what was a training dive without drills? We exited the cave almost two hours after we had descended below the surface, our longest dive to that point. We had one more dive to do before completing the requirements for our Trimix diver certifications. That would have to wait for another trip.

We continued diving each of our remaining days in Florida. We concentrated on exploring and learning the passages in Jackson Blue. We ventured into the Horseshoe Circuit, but this time from the opposite end. Jen decided to accompany me this time. The circuit was a bypass around the chimney fissure, beginning at the top, to the left of the fissure, looping out, and ending in the large room at the bottom of the fissure.

As we moved through the passage, we encountered another team of divers coming toward us. The Horseshoe Circuit is not a large tunnel, so we had to move aside to let them pass by us. Remember that I mentioned one of the rules of cave diving is the exiting team always has the right-of-way. Unfortunately, the exiting team left a wake of silt behind them. We couldn't see anything but dust hanging in the passage. There was no point in going into it blindly, so we turned around. We returned to the primary guideline and descended through the chimney fissure.

We went into the Parallel Line passage again. Not far from where it joins back to the main passage, to the left of the gold line, we found another line leading up into the ceiling. It was on the opposite wall behind a rock formation that looked like a chicken and had been named Chicken Head Rock. You might recall reading about it in the second book of the *Beyond* thriller series, *Into the Darkness Beyond*.

I went up into the crack in the ceiling while Jen waited next to the chicken head, but I didn't get far. I got wedged in between the two walls. At that moment, I realized that backmounted tanks were going to be too limiting. I had seen another diver in sidemounted tanks, and my interest was piqued. I wanted to try this new configuration. I intended to experiment with it when we returned to Arizona.

97

The next day Jen and I did a different type of dive. I read about a club of sorts called the Chemical Light Society. It wasn't really a club, but rather a small group of divers with a private subforum on one of the cave diving internet forums. In order to receive access to this subforum, you had to do a cave dive using only chemical lights for illumination. Chemical lights are those glow sticks that you crack so they light up. It was an interesting concept.

Jen and I bought six glow sticks, three for each of us. We had to have our backup glow sticks after all. Because we had done so many dives in Jackson Blue, we opted to do the dive there. We entered the cave and cracked one glow stick each. The two additional glow sticks remained in our pockets. Of course, we also had our primary and backup dive lights just in case.

At first, we maintained contact with the guideline. As our eyes adjusted, we were able to see more. We discovered that when we held the glow sticks out in front of us, we could see several feet ahead. It was amazing how well those chemical light sticks illuminated the cave. We swam just beyond the first line intersection. The dive went well. It was peaceful and calming. We couldn't see a lot of the passage around us, but we saw enough. The chemical lights forced us to maintain focus on the guideline and helped us learn it better. The dive was a little eerie but relaxing at the same time.

For our next dive, we did the circuit between the first and second intersections of the primary guideline again. We focused on learning the main passage and where the offshoot tunnels were located. We wanted the cave to be as familiar to us as the neighborhood where we lived. Sadly, that was the last dive of the trip.

I did have something to look forward to. I was planning to experiment diving with sidemounted tanks in one of the Arizona lakes. I had seen enough of it and did some research on the internet. I had dive equipment that I could modify and create my own frankenrig. I wanted to know what diving sidemount felt like before we spent a bunch of money on new equipment. There might have been a chance I didn't like it. That was doubtful.

I built my frankenrig and about two weeks after returning to Arizona, I headed into Lake Pleasant with a friend. It felt great! I liked having my scuba tanks mounted at my sides instead of on my back. It felt so much better and less constricting. While it was far from perfect, it was liberating. There were issues with the set up. I didn't have the proper length hoses, and I hadn't set the rig up correctly. I placed the buoyancy wing on top of the harness instead of beneath it, so the sides of the wings flapped up like a taco. This experience is why I always tell divers not to try to build their own sidemount rig before they've obtained experience sidemount diving. It didn't affect my trim or buoyancy or how I felt in the water. It just didn't look great and wouldn't do me any good in tight spaces. It was an easy issue to correct, and I made adjustments after the dive.

The next day, I did another dive in sidemount. The adjustments I made to the harness and wing worked. The wing stayed down and wrapped around my torso instead of tacoing up. The tanks remained horizontally trimmed. It felt even better than it had the day before. I knew at that moment that I wanted to dive sidemount rather than backmount. I started researching the different sidemount rigs available. There were only two, so it went quickly.

Unfortunately, purchasing a sidemount rig would have to wait until we returned to Florida. Divers in Arizona didn't know what sidemount diving was. They barely knew what cave diving was. Most of the divers were strictly recreational. The ones that weren't were barely technical. One day we were at our local dive shop talking to one of the divemasters about our cave diving training. He mentioned one of the shop's instructors was a technical diver and introduced us to a couple of divers who had been diving with him. They began an animated tale about a visit to Peppersauce Cave, located in the Santa Catalina Mountains north of Tucson.

They visited Peppersauce Cave with Kevin, the technical diver, after Kevin had told them about a sump he had found. The three of them went into Peppersauce Cave, to the sump, and entered the water. They were using single tanks, but Kevin, the technical diver, *had a stage tank with a nine-foot hose so they were okay*. It took every bit of self-control to keep from laughing at that statement. You see, there is no such thing as a nine-foot hose. Sure, it can be custom ordered, but it's not industry standard. Also, no technical diver in his or her right mind would attempt to dive a sump with a single tank, even with a stage tank. It was a big risk. I doubted whether any of them knew much about technical diving.

Eventually, Jen and I visited Peppersauce Cave and found the sump. It was a small body of water about nine hundred feet from the opening. There were several areas where we had to climb up and drop down to continue through the passage. When we arrived at the sump, the water was about an eight-foot drop from the shelf we stood on. I couldn't imagine three divers hauling tanks and scuba gear all that way. It would have taken several hours. They also wouldn't have all been able to fit into the sump. It was barely large enough for one diver, never mind three. They would have silted it out immediately. It made for a good story, and we still laugh about it today.

* * *

A couple of months after returning to Arizona, we went on our first trip to dive the caves of Mexico. It was only three days of cave diving, but we fell in love with the Mexican caves and wanted to see more of them. They were absolutely amazing. They weren't better than the Florida caves. They were just different. Florida caves were formed underwater. The movement of water through the passages carved out the tunnels and created the formations. The caves in Mexico were formed when they were exposed to air. They contain stalactites and stalagmites that resemble the formations we see inside of the cave at Florida Caverns State Park in Marianna. When sea levels rose, the Mexican caves were submerged.

We returned from Mexico missing the caves even more. We still didn't know when we would return to Florida because Jen was waiting to find out about her school schedule. About a year earlier, Jen decided to pursue a career in nursing after working in healthcare for more than ten years. She completed her prerequisite classes at the local community college the semester our first trip to Mexico happened and applied to the local nursing program. She was accepted. The problem was that everyone who applied was accepted. Everyone was placed on a waiting list, first come first serve. Jen's name was on the list, but we learned she wouldn't begin the program for five years. The waiting list was that long!

We were planning to move to Florida after Jen graduated from nursing school. If we waited, we would be in Arizona for another seven years. That wasn't acceptable. We researched our options and found several nursing school programs in Florida within an hour's drive of our house. Jen applied to three of those and was accepted into all three. Chipola College, located in Marianna, Florida, only ten minutes from our house, was one of the programs she had applied to. The semester began six weeks later. We had five weeks to pack and load the van and trailer for our final trip. We weren't visiting Florida this time. We were moving there!

14

Meet my dive buddy, Al

We had to tie up loose ends in Arizona and finish the scuba courses we had scheduled with students. At the beginning of August, we said goodbye to our home in Tucson. This was going to be our longest drive yet. We were caravaning across the country. I was driving the van and Jen was driving the truck. We had completed the drive several times but always in the same vehicle taking turns behind the wheel. This was the first time we were going to each be driving straight through.

The drive took a lot longer than usual, but we expected that. We finally pulled into our driveway sometime after midnight. I'm sure the town was abuzz about the caravan of trucks and trailers arriving in the middle of the night. They probably thought we had hit Fort Knox and took every last gold bar. At that point, we didn't care what they thought. We were just happy to be in our new home.

Other than a quick dive in Jackson Blue a couple days after we arrived in Florida, our first week was spent unpacking everything we owned from the van, the truck, and the trailers. Finally, the weekend before Jen started the nursing program, we took a break from settling in and headed to Morrison Spring. This would be our third visit to the spring. It had been flooded during the previous two visits, so we hadn't been diving in it yet. That's right. A spring basin full of water was flooded. You might wonder how that can happen. It does and it's not uncommon. In fact, Morrison stays flooded almost as much as when it's not.

There's always water in the spring. After all, that's what comes out of it. When we say it's flooded, it's much the same as when we say a river is flooded. The water level rises enough to crest the banks and flood the surrounding areas. Something similar happens at many Florida springs, Morrison being one of them.

Morrison Spring feeds the Choctawhatchee River. When it rains enough, the river floods. This happens several times each year. The banks are only suggestions. Some of them are tall enough to contain the rise. Other areas allow the surrounding land to be overcome by the river and create swamps.

Around the springs, the tannic river water backs up into the spring runs. The river water is usually slightly brown because of all of the tree roots along the banks. As the water rises, the shallower levels of water turn tannic brown. The higher the water level, the more opaque the water becomes. The current coming from the spring mixes with the brown water and turns the normally crystal-clear spring water into the same tannic brown tint. The higher the water level, the more tannins make their way into the basin and the more difficult it is to see through. When this happens, we say the spring is flooded.

The water flowing out of the spring remains clear because it's coming from the hidden rivers deep beneath the ground. However, there's not enough of it to keep the river water out of the spring basin. I ventured into Morrison Spring once when it was partially flooded. The river was just starting to back up into the basin and it was more of a tea color than a coffee color. Not only was the visibility affected, but the temperature was as well. We happened to be there during the colder months when the river water drops in temperature. On that day, the water temperature in the spring basin was about ten degrees cooler than the usual sixty-nine degrees we were accustomed to. At the cave opening, fifty feet below the surface, not only was the visibility clear, but the water temperature was back to the expected sixty-nine degrees.

The water layers in the shallower depths were tannic enough that sunlight was not able to penetrate more than fifteen feet below the surface. Even at fifteen feet, we only had a glimmer of light. Morrison Spring is normally considered a cavern dive because daylight reaches into almost every corner inside. With the tannins blocking the sun from penetrating deeper than fifteen feet, Morrison was effectively a cave dive. Nothing changed about it other than daylight wasn't able to penetrate into the cavern like it normally did. That meant cavern divers could not dive Morrison until the water became clear and light was able to reach into the cavern. They would be violating one of their limitations if they did.

While Morrison Spring is one of thirty-three 1st magnitude springs in Florida, which means it discharges at least sixty-four million gallons of water per day, there is no accessible cave there. At least, there hasn't been one for several decades. Sheck Exley, the cave diver who created the cave diving training guidelines that cave divers follow today, was one of the first people to dive in Morrison cave. He explored, mapped, and surveyed it, reaching two hundred and forty feet of depth before arriving at a mud restriction. This was back in the days before divers were using Trimix to counteract nitrogen narcosis. Sheck did his dives breathing air! Narcosis affected me at one hundred and forty feet. I couldn't imagine how he must have felt at two hundred and forty feet.

Not long after Sheck explored Morrison Spring, a couple of open water scuba divers went into the cave, were adversely affected by nitrogen narcosis, and died in its depths. They were using single scuba tanks and went too deep. The effects of nitrogen narcosis took over, leaving them disoriented, and they breathed through the air in their tanks, drowning near the bottom of the cave.

There are reports that more than twenty divers died inside of the cave at Morrison. This led to Walton County's Sheriff Anderson, who happened not to like cave divers, to take action. Sheriff Anderson wasn't the only one that didn't like cave diving. It was not liked by many at the time. There are still people today who think it should be outlawed. Fortunately, they are in the minority. Sheriff Anderson decided to do something about the deaths happening in the caves in his county. He sent a couple of divers with explosives into Morrison Spring. They set them, exited the cave, and detonated them. The explosion caused part of the cave to collapse, blocking the passage to the deeper section.

There are a couple of areas where the water flows out from the depths of the hidden cave. There have been divers that have tried to bypass the large boulder that blocks the passage. I'm one of those divers. The current is too strong, and the opening is too small. It's simply not possible. It would take more explosives to blast an opening through the collapsed limestone. To this day Morrison remains a cavern with no access to the cave hidden below it. While it's sad, it doesn't detract from its allure. Morrison Spring is one of the most beautiful cavern dives in the state. Divers can reach a depth of about ninety feet and swim with the dozens of Florida freshwater eels that inhabit its dark recesses.

When we arrived at Morrison Spring on this third visit, conditions were perfect. The basin was clear. From the surface, we could see where the floor dropped down toward the opening. We quickly geared up, excited to finally be able to dive the spring. What made it even better was that this was when Morrison was untouched. There was no boardwalk. There was no paved parking lot. We were able to park the van on the beach right next to the water. As of this writing, entry is limited to fifty-eight vehicles and the line into the park often extends more than half a mile. We had an amazing dive that day and finally got to see what was so special about this spring.

After our dive in Morrison, Jen and I headed back to Jackson County and went diving in Jackson Blue that afternoon. It was our final weekend before Jen returned to school and we were taking advantage of it. For the first time, we made it beyond the second line intersection. We swam another three hundred feet to the Hall of the Mountain King, a beautiful room that deserved such a majestic name.

The name comes from a piece of orchestral music composed by Edvard Grieg in the late eighteen hundreds. When the first explorer entered that magnificent room, that must have been the image and music that came to mind. The room is about one hundred feet long, thirty feet from floor to ceiling, and forty feet wide. There are a couple of large mounds in the second two-thirds of the room that are ten to fifteen feet tall and resemble mountains. It's quite a sight. I can only imagine what it must have felt like to be the first person to enter that room.

The next day Jen started nursing school. I had a few days off from work and wanted to dive. At this time, there were only a couple of other cave divers living in Jackson County. Finding a dive buddy was difficult. We had cave divers visiting the area occasionally but mostly on weekends. Jen and I were often the only ones at Jackson Blue during the week. I had done some solo diving in Arizona, but I had never done a solo cave dive. That was about to change.

On Jen's first day of class, I went to Jackson Blue prepared to dive by myself. Well, not exactly by myself. I brought along Al. That's A L, not A one. Al is the nickname I gave my aluminum eighty cubic foot scuba tank. That was my buddy bottle. I carried the scuba tank with me with no intention of breathing from it. Al was simply a redundant source of air in case I ran into trouble. I planned an easy dive with Al. It was one I had done on several prior occasions. I did the gold line circuit. I had done several dozen cave dives in Jackson Blue by this point, but I had no misconceptions that diving solo was without risk. I wanted to dive, though, so I took measures to minimize the risk.

It was a fantastic dive. Al was just along for the ride. Al was the perfect type of buddy. I knew where he was at all times without having to look for him. And Al was there with the sole purpose of supporting me. I didn't turn around because of the pressure in my scuba tanks. I never got close to my turn pressure. I turned because I had gone as far as I planned to go during my first solo cave dive.

One of the most amazing things about the dive was how much better my air consumption was. My respiratory rate was much slower. I breathed a lot less air. Not having Jen in the cave with me to keep track of and worry about made me more relaxed. Not that she made me nervous, but keeping track of any dive buddy will cause more movement and result in muscles demanding more oxygen. I moved through the cave slowly and looked around. I saw more than I had seen on previous dives. I discovered that I really liked cave diving solo.

A couple of days after my solo dive, I had another first. I went cave diving in sidemount configuration. I borrowed a sidemount rig and a set of sidemount scuba tanks. This was not only my first sidemount cave dive, but also my first time using steel sidemounted tanks. I did a conservative dive and remained in the cavern zone. I felt that would be safer being that I was in a new equipment configuration.

The scuba tanks most divers use are aluminum and have a volume of eighty cubic feet when filled to a pressure of thirty-one hundred psi. They are lightweight compared to steel tanks, especially in the water. Underwater, they range from three to four pounds negative buoyancy when full to one pound negative to neutral buoyancy when empty. While they are easy to carry around in the water, the bottoms begin to float after only a few hundred psi of air is breathed from them.

Steel tanks are a bit different. Most are twelve to fifteen pounds negative in the water when full and one to two pounds negative when empty, although it's rare that they get close to being empty. When cave diving, we plan and execute our dives so that we don't surface with less than one third of the air pressure that we begin with. Unless something goes wrong, we always surface with more than one thousand psi in our scuba tanks. I usually surface with half of the air in my tanks.

I was diving in a wetsuit, and I was extremely foot heavy on this first sidemount dive in the Jackson Blue cavern. The difference between steel and aluminum scuba tanks was very apparent. My feet kept dropping low, and I struggled to maintain my horizontal trim. I managed to reposition the tanks and felt better, but I still felt foot heavy. I knew I was going to have to make adjustments.

Jen was off from school the next day, so we went to Jackson Blue to do another dive together. I was starting to learn the cave. I was beginning my transition from being a tourist cave diver to being a resident cave diver. I've previously mentioned pulling and gliding along the cave. Remember the liquid skin story? I was learning that pulling wasn't necessary, even in high flow caves such as Jackson Blue.

Jackson Blue is a first magnitude spring, typically discharging significantly more than sixty-four million gallons of water a day into Merritt's Mill Pond. This means the current is strong and can be difficult to swim against. Up until this point, I had been pulling my way into the cave as I was taught to do in high flow systems. I didn't like touching the cave, so for the first time, I did a cave dive in a high flow system without touching it. I swam the entire time and made it to the fifteen-hundred-foot marker. I didn't even have a stage tank with me.

I did this by reading the cave. I had done enough dives in Jackson Blue that I was starting to notice things. Most of Jackson Blue has bare limestone floors because the water current pushes the sediment that would normally be there out of the cave. During my previous dives in the cave, I noticed there were trails of sediment on the floor in certain areas. These weren't trails of just a little sediment. They were thick layers of sand and mud. One such area was located in the Rock Garden immediately after the Deco Room. There's a path of sand along the wall to the right that extends to the beginning of the gold line. When I hovered a foot or so above the sand, I noticed that I barely felt any current. I could swim without struggling against the flow. I no longer had to pull myself along that section of the cave.

Once I reached the gold line, I saw a formation ahead in the tunnel and used it to shield myself from the current. I remained low so that I was swimming below the top of the formation. When I reached it, I looked for another area of the passage that could shield me from the current. There were several areas along the cave where this was possible. I continued to leapfrog from formation to formation as I penetrated the cave, never touching it. I didn't have to change my position in the passage all that much. I just had to be closer to the floor, the ceiling, or one of the walls. I had to look for the flow and stay out of it.

Jen had the next two days free, and we returned to Jackson Blue with sidemount equipment. I wanted to experiment more as well as get Jen to try it. I adjusted the bands on the scuba tanks and had positive results. My feet didn't feel as heavy as they had during that first dive. I was no longer struggling to maintain horizontal trim. I used what I learned from my previous dive to set Jen's equipment up so she could have a good first experience. She was in trim and felt comfortable. She loved how sidemount felt. We swam to the first intersection, the limit we set for ourselves since we were in a new configuration. Jen was hooked.

The next day, we went back to do another dive in sidemount, this time using our own sidemount rigs. With the dives I had done in Arizona and the couple of dives in Florida, I was convinced I wanted to dive sidemount regularly. Jen was also happy with it, liking it much more than having tanks on her back. We were ready to invest in equipment.

This time, we did the gold line circuit and swam to the second line intersection. On the way out, Jen and I got video of each other in our new sidemount rigs so we could see what we looked like. I especially wanted to see how the scuba tanks were trimming out along my sides. They looked great and remained in line with my body. My horizontal trim was nearly perfect. It was only my fifth dive in sidemount, counting the two in Arizona, and I couldn't be happier with the results.

A few days later, after working a shift to help pay for the new scuba equipment, I was back at Jackson Blue for another dive in sidemount. Jen was at school, so I went solo. I brought a set of aluminum eighty cubic foot scuba tanks to try out because I hadn't disassembled my backmount tanks yet. The bottoms of the tanks began to rise. I contemplated putting weights on the cam bands to keep the tanks weighted down. Back then, this was common practice. Now, it's frowned upon, especially when cave diving. There are still sidemount cave divers that place weights on their aluminum sidemount tanks, but it's not as prevalent as it used to be.

I traded one of our sets of backmounted scuba tanks for a set of steel tanks that we would use for sidemount diving and disassembled the other set of tanks. Jen and I returned to Jackson Blue to dive sidemount in our own steel tanks for the first time. I had learned quite a bit about how I needed to configure the equipment by that time and the tanks trimmed out nicely. We were happy with the results and with our decision to dive sidemount. I was also ready to start going into smaller spaces, but first, we wanted to explore other areas of the Florida panhandle.

Jen and I continued to explore Jackson Blue on the weekends between my work shifts and her school week. The Florida panhandle was experiencing a drought and the current in Jackson Blue was decreasing in intensity. It seemed like we were able to swim a little farther into the cave on each subsequent dive. Jackson Blue no longer felt like a first magnitude spring. We swam a little beyond the third gold line intersection nineteen-hundred-feet from the opening. This was a huge accomplishment and the farthest we had been in a cave.

The next day we were back and made it to the third intersection again. We didn't expect that. The day before we had been in backmounted tanks and used stage tanks. This time we were in sidemounted tanks and didn't have stage tanks to breathe from. We discovered that being in sidemount configuration reduced our breathing rates. We swam the same distance breathing significantly less air. We created less drag with the tanks at our sides rather than on our backs and exerted less effort to swim. That meant our muscles required less oxygen and we breathed slower. The transition that was occurring was amazing.

A few days later, we took a stage tank with us for the first time in sidemount and made it to the fourth intersection located two hundred feet beyond the third one. This was similar to the circuit between the first and second intersection. At the fourth intersection, we encountered a traffic light propped on the rocks. It was a single red light as commonly used in the 1950s. We were at the beginning of the infamous Trash Room located twenty-one hundred feet from the closest opening.

The Trash Room is a section of Jackson Blue that extends about two hundred feet from the traffic light. If you've read my thriller, *Into the Darkness Beyond*, you already know about this area. The Trash Room was created when an old sinkhole existed there. The sinkhole has since filled in from years of dirt, leaves, and branches falling into it. There's a vertical crack near the Trash Room named Mystery Sink that was likely the tunnel that led to the sinkhole at some point many decades ago. I've gone into that crack, and it gets too small to pass through at about fifteen feet of depth. The trash would have definitely fit, though.

Jen and I were thrilled to have made it so far into Jackson Blue only a little more than a month after moving to Florida full-time. The transition from tourist cave divers to resident cave divers was taking place. We were not only learning the cave, but we were becoming more proficient cave divers. It seemed like it happened quickly, but we were diving quite a bit. We did sixteen dives in Jackson Blue that first month after moving to Florida. That was in addition to the other dives we had done.

We were ready for a change in scenery, though. We wanted to visit Peacock Springs State Park. It had been more than a year since we were diving in Peacock I, and we wanted to check it out without having to keep an eye on an instructor that would give us drills to do at any minute. The next day, we got up early and drove the two and a quarter hours to Luraville to see more of the hidden rivers beneath the state park.

15

Peacock and the Canyon

I dedicated the rest of the year to becoming more familiar with the hidden rivers of Florida and building my cave diving experience. Fortunately, Jen's first semester did not require all of her time and attention, so she was able to join me on many of those dives. When she wasn't with me, I kept my solo diving conservative. I spent most of my time in Jackson Blue and didn't go beyond the second line intersection. I wanted to be in familiar territory where my chances of surviving any issues were greater. That didn't last long. I found myself wanting to see other caves. Caves that Jen wasn't interested in going into. Either they were too small for her liking, or the visibility was too poor. I'm getting ahead of myself.

As I mentioned, we returned to Peacock Springs State Park to dive Peacock I. We hadn't been in that opening in more than a year and a half. We had done only one dive there outside of class. That was the dive to Pothole Sink. Other than that, our focus was on our training. While we had seen the cave, we hadn't really *seen* it. We weren't familiar with it. It was merely a venue for the training dives. We were looking forward to this new experience.

There's definitely a difference between doing a training dive and a tourist dive. During a tourist dive, we get to see the cave. We can enjoy it and the beauty within. Training dives, on the other hand, demand strict focus. They require paying attention to the other students in the class as well as to the instructor. This meant that we couldn't focus as much on the cave as we should. Sure, we saw the cave. We just didn't have the opportunity to learn it. This was our objective upon returning to Peacock Springs State Park. We wanted to learn the cave like we had been learning Jackson Blue.

We woke up early and hit the road shortly after sunrise. This was a feat in itself because I'm not a morning person. I worked night shift most of my life, and when I wasn't working, I was up late. It has always taken me a couple of hours to get sufficient caffeine in my system to start moving. Mornings and I have never gotten along well. This is probably one of the reasons I like cave diving so much. There's no schedule to adhere to. I didn't have to be at the dock in time for a boat to depart at eight o'clock. I could cave dive whenever I wanted as evidenced by the late evening dives we did during previous trips.

We arrived in Luraville by nine, or rather eight our time. The eastern/central time zone line is on the eastern border of Jackson County. We crossed into eastern time zone twenty minutes after leaving our house. Because the state park closed at sunset, we had to be there early if we wanted to do more than one dive and not feel rushed. We set up our equipment, dropped into the water, and headed toward Olsen Sink. We passed Pothole Sink along the way and still couldn't see light streaming into the tunnel. We continued and about half an hour later, we swam around a corner and saw rays of sunshine illuminating the passage ahead of us. We were at Olsen Sink. We had just completed our first traverse. We entered one opening and swam to another.

We swam to the end of the line and I deployed a jump spool from it to the surface. There was another gold line on the opposite side of the sinkhole and we didn't want to get confused when we descended back to the line to swim out. That could be a fatal mistake. We surfaced for a few minutes to look around. It was beautiful. We were in the middle of the woods, surrounded by trees. There was a primitive trail that led to the sinkhole, but nothing else. The observation deck hadn't been built yet. It felt like we were miles from civilization. I guess technically we were. It seemed like we were even farther away, though.

We descended below the surface and swam back a couple of hundred feet to a passage named the Crossover Tunnel that connects the Olsen line to the Peanut line, the other gold line passage that begins in the Peacock I cavern. The Crossover Tunnel forms the base of the triangle. Except it wasn't shaped quite like a triangle. Just like the rivers we can see at the surface, the hidden rivers also meander along the path of least resistance when they form.

We set a jump spool line and made the traverse from one gold line to the other. When we arrived at the Peanut line, we set another jump spool line and continued to the left, toward the exit. We were about one thousand feet from the Peacock I opening. We continued swimming through the passage and made it back to our starting point. We saw a new sinkhole, completed a traverse, and swam our first major circuit in a cave. This wasn't like the two-hundred-foot circuit between the first and second line intersections in Jackson Blue. We entered and exited the same opening without going through the same passage twice, and we did it without ever reaching the turn pressure in our scuba tanks.

We returned to Peacock I after lunch to swim to the Peanut Restriction. Located about eighteen hundred feet from the Peacock I opening is a restriction somewhat shaped like a peanut. I didn't see the resemblance. Maybe I was looking at it from the wrong angle. Or maybe it just didn't look like a peanut any longer. We made it to the restriction and continued through it. Even Jen, who doesn't like small passages, went through. A few feet later we were at the end of the gold line and looking at a perpendicular gold line fifteen feet away. That line connected Olsen Sink, which we had been to during our earlier dive, and Challenge Sink, which was closer to the Orange Grove opening.

Peacock Springs is similar to the hidden rivers of Mexico. It has several openings, seven not counting the Peacock II opening, all within the same cave system. The tunnel that once connected Peacock II to Peacock I collapsed, blocking the passage. The cave has four gold lines – the two gold lines that begin at the Peacock I opening, one that connects the Orange Grove opening to Challenge Sink, and one that connects Olsen and Challenge Sinks. The four sections of gold line replaced the white line in the cave in 1989 following Debra Reeves' death.

After seeing the Olsen/Challenge gold line, we turned around and swam back to the Crossover Tunnel. Our jump spools were still in place from the previous dive, providing us with a continuous guideline should we have had to turn around. That is one of the most important rules of cave diving. We always ensure that there is a continuous guideline to the surface. It was our lifeline out of the cave.

I'll reiterate that the lines aren't there for us to follow into the cave. They are there to follow out of the cave should we lose visibility. Sure, they help guide us through the passages, but as we became more familiar with the caves, the lines only became an occasional reference, not our road maps. This was one of the differences between being a tourist cave diver and a resident cave diver. We were learning the caves, not learning the lines. However, should the visibility in the cave suddenly become diminished or non-existent, the lines assured us that we could make it to the opening and back to the surface.

During our morning dive, when we swam the circuit, we left the jump spool lines in place at both ends of the Crossover Tunnel. Had we not done that, we would have been without a continuous guideline back to our point of entry. Neither end of the Crossover Tunnel line intersects the gold lines. The gap is only a few feet long on the Olsen line end, but it's about fifteen feet long on the Peanut line end. Fifteen feet is a long way to move in a cave when you don't have visibility or a continuous guideline. I couldn't find the line only ten feet away from me in Devil's during our training.

While we were closer to the Peacock I opening when we swam from the Crossover Tunnel to the Peanut Line, Jen and I had never seen the passage between the Crossover Tunnel and the Peanut Line breakdown four hundred feet away. We didn't know what it looked like. If we had an emergency that required us to exit, the best course of action, the only course of action our training allowed, was to turn around and head out the way we had come. We had to do that even though we were significantly closer to Peacock I along the Peanut Line. Turning back meant it might take us twice as long to exit the cave and surface, but as long as we were following our air management rules, we would have enough air to exit the way we had come.

This is why cave divers use the rule of thirds to plan cave dives. We plan on using one third of our starting air pressure to penetrate the cave and one third to exit, reserving the final third for emergencies. If we have an issue within the first third of our air, we have enough air to turn around and exit where we entered from, even if one of us loses all of the air in our tanks. This is all in theory. In reality, we would likely be breathing a little faster than normal in an emergency situation and it wouldn't be enough. This is one reason I never dive thirds.

If I start with thirty-six hundred psi in my tanks, I will not penetrate until my air pressure is twenty-four hundred psi. That doesn't leave me enough reserve air. Instead, I'll turn around when my tank pressure is twenty-six hundred psi. I use one thousand psi for penetration, one thousand psi to exit, and sixteen hundred psi in case of an emergency. That's more than one and a half times the amount of air used to swim into the cave. That buffer makes me feel a lot better about things. I'd rather have that additional six hundred psi for emergencies than increase my penetration pressure by two hundred psi because that extra bit isn't going to get me much farther into the cave. If I want to go farther, I'll bring an additional tank along.

The nice thing about a cave system such as Peacock is that we have multiple openings that can be used during a dive. We don't normally plan a dive with this in mind because we never know when conditions might change. We had just been to Olsen Sink a few hours earlier and verified that the line and opening were intact. We knew the gold line ended below the surface at Olsen Sink and not a hundred feet away from it with no daylight visible. If we had an emergency near Olsen Sink, I would exit there even with enough air to swim to Peacock I. I would still be taking a risk, although not quite as much of one. Caves can collapse and block exits, but that goes for any route.

If we had never been to Olsen Sink, it wouldn't be a viable option. We would have to continue to swim twelve hundred feet from the Crossover Tunnel to Peacock I, even with Olsen Sink only two hundred feet away. Why? If we were unfamiliar with an opening, then we wouldn't know what to expect. What if we turned left toward Olsen Sink and one hundred feet later, we arrived at the end of the line and saw no daylight streaming into the cave? We could deploy a line from one of our safety spools, spools that we carry with us for such occasions. But what if we did that and the passage split into two and we still couldn't see daylight? How would we know which way to go?

Some will claim it's only two hundred feet. It's worth the risk. However, if you planned your dive correctly, and followed the plan, you would have enough air in your tanks to get both you and your dive buddy out by going the way you came, even if it was one thousand feet farther. If you swam toward Olsen Sink and couldn't find it, you would have wasted time and your limited air supply. By the time you turned around to head out the familiar way, your air supply might not be enough to get you out of the cave. Always go the way you know.

We retrieved our jump spools on the way back to the Olsen line. Twelve hundred feet later, we surfaced. We had just swum four thousand feet in Peacock Springs. At the time, Peacock Springs cave system had just over nineteen thousand feet of lined and surveyed passages. Including what we saw from the Orange Grove opening during training, we swam through about one fourth of the entire cave. We still had a long way to go to see it all. The day trip to dive Peacock was not only fun, but also productive.

* * *

About a week later, we planned a dive in Jackson Blue to visit King's Canyon, a fissure tunnel that runs parallel to the Hall of the Mountain King. Jen and I headed into Jackson Blue and swam to the Hall of the

Mountain King where we set one of our jump spool lines between the gold line and the white line leading to King's Canyon. We followed the new line and about two hundred and fifty feet later, we encountered a line intersection. We could continue forward into a smaller passage or go straight up into a fissure canyon. We had arrived at King's Canyon.

We ascended thirty feet shallower alongside the vertical line until we encountered another intersection of lines. King's Canyon is forty-five feet tall and two hundred feet long, so we were in the upper third of the passage. What the canyon has in height, it lacks in width. There are places where we could easily touch the walls on both sides with outstretched arms. There were some places where we didn't have to stretch our arms out to touch the walls. In other places, we had to rotate sideways to squeeze our sidemounted tanks through.

We slowly swam along the passage, mesmerized by its beauty. It was like no other cave passage we had seen during our short time cave diving. It was amazing that the earth could crack open and produce such a beautiful passage. King's Canyon became my favorite passage and still ranks in the top five most beautiful areas I've seen in a cave. That includes caves in Mexico and Europe.

Jen started clinicals at school and her diving availability was less frequent, leaving me to fend for myself in the caves. I returned to Jackson Blue a couple of days later for a solo dive, still keeping my solo activities conservative and turning at the second line intersection. I knew that passage well and felt comfortable diving it alone. I did this for two days, making adjustments to my sidemount diving equipment.

This was how it began. I became motivated to learn more about diving sidemount. There were very few sidemount diving instructors at the time. I didn't know any that were actively teaching the class. Many of the sidemount diving instructors I knew of didn't dive sidemount regularly. They were simply card-carrying instructors. There weren't many sidemount divers, either. It was rare to see anyone else in sidemount configuration when I was diving. Most of the sidemount divers were older explorers with frankenrigs. That meant I had to experiment with the equipment myself.

I made adjustments regularly, one at a time, to see how the changes felt. I kept it simple so I could see how each change affected my trim. That meant more diving. I read as much as I could find on the internet, came up with my own modifications, and made changes during almost every dive. I wanted my sidemount equipment to be configured perfectly for me and the diving I was doing, so I spent a lot of time experimenting. This kept me focused on my equipment and helped to rein in my desire to go beyond the second line intersection alone.

Jen and I returned to King's Canyon a couple of weeks later with Mark, a friend of ours. We swam to the line intersection at the bottom of King's Canyon. Mark signaled us to turn around. He didn't feel comfortable with the size of the fissure above us. It wasn't tiny by any means. If Jen swam through it, it was a decent size. Mark hadn't been cave diving very long and was being cautious. We were fine with it. There was no shame in turning a dive when you weren't feeling it. Another rule we follow in cave diving is that anyone can call any dive at any time without question. Mark called the dive, so we turned around and began our exit. King's Canyon would be there next time.

Jen and I returned for another dive after refilling our scuba tanks. We wanted to see how far we could penetrate. We were still in drought conditions and the current in Jackson Blue was greatly diminished. It felt more like Hole in the Wall and Twin caves than a first magnitude spring. We got in the water, each with a stage tank, and began our swim. About forty minutes later, we arrived at the traffic light with a hundred psi of penetration left before we had to turn. We were about to see the Trash Room for the first time.

16

Three strikes and you're out…or is it five?

I couldn't stop thinking about the traffic light in Jackson Blue. I wanted to return, go beyond it, and explore the Trash Room. I wasn't sure if it was possible without a dive propulsion vehicle, or DPV. The traffic light was twenty-one hundred feet from the opening, and the Trash Room encompassed the next two hundred and fifty feet. That was a long way to swim. With Jackson Blue being a first magnitude spring and having a strong current, swimming that distance didn't seem feasible. Except it hadn't rained in Jackson County in several weeks. We were in a drought and the current flowing out of Jackson Blue had decreased in intensity significantly. It was almost indiscernible. Swimming in Jackson Blue was like swimming in Hole in the Wall or Twin caves.

Jen and I didn't have DPVs. We couldn't budget the money for them just yet. We had spent a lot on our new sidemount equipment and tanks, and DPVs were expensive. A new DPV was priced at several thousand dollars. A used DPV would cost us a few grand. Times two. We were stuck swimming. There were many passages to see in the first couple thousand feet of the caves near us, so it wasn't that disappointing. We also had caves farther away that we could explore. There was a lot to keep us busy, but I really wanted to see the Trash Room.

We had set out on that dive in Jackson Blue with no expectations. We swam and looked around while I noted potential offshoot tunnels to explore. I didn't venture into any of them. There would be time for that on the way out. We began the dive breathing from our stage tanks.

When the pressures in those tanks were at two thousand psi, we unclipped them from our harnesses and secured them to the gold line. We would retrieve them on the way out. We continued our swim, and forty minutes after we began the dive, we were there.

We checked our pressure gauges and had enough air to continue farther into the cave. We had enough air to finally see the Trash Room. Excited, we swam past the traffic light and entered this section of cave for the first time. There was so much trash strewn about the tunnel. We saw old glass bottles, tin cans, shoes, and a variety of other unidentifiable refuse. It was scattered throughout the passage. It didn't look like a landfill. Every inch of the floor wasn't covered with trash. However, there were pieces of trash every few feet. It spanned the twenty-five-foot width of the passage and continued farther into the cave.

Jen and I slowly moved through the section examining every piece of trash that we saw. We didn't make it to the end of the trash, but we probably saw about half of the Trash Room before we had to turn around. I didn't want to leave. I wanted to keep going and see it to the end. I wanted to continue deeper into the cave and look around the next corner. It took every bit of self-restraint to turn around. I couldn't believe that we had made it so far while swimming. It was unheard of. The end of the gold line in Jackson Blue is forty-six hundred feet from the opening. The main passage continues another few hundred feet, but it's white cave line from that point. We made it almost halfway to the end of the gold line. It was my fortieth dive in Jackson Blue.

On the way out, we peeked into some of the offshoot tunnels. One of the lines I found led to the Queen's Bypass tunnel on the opposite side of King's Canyon. It provided a bypass between the Hall of the Mountain King and the left side of the first gold line circuit. I made a note of it for a future dive. There was still so much to see in that cave.

Three days later we returned to Jackson Blue to try to make it to the Trash Room again, only things didn't start well this time. We should have called the dive before we even entered the water. We had three tank pressure gauges leaking air. I had to replace the o-rings. Then, my stage tank regulator began to free flow, and I had to make adjustments to it. I made the repairs and after a twenty-minute delay, we finally began our dive and had another issue.

My primary dive light powered off as we were moving from the Deco Room to the Rock Garden. We turned around and surfaced so I could figure out what was wrong with it. Fortunately, it was easy to repair. It was a third strike. Or was it the fifth? It depends on whether you count the leaking pressure gauges as one or three. We should have called it a day. We didn't. We headed back toward the cave opening a second time. I had two backup lights on me. If the primary light failed a second time, I could turn around and exit while using one of them.

When it came time to remove the stage tanks to leave them secured to the guideline, I had difficulty removing mine. I struggled until I was able to unclip it. Apparently, I had clipped it to the wrong D ring, and it was trapped by one of my sidemount tanks. Strike four, or seven. I wondered what more could go wrong. I shouldn't have done that. I should have signaled Jen to turn around. I didn't.

We made it past the third line intersection and took the upper route toward the traffic light. When I got to the point where we had to descend to the level where the traffic light was located, I couldn't equalize the air spaces in my ears. I tried to descend, but the pressure in my ears was too great and I had to stop. We still had three hundred psi left in our tanks before we had to turn around. We would have made it through the Trash Room and beyond. We might have even made it to Stage Rock. It wasn't happening, though. Strike five, or eight, finally convinced me to turn around. I had already pushed my luck too far.

I signaled to Jen, and we began our swim out. An hour and forty-five minutes later, we surfaced. Despite all of the issues that occurred, we survived the dive. It was a good dive, even if we didn't make it as far as we had hoped. Even if we didn't see the Trash Room. The saying goes that a bad day diving is still better than a good day at work.

I wanted to see a new cave, so we decided to travel two hours east to dive Madison Blue, located in Madison County. We were heading back to eastern time zone which meant we had to get up early again. To make things worse, the state set a limit on the number of cave divers allowed into Madison Blue cave at any given time. I don't know if it was to limit the environmental impact or because some of the passages were smaller. Regardless of the reason, no more than six cave divers were allowed to be signed in to dive at the same time. If you happened to arrive after the quota was met, you had to wait until enough divers exited the cave and signed out of the park before you were allowed to sign in to dive. That or go somewhere else. It was a weekday so we were hopeful it wouldn't be an issue.

Madison Blue has a lot of offshoot areas near the beginning of the cave. It's more of a maze there than farther in. There are two openings, the larger main opening where a majority of the water flows out into the spring basin, and a smaller, offset opening named the Rabbit Hole. The Rabbit Hole was the preferred entry because the current was less intense. Madison Blue is a first magnitude spring.

We stayed near the front of the cave for the first dive, exploring the offshoot tunnels a few hundred feet in. We did a tour of the Godzilla Room, identifiable by a small Godzilla action figure tied to the line, and the Banana Room, not to be confused with the Banana Room in Jackson Blue. Both are so named due to their curved shapes. After the Banana Room, we headed to the Century Tunnel, another popular name for cave passages. Hole in the Wall and Twin both have Century Tunnels, as well as another lesser-known cave in Jackson County. These tunnels were so named because they averaged one hundred feet of depth.

During our second dive, we swam toward a passage named Rocky Horror, named after the late-night picture show that used to be popular in the 1970s and 1980s. I don't think this tunnel was so named because of anything in the movie, though. The passage is narrow, rocky, and extends a few hundred feet with a lot of switchbacks. It zigzags left and right frequently. Every few feet, the tunnel curves one way or the other.

Most of the tunnel is too small for two divers to pass by each other or to even turn around. This means if two teams encounter each other going in opposite directions, there would be a problem.

To deal with this, an interesting system was devised and placed at the beginning of this tunnel to alert other cave divers when there is already a team in Rocky Horror. A clipboard with a metal clip on top and the words IN and OUT written on it is secured to the line. When a dive team arrives at the clipboard, if the clip is in the IN box, that means other divers are in that section (as long as the clip was properly positioned) and alternate plans should be made. If the clip is in the OUT box, protocol dictates it must be moved to the IN box before entry can be made. There's no sign at the park alerting divers to any of this. We know about this system through word of mouth.

Unfortunately, Jen and I didn't make it to Rocky Horror. We got to a location on the map known as Potter's Delight and turned around. We didn't have stage tanks with us and had been swimming slowly because it was our first time there. We also missed the jump to the offshoot tunnel leading to Rocky Horror initially and had to backtrack. By the time we found it, it was time to turn around.

About a week later, we returned to Jackson Blue and finally made it to the Trash Room again. Not only did we get there, but we made it to Stage Rock, located about two hundred feet after the last piece of trash. The passage beyond the Trash Room gets larger. The ceiling is higher, and the walls are wider apart. This results in the current not being as strong. In turn, the floor is covered in sediment and there are limited places to leave stage tanks. We don't want to place them on the sediment covered floor, creating silt clouds and leaving marks. Instead, we find areas that are more appropriate for leaving stage tanks. One of these places is located about twenty-six hundred feet from the opening and is named Stage Rock (also a popular name in caves).

Jackson Blue Stage Rock is more of a slope than an actual rock. The wall on the left side juts out toward the middle of the passage and slopes down to the floor. The slope is minor, less than ten degrees, making it a perfect place to set stage tanks. It's high enough off of the floor, creating a sediment-free space measuring about fifteen feet long by five feet wide. Three or four stage tanks can easily be secured to the line without disturbing the silt in the rest of the passage. Stage Rock was the farthest we had been, and we got there swimming with only one stage tank in addition to our sidemounted tanks. I was excited to have swum so far into Jackson Blue. It was unheard of!

We returned to Peacock Springs State Park to do the final dive required to complete our Trimix diving certification. The plan was to dive Lower Orange Grove again, so we arrived the day before to reacquaint ourselves with the area. We descended into the Orange Grove sinkhole and attempted to find the opening to Lower Orange Grove. It had seemed so obvious when we were previously there, and I was certain I could find it. We spent almost an hour looking but were unsuccessful. I squeezed into tight holes and reached a depth of one hundred and twenty-eight feet, but the entrance remained hidden.

We were back the next morning to meet our instructor. We got in the water and followed him to the bottom. He took us straight to the opening and into the cave. I had been near it and had even gone into it but zigged when I should have zagged in the corkscrew and ended up in a small cubby hole instead of the main cave passage. I made a mental note of the route we took for future reference. I should have written it down because the next time I tried to find it, I had difficulty again.

We continued into Lower Orange Grove, reaching a depth of one hundred and fifty-nine feet. After this dip, we followed a slope up about twenty feet and arrived at a line intersection. The line split to the left and to the right. We chose to go to the right. We were in what used to be a large room. The ceiling in the center of the room collapsed long before anyone had ventured into it and left a trail around its perimeter.

We slowly made our way along the trail, arriving at the intersection again just as we were about to reach our turn pressure. We knew it was the same intersection because of the non-directional line markers we placed there. Rather than turn around and go back, we grabbed our markers, turned to the right, and swam back toward the small cave opening. We exited the cave and began our decompression stops. We had completed another circuit and finally met the requirements for our Trimix diving certifications.

After lunch, Jen and I returned to Peacock I without our instructor for another dive before heading home. We explored the Peanut Restriction line, making it to the end again. This time we set a jump spool line from it to the Olsen/Challenge line and swam about fifty feet toward Challenge Sink before turning. As we were swimming back, we found very distinctive letters carved into the sediment on a mound in the floor. Someone had written the initials "DIC" into the mud.

There had been sightings of similar cave vandalism elsewhere. Cave divers were discussing the damage on the cave diving social media forums. The worst incident of this graffiti occurred in Cow Spring, a cave located in Luraville. In Cow, the initials were carved into the clay banks in the main passage. The clay banks are beautiful multicolored walls along a section of the main tunnel. They occur in a bend in the tunnel where the current has blown away the sediment and revealed the clay beneath it. The clay banks are made up of multicolored layers about six to eight inches tall and extending more than thirty feet in length.

For some reason, a cave diver thought he could bring the essence of Banksy into the cave and decided to leave his mark by carving the initials into one of the banks. The letters were about four inches tall and very obvious. Cave divers reported seeing DIC also carved into the floor in Devil's Spring cave. My discovery of it in Peacock Springs was the third such report of this vandalism.

I took photos and video of the graffiti and then used my hand to fan the floor and stir up the sediment in an attempt to fill the area where the letters were carved. I was careful not to touch the floor, just fanning my hand an inch above it. I waited for the silt to settle and noted that the letters were filling in. I fanned my hand over them a second time, making them barely discernible. I fanned it once more and waited. I repeated this until the letters were completely filled in and the floor was restored to a somewhat undisturbed state.

The process of restoring the clay banks in Cow Spring was not so easy. There was no sediment to fan. The clay had been carved out, likely fallen to the floor, and pushed away by the current. Fortunately, a cave diver who visited Florida a few times a year was an artist who worked with different types of media, including clay. His name happened to be Michael Angelo. He was destined to be an artist. During his next trip to Florida, he did a dive in Cow Spring to assess the damage and obtain a sample of the clay so he could attempt to match the color and consistency. He was going to try to repair the damage.

The main issue was matching the colors of the clay he was using as a filler to the colors of the clay in the banks. The bank was striped with a variety of dark and light shades. The letters were carved across multiple layers of the bank, so it wasn't going to be an easy operation. Making it even more challenging was the current moving through the cave. It was stronger in the area of the clay banks, and maintaining position without further damaging the cave while doing such delicate work would prove difficult. A plan was formulated that would include three divers and multiple dives to complete the restoration.

The repair was successful after three days, multiple dives, and more than thirty hours devoted to the project. The letters could still be seen, but only if you knew where to look and focused on them. They were not noticeable when just passing through. Over the years, the current has completely erased any signs of the letters having been there. It would have taken decades, if not centuries, had it not been for the efforts of the divers that worked on the repair project.

The identity of the diver who vandalized the cave was learned. Whether he felt guilty or was pressured by his friends, he came forward and confessed his actions. He wasn't from the United States, so the state of Florida prosecuted him in absentia under Florida statute 810.13 – cave vandalism. He is no longer allowed to visit the country. That's what happens when you vandalize a cave in Florida.

17

I don't need to see where I'm diving

Jen and I were enjoying getting to know Jackson Blue, but we wanted to see other caves located in Jackson County. I had learned about a place called Spring Lake, located south of Marianna, and home to eight freshwater springs, many of them large enough to dive, and most of them interconnected. Unfortunately, the lake is surrounded by private property and access is currently restricted. At the time, we did have one point of access at the end of Mystery Springs Road through a county-maintained boat launch.

Spring Lake isn't really a lake. It's more of a marsh. The area near the boat launch is very shallow, only inches deep in most places. It was more of a kayak or canoe launch. There was a narrow body of water that could be followed, but there were also several downed trees making it difficult to pass. This was before Hurricane Michael, and I can only imagine what it looks like now.

The first part of the lake near the boat launch was shallow enough to walk through. The bottom was comprised of sand and provided solid footing. As we got farther from the launch, it got deeper, and the bottom became soft. Every step resulted in sinking knee deep into muck.

The closest spring to the Mystery Springs Road boat launch was Black Spring, located a few hundred feet away. It might as well have been a thousand feet. It took us half an hour to get to because of the muck and the downed trees. We brought our canoe and used it to transport our dive equipment but walked alongside it as we made our way through the marsh. We couldn't take the canoe all the way to the spring because of the trees blocking the path. Jen and I pulled the canoe as far as we could and tied it to one of the trees that sat too high to get the canoe across. We walked and swam the rest of the way. The water was dark and murky, and the thought of alligators was in the back of our minds. We didn't find any alligators and only knew we had found the spring basin when the bottom dropped out from beneath us.

Black Spring was appropriately named. I couldn't see my hand six inches beneath the surface. I was hopeful that it was similar to Morrison and the water flowing from the spring was clear. I returned to the canoe, put on my dive equipment, and dragged the scuba tanks behind me until I was at the basin. It was slow going. Jen wasn't interested in descending into the black murky basin where there might be an alligator hiding and waiting for its next meal. Gator be damned, I wanted to see a new cave. I was either determined or stupid. Probably a little bit of both.

I descended into the black water, hoping I didn't land on top of an alligator. I told myself the water was too cold for them, but I wasn't certain. I spooled line from my primary reel as I followed the slope deeper, all traces of light swallowed by the muck. I found the entrance by pure luck. The water in the basin was a few degrees warmer than the water coming out of the cave and I managed to cross into the path of cold water. I followed the cold stream into the cave and somehow found a guideline tied to the wall on the left just inside. At least I think it was inside of the cave. I hadn't seen daylight since I had gotten five feet below the surface.

I secured the line from my primary reel to the guideline and formed a circle around the line with my thumb and forefinger. I slowly made my way into the cave only knowing where I was because I could feel the line between my fingers. I arrived at a line intersection about two hundred feet from the opening and decided to turn around. The visibility hadn't improved. I couldn't see anything other than occasional glimpses of the wall to my left and the line in my hand. It didn't make sense to keep going. On the way out, I could no longer see the wall. My exhalation bubbles had dislodged the sediment from the ceiling and made the bad visibility even worse. It wasn't much of a cave dive, but it was a great adventure. And I didn't have to wrestle any alligators.

With one adventure behind us, Jen and I spent the next few dives in Jackson Blue happy to be in clear water where we didn't have to fight our way through muck and over downed trees. We were also thankful that we didn't have to worry about an alligator rising from the dark recesses. We returned to the Horseshoe Circuit, finally having it to ourselves and swam the entire length from the top of the chimney fissure to the bottom. It wasn't too small for Jen after all.

We returned to the Squirrel Passage now that we were diving in sidemount configuration and made it past the restriction, emerging at the other end of the line. I swam from the small tunnel into the large main passage of the cave and spotted the gold line twenty feet away. Jen followed me out into the room and began to signal wildly. She was wide-eyed and pointing around the room. Either an alligator had followed us into the cave, or she had just made a discovery.

It took a moment, but I finally understood what Jen was trying to tell me. She thought we had discovered a new section of the cave. She hadn't studied the map and thought the room we were in was a different section of the cave, possibly a previously unexplored section. I aimed the beam of my dive light at the gold line and gave her the signal for line. She still didn't see it. To be fair, the faded yellow line blended with the color of the limestone behind it. I swam to the line and grabbed it. That's when she realized where we were. Her shoulders slumped in disappointment as she realized we hadn't discovered anything.

* * *

Ever since finding the line leading to Queen's Bypass, I had wanted to check it out. We headed there with Mark. We entered the bypass from the Hall of the Mountain King and swam with the flow of the water at our backs. When we reached a restriction about two-thirds of the way from where we left the main passage, Mark signaled that he wanted to turn around. The size of the passage was not large enough for his comfort level. We didn't know it then, but we were less than two hundred feet from the end of that line and the left side tunnel between the first and second line intersections.

A few days later, Jen and I returned to Jackson Blue to explore more offshoot tunnels, and I encountered my first true sidemount restriction. I also had my first real *oh shit!* moment. This was worse than when I got wedged in the horizontal crack in Orange Grove Sink. I found a line leading into the restriction about a hundred feet past the first line intersection in the right tunnel. The restriction was wide enough to pass through, but the vertical clearance was minimal. I set a jump spool line and squeezed through, my back rubbing the limestone above and my belly moving through the mud on the floor. I didn't bother looking back to see the mess I was making.

After a minute or two, the tunnel increased in size. The line came to an end tied to the ceiling in a decent sized room. I looked around, wanting to continue, but I would have had to deploy another line, and Jen was waiting for me on the other side of the restriction. I placed a personal marker on the line a few inches from the end for future reference and turned around. That's when I saw the giant silt cloud that had enveloped the tunnel I had just come through. The tunnel I had to swim back through to get to Jen.

The silt I disturbed in the restriction had followed me through the tunnel. I hadn't thought about the direction of the current and that it was pushing the silt through the passage with me. I had no other choice, so I made contact with the line and swam into the silt cloud. I closed my eyes to fend off the disorientation that would follow if I kept them open. When your eyes are open, your brain expects to see something. Swimming through a silt cloud creates disorientation because you don't see anything. Closing your eyes removes the expectation your brain has and makes moving through the passage much easier from a psychological perspective.

I occasionally opened my eyes to see if the silt had cleared. It hadn't, but I didn't expect it to. I maintained contact with the line with my left hand and held my right hand in front of me to protect my head from hitting the ceiling. About a minute later, my right hand encountered a wall. I moved my hand around, searching for the restriction I had passed through. I couldn't find it. The line was beneath me, so I knew I was in the right place, unless it had moved.

I thought I might have been angled wrong, so I backed up and repositioned. I moved forward and my hand hit the wall again. I searched in front and to the side but couldn't find the hole I had come through. I backed up and approached it again but continued to hit rock. I could feel the panic rising. I tested the tension on the guideline. It wasn't slack. I told myself the restriction had to be there.

I backed up and tried again, this time getting lucky and finding the restriction. I had been holding my right hand too high and kept feeling the ceiling where it dipped down to form the restriction. I hadn't thought about how low it was. I was relieved that I was leaving the silt cloud behind and rejoining Jen in the main passage rather than dying in the silt filled passage. Once at the end of the line, I retrieved my jump spool and gave Jen the dive is over signal. That was a little too close for comfort and I was ready to be back on the surface.

As Jen and I swam out, I noticed a marker hanging from the ceiling to my left. I stopped to inspect it and recognized it as the marker I had just left a few minutes earlier. I looked around and realized we were in the tunnel I had been in when I turned around. I hadn't realized that I was in the main passage. The gold line was ten feet away against the opposite wall and, just as happened to Jen, I didn't see it because it blended in with the floor. Had I known that I was in the main passage, I would have swum along that to return to Jen rather than going through the silt cloud.

As we were heading out, Jen fell into her usual practice of searching for offshoot tunnels. Every time she stopped to look at something, I signaled her and indicated I wanted to continue exiting. Jen didn't know how badly I wanted to be out of the cave. All she saw was our usual hand signal to turn around and she treated it as a normal exit, taking her time to explore. I signaled her three times before she realized I was done. She finally focused on swimming out of the cave, and we expedited our exit. Once we were back at the surface, I told her about my experience with the restriction. She was thankful she hadn't followed me and apologized for delaying the exit. It wasn't her fault.

Prior to this, we used a closed fist with the thumb up hand signal (just like the Fonz, except without the ayyyyyy) for turning around and exiting the cave. There was no way to distinguish between a normal exit and an expedited exit. We had one signal, and we had to figure out what kind of exit we were going to do. That was how we were trained. During our dive debriefing, we devised a way to differentiate between the two. We would use the Fonzie signal to communicate an expedited exit. Turn around and swim at a slightly faster than casual pace toward the opening. No exploring. No passing go. No collecting two hundred dollars. For a casual exit, we would point an index finger up and twirl it in a circle to indicate turning around. That signal meant we had reached one of the turn indicators – tank pressure, penetration distance, depth, etc. – and we could then take our time exiting the cave. We've used those hand signals from that day forward with no further confusion.

A few days later, we returned to Jackson Blue. When we reached the area where I had left the marker the last time, I stopped and set a jump spool line to it. A couple of minutes later I arrived at the restriction, seeing it for the first time from this approach. I finally understood why it had given me so much difficulty. The restriction was a small hole located at the bottom of an arch. My hand had been feeling the area above. The hole was about half a foot lower. This time, I could see the restriction and it gave me no issues. I slipped through back into the main passage and met Jen on the other side.

I had conquered the first restriction that gave me pause and made me rethink my choice to dive in sidemount restrictions. It was a good lesson to learn. I knew I had limits. And I knew that persistence would get me out of almost anything. This would be a lesson I referred back to many times over the years. I'd often ask myself *what the hell am I doing here* during a dive. It kept me grounded and prevented me from becoming complacent. Complacency is what gets you killed in cave diving.

A couple of years later, I returned to that restriction, and it no longer seemed very small. It still couldn't be passed in backmounted tanks, but it didn't give me pause. I had been through smaller restrictions since. With time, perspective changes. Mine certainly had. Seeing that restriction after a couple of years was the first time I realized that. It taught me to revisit areas that I once thought might be too small because they might not seem so small after more experience. It was a good lesson, and one I'll never forget.

18

We're gonna need scooters!

I spent a lot of time in Jackson Blue over the next few months and became very familiar with it. I began recognizing the passages I was swimming through. I knew where I was simply by looking around. The guideline became a reference I rarely used. It was there in case something happened to the visibility, but I didn't need it otherwise. I felt the most comfortable and confident when diving Jackson Blue. It became a second home. I poked my head into every nook and cranny I could find, looking for hidden offshoot tunnels. I didn't care if they had line in them or not. I just wanted to see as much of the cave as I could.

I found a lot of new passages in Jackson Blue that weren't denoted on the published map. Some of them had guidelines in them. Others did not. I sketched the new findings on my personal map and highlighted the tunnels as I explored them. The first two thousand feet of my map was quickly turning yellow. I continued to explore King's Canyon and Queen's Bypass, the two most significant offshoot tunnels closest to the opening of the cave. I learned that there was a lot more to King's Canyon than the map revealed.

The drought continued for a few months longer. The current was almost at a standstill. Jen and I went diving in Jackson Blue one day with a third diver. We swam to the traffic light, through the Trash Room, to Stage Rock, and another hundred feet beyond that. It was the farthest we had gotten in the cave. Twenty-seven hundred feet! We were more than half a mile from the opening and had done that by the power of our fins using only three scuba tanks each.

I was reaching my limits. I had visited every offshoot passage along the first twenty-six hundred feet of the cave multiple times. There was nothing new to see within swimming distance in Jackson Blue. I enjoyed my dives there, but I wanted to see other caves. The problem was that Jackson Blue was the only land accessible cave within an hour's drive of where we lived. It was time to get a boat.

We acquired an old canoe. It wasn't large by any means, only twelve feet in length, but it was big enough to fit both of us and our scuba diving equipment. All of that weight in the canoe didn't leave much freeboard. It stayed afloat, though, and got us onto Merritt's Mill Pond and the Chipola River. The canoe gave us the freedom we needed to see other caves.

For our maiden voyage, we went to Twin Cave. There was a primitive access point to the pond that was almost directly across from the dock, so it was an easy paddle. I put the canoe in the water and took it for a test run to make sure it was watertight and wouldn't sink. The inside of the boat remained dry, and I stayed afloat. Back on shore, we loaded our dive equipment and paddled to the dock. The canoe didn't move quite as fast with two people and two hundred pounds of scuba equipment, but it got us there.

The last time we had been diving in Twin, we barely made it beyond the eight-hundred-foot distance marker. After our recent dives in Jackson Blue, we knew we could get much farther. And we did. Our transition from tourist cave divers to resident cave divers was progressing. Jen and I swam along the Subway Tunnel and encountered a pleasant surprise one thousand feet from the opening. The floor of the tunnel dropped away into a large fissure. It disappeared and cracked open, leaving in its place a long, narrow slit that led into the darkness below. The crack was about twenty feet long and six feet wide. Our ten-watt HID dive lights weren't powerful enough to allow us to see the floor at the bottom of the fissure. It was just a dark void inviting us to explore it.

I looked into the abyss, wanting to answer its call and descend into it. The Subway Tunnel continued forward beyond the fissure, though. There was a choice to be made. My desire to continue forward overpowered the desire to go deeper. I wanted to see what lay ahead. Jen and I continued swimming into the small tunnel. The passage beyond the fissure got fifteen feet shallower and narrower. It was large enough to swim through comfortably, but an errant kick of the fin could easily disturb the thick layer of sediment that reappeared on the floor after the crack. The visibility could have easily gone from perfect to a total silt-out. We moved slowly, not wanting to experience that.

About two hundred and fifty feet later, we arrived at the top of another fissure. It wasn't as large as the first one, but we still couldn't see the bottom. It measured about ten feet long and was narrower. I had to turn so the tank on my right side was slightly lower than the tank on my left in order to descend into the crack. I would have been able to go straight down if I had tanks on my back instead of at my sides. Unlike my scuba tanks, those days were behind me.

I descended into the fissure and arrived at the bottom sixty feet deeper. I was almost one hundred feet deep. It wasn't a straight drop, and I lost sight of Jen's light. Jen had issues equalizing her ears, so she remained at the top of the fissure. My eyes traced the path of the guideline and saw it disappear into the darkness to my right. The passage it went into was about four feet tall and fifteen feet wide. According to the map, I was at one end of the Training Room.

I resisted the urge to continue, turned back, and ascended to reconvene with Jen. I followed her back to the first fissure and we stopped so I could check it out as well. Once again, I descended while Jen waited. Because this fissure was bigger than the previous one, we maintained visual contact. At the bottom, the gold line disappeared into a restriction, heading in the same direction as the gold line sixty feet shallower. It looked like the tunnel was directly below the small tunnel we had just swam through. I was tempted to go through the restriction and see what the passage looked like beyond it, but Jen was waiting for me. She wouldn't have been pleased if I disappeared. I turned away and began my ascent to the Subway Tunnel.

Jen and I continued to visit Peacock Springs State Park on occasion. We weren't bored with the caves in Jackson County. We just wanted to get experience diving as many caves as possible. We wanted to explore every cave in Florida. During one of the Peacock trips, we entered the cave through the Orange Grove opening and swam to Challenge Sink, eighteen hundred feet away. Once there, we surfaced for a quick look. It was worth the time and effort. Challenge Sink is one of the prettiest sinkholes I've seen. We floated on the surface rotating around and taking it all in. We were in the middle of the forest, six feet below ground level, on the other side of the road from the park entrance and Orange Grove Sink. Challenge Sink was appropriately named. It would be difficult to exit from. The walls were steep and slick. Exiting was possible, but we'd have to leave our tanks in the water until we could get ropes to pull them up. We had no plans to do that, but it was nice knowing we had another option to exit in the event of an emergency.

A few years later, we heard about another cave diver that had an issue with his scuba tanks near Challenge Sink and used it as an emergency exit. He should have had sufficient air in his tanks to turn around and make it to Orange Grove, but the option to surface sooner was there and he took it. I can't say I would have done it any differently.

As I mentioned, Challenge Sink is located across the street from the main area of the park. It's on state park land, but the state doesn't want people entering Challenge Sink. They prefer to preserve the natural habitat around it. It can't be seen from the road, and there aren't any roads or trails leading to it. The cave passages on both sides of Challenge Sink pass below the road between it and the main area of the park. Anytime you're driving along 180th Street and passing the entrance to the Wes Skiles Peacock Springs State Park, keep in mind you're driving over cave passages only sixty feet below the road. You might even be driving over cave divers in those passages.

* * *

Drought conditions came to an end. It didn't just start raining. The drought ended in typical Florida style. There were torrential rainstorms in Jackson County that lasted thirty-eight hours. The rain began Thursday night and didn't stop until Saturday morning. A total of twenty-three inches of rain dropped in the area during that thirty-eight-hour period. Streets flooded. Citizens Lodge, one of the parks bordering the Chipola River, flooded. It wasn't just the park that was underwater. The building located on the other side of the park from the riverbank had water intrusion. More than three quarters of the park was submerged! The amount of rain we had was incredible. It wasn't even hurricane season. This happened in February of 2008.

Jen and I had lived in Arizona for many years and were used to monsoons rolling in during the afternoons and dropping enough rain to flood the desert washes. This was different. It was dark and dreary, and the rain kept coming. We stood under our carport and watched the entire length of our driveway flood. Areas of our backyard were underwater. We had to walk our dogs in the carport to keep from having wet dog smell infiltrate the house.

Saturday morning, we woke up to a clear, sunny day. There wasn't a trace of clouds in the sky. If it wasn't for our flooded backyard and driveway, we wouldn't have known it had been raining for the past day and a half. We checked the property to make sure nothing had floated away and left to go cave diving. What else would a cave diver do on a beautiful, clear Saturday morning? We were fairly certain that our days of swimming far into Jackson Blue were behind us. There was no way the amount of rain we experienced hadn't affected the current. We drove to the sheriff's office to sign out the key, and the deputy signing us in warned us that other divers had been there earlier and returned shortly after stating the cave was blown out. He said the visibility was non-existent. I didn't believe him. I thought he had to be exaggerating. Jackson Blue never got blown out.

We took the key and headed across town. I had to see it for myself. Once at the park, we walked to the water's edge. I couldn't believe my eyes. The basin was a dull green color resembling pea soup, and we couldn't see the sandy bottom only three feet below the surface. Jackson Blue had really blown out. Even worse was that we could see a boil on the surface in front of the cave. That was the first time we had seen evidence of any kind of current coming from Jackson Blue. The presence of the boil confirmed that we would no longer be swimming to Stage Rock with three scuba tanks. I didn't know if we would make it to the Hall of the Mountain King. We had only been living in Florida for six months and conditions had changed drastically.

Rather than enter the pea soup spring basin, we decided to give it a couple of hours to see if the newly recharged aquifer would clear the visibility. It was before noon, and we could wait until afternoon to go diving. We drove around Jackson County for the next couple of hours to see what the rain had done. We had seen large ponds of water along the road during our drive from home to the park. We drove to Citizens' Lodge and were in shock when we saw most of the park underwater. The building that was located almost half a mile from the riverbank was surrounded by water. The area of the park between the building and the river had turned into a lake. We drove to a couple of boat ramps and saw that they were flooded as well. The river had crested from its usual six feet to more than twenty-four feet in a two-day period. It was absolutely incredible. I wouldn't have believed it if I hadn't seen it for myself.

We returned to the park about three hours later, hoping the basin had begun to clear. The appearance hadn't changed at all, but we decided to go diving anyway. I wanted to see if the conditions we were seeing in the basin were being caused by the water coming from inside of the cave or if it was the pond water backing into the basin and the cave. Although, the boil seemed to already discount the latter.

The water felt colder than usual, and I became hopeful that we were seeing pond water intrusion. It was February and the pond was typically several degrees colder farther from the springs. The spring water was always sixty-nine degrees Fahrenheit/twenty degrees Celsius. I was hopeful that the visibility would be clear inside of the cave. I tied one end of my primary reel around the ladder rail next to the diving platform. Jen and I had been diving Jackson Blue enough that we hadn't used a primary line in several months, but we felt it necessary considering the conditions.

One of the rules of cave diving is to always have a continuous guideline to the surface. We did that at every other cave. However, we were extremely familiar with Jackson Blue and knew we could get out of the cave from the beginning of the gold line, even in poor visibility. We had tested that by securing the line from one of our safety spools to the gold line, closing our eyes, and exiting the cave by feeling our way out. All one has to do is follow the wall to the left. There's nowhere else to go except out of the cave. Besides, prior to the torrential rains, Jackson Blue had always been clear. It had never blown out.

Why did we place a line in the cave for this dive if we didn't normally use one? We did it so we could stay together. The visibility in the basin and in the cavern was so bad that we couldn't see each other when we were only two feet apart. I could barely see the beam from my dive light in front of me. I ran the line into the cave and Jen followed behind by maintaining contact with the line. I easily found the gold line, even with the visibility as bad as it was.

When we reached the top of the chimney fissure, I stopped for a moment to check if I could feel any water movement. It was strange because there was a distinct boil on the surface outside of the cave but minimal flow inside. I watched the particles in the water and saw them slowly heading toward the opening. There was current, but it wasn't that strong, and the direction of travel did not bode well for our chances of getting clear visibility anytime soon. We were two hundred and fifty feet inside of the cave and the visibility was still bad. It wasn't likely that it would clear no matter how far we went. We continued anyway. We were too curious not to.

We descended the fissure and the visibility seemed to clear slightly. It opened up from about a foot of visibility to four feet. It still had a green tint to it and was very hazy. It was as if we were moving through a thick fog. We continued to the first line intersection nine hundred feet from the opening. The visibility never improved. It was just as green and hazy. Jen and I turned around and headed out, wondering how long the bad conditions would last. This was the first time such a thing had happened as long as anyone could remember. Jackson Blue had never experienced a weather-related visibility blow out. Almost twenty years later, I've never seen it happen again.

Jen and I woke up the next morning anxious to see if conditions at Jackson Blue had improved. When we arrived at the park, we looked into the water. This time, we could see the sandy bottom of the spring basin. The water was hazy, but conditions had improved. It was no longer green. It was more like a fog. We did a short dive into the cave to see what it looked like inside. This time we didn't need the primary line to stay together. We could see about twenty feet in front of us. It was still far from being its usual perfect visibility.

About a week later, we returned to Jackson Blue. The water clarity had still not returned to normal. The visibility was about twenty feet but wasn't as hazy as it had been the weekend before. What was also not back to normal, or at least the normal we had experienced during our first six months of living in Florida, was the intensity of the current. The water flowing out of the cave was ripping! That boil we had begun to see a week earlier looked more like the surface of a jet tub. The current was so strong that we had to pull ourselves into the cavern. We couldn't kick our fins hard enough to counteract it. All of that time I had taken to learn the cave and how to swim through it without touching it was quickly wiped away in one weekend. There were no areas of the cave that a diver could hide from the current. It was everywhere. It felt like we were swimming in a firehose.

Once we got into the Rock Garden, we descended until we were just above the sandy path on the right and partly shielded from the current.

We still had to work hard to swim against it. It was no longer possible to coast through that section. At the beginning of the gold line, there was nowhere to hide. The current was everywhere. We moved through the passage carefully selecting handholds to use to pull ourselves along. It was slow going. The current was kicking our butts. It took nearly half an hour, but we made it to the first line intersection. That normally only took us eighteen minutes. We went to the left into the larger of the two tunnels because the current coming from the other side was too strong. The left side wasn't much better. The current was strong no matter where we went.

When we arrived at the second line intersection, I signaled Jen to turn around. I had enough. I was tired and out of breath and wanted to ride out with the current that was working so hard to keep us from going farther into the cave. When we returned to the basin and surfaced, the first words out of my mouth were "We're gonna need scooters!"

We hadn't planned on making such a large purchase so soon after moving to Florida. Jen and I thought we could spend a couple of years exploring and learning the cave passages within swimming distance. We still had Hole in the Wall and Twin, but Jackson Blue was the most convenient and we enjoyed diving there. I had already explored every offshoot tunnel I could find in the first twenty-six hundred feet of the cave. With the current as strong as it was, I could no longer swim beyond eleven hundred feet.

That evening I browsed the eBay listings. New scooters were too expensive, especially considering we needed two of them, so I looked for used. I found a Mako DPV for under a thousand dollars. That was much easier to swallow than ten thousand dollars for two new DPVs. The Mako wasn't top-of-the-line, but it was appropriate for cave diving and would do until we had enough money to buy new. I clicked the buy now button, and we anxiously awaited the arrival of our first DPV.

In the meantime, we borrowed a couple of Mako DPVs from a friend of ours. We wanted to get some practice while we waited for ours to arrive. We went to Jackson Blue and practiced with the borrowed

DPVs in the spring basin before venturing into the cave. At that time, the basin was not overgrown with eel grass like it currently is, so there was a lot more room to maneuver. Once we felt comfortable with the DPVs in the basin, we turned toward the opening and headed into the Jackson Blue cavern. We zoomed in and out of the Deco Room, getting a feel for being propelled through the water by large DPVs. We had used smaller SeaDoo scooters in the Arizona lakes, but these were much different. They were bigger and more powerful.

Once we felt comfortable in the Deco Room, we decided to head farther into the cave. That might not have been the brightest idea. We went to the top of the chimney fissure, scootered down to the deeper section, and continued toward the first breakdown. Jen and I were side by side, moving quickly through the tunnel. I turned to look at Jen and noticed that she was a little too close to the ceiling. Before I could react and signal her to stop or point the nose of her DPV down, she smacked her head on the limestone surface. We stopped and hovered for a moment. I watched Jen carefully, ready to grab her and drag her out of the cave if she lost consciousness. Fortunately, she didn't. She recovered and we turned around, heading out slowly. Helmets were in our future.

More than two weeks had passed since the storm, and Merritt's Mill Pond was still murky. I was curious about the conditions at Twin Cave. Jen had a slight headache, but she wasn't feeling nauseous and wasn't drowsy. She hadn't hit her head hard enough to cause a concussion and didn't have any scrapes, just a small bump. It had merely stunned her. I left her on shore for a few minutes while I scootered toward Twin cave to check the conditions there.

It took me a lot longer than I expected to get to the cave opening. I thought it might take ten minutes, but it took double that! The water in the pond was murky and got worse the farther I went from the Jackson Blue spring basin. I finally arrived at Twin Cave and peeked inside. The visibility was less than five feet. I secured the tow rope of the DPV to a hole in the limestone and ran a guideline to the gold line two hundred feet in. The conditions didn't change. Visibility was worse than it had been in Jackson Blue the first day after the storm.

It was about a month before the visibility in Jackson Blue started to return to its normal near perfect clarity. Rain was minimal, yet the current seemed to get stronger. There were discussions on the social media sites about the conditions. In one of the threads, I learned that the current at Jackson Blue had been much stronger years earlier. One diver stated that he could only reach the first line intersection with a set of double backmounted tanks, a stage tank, and a DPV while also kicking his fins as hard as he could. I couldn't imagine having to fight that hard to travel nine hundred feet. It didn't sound fun. I'm pretty certain I would have found a different hobby if that was how all caves were.

19

Zoom! Zoom!

The Mako DPV we found on eBay arrived. I was excited to finally have a way to fight the strong current in Jackson Blue. It hadn't shown any signs of easing off. If anything, it continued to grow more intense. Swimming in that cave was no longer fun. I continued my search for a second DPV, found one for about the same price, and clicked the purchase button. In the meantime, we borrowed our friend's Mako DPV and headed to Jackson Blue for our new DPV's maiden voyage, well, maiden voyage with us anyway. We took it around the spring basin for a few laps before venturing into Jackson Blue again. This time, we wore helmets.

We made it to the Hall of the Mountain King before turning around. We would have continued farther into the cave, but the visibility in the Hall of the Mountain King was less than five feet. It had been more than a month since the rainstorm, but I didn't think this was residual effects. There were other divers in the cave, and we suspected they were responsible for stirring up the sediment.

We returned to Twin cave to see if conditions had improved and were pleased to see they had. It was hazy, but much better than when I last saw it. We swam the Subway Tunnel, descended into the first fissure and continued following the gold line. We were one hundred feet deep, and it felt like we were inside a maze of catacombs below an old European castle. They were wide and low and dusty with several offshoot tunnels on both sides. I kept expecting to see a crypt with a dead bishop or cardinal inside.

We moved through these catacombs, soon arriving in the Training Room. There was a set of line arrows on the guideline pointing in opposite directions. One pointed back the way we had come, and the other pointed in the direction we were going. We were at the midway point of the circuit. We could go back and ascend through the fissure we had descended, or we could continue straight and ascend through the other fissure. It would be the same distance to the opening regardless of which way we went. We chose to continue forward.

The Training Room was a long rectangular passage about four to five feet tall and twenty feet wide. There were no offshoot tunnels or unique formations. It was just a wide corridor through the earth. It felt like a crawlspace under a house. At the end of the Training Room, I recognized the bottom of the other fissure, so Jen and I ascended to the small tunnel above. We continued toward the first fissure and, as we approached it, I saw bubbles rising from divots in the floor. Our exhaust bubbles had penetrated from the catacombs sixty feet below. They had made their way through long fistulas connecting the two tunnels. I was amazed at how porous the limestone was.

A minute later, we were at the top of the first fissure. We had completed the gold line circuit in Twin Cave. We continued through the Subway Tunnel and had plenty of air in our scuba tanks when we surfaced. We decided to paddle to Shangri-la, a cave located in one of the bluffs between Twin Cave and Jackson Blue. This is one of the prettiest locations on Merritt's Mill Pond. It's set back in the banks of the pond in a shady area of cypress trees. The opening of the cave is at the base of a limestone wall that contains holes that lead to the underwater cave. There's an *island* offset to the left in front of the opening. It's quiet and one of the most relaxing areas on the pond. The county has since built a boardwalk from Blue Springs Recreation Area to Shangri-La and that may change, unfortunately.

We tied the canoe to one of the cypress trees and stepped into the shallow water. Shangri-la is mostly a cavern dive. There's a cave in there, but I didn't venture into it for another few years. I'm not sure how many people have been in that cave, but I'd guess I could count them on one hand. The passage is very small and requires pushing a scuba tank, sometimes both, in front to get through some sections. I tried to go into the cave that day, but the passage beyond the cavern was too small for my comfort level. We were also using the air left over from our dive in Twin Cave and I didn't feel comfortable pushing into such a small restriction without full scuba tanks.

After lunch, we headed to Jackson Blue for another DPV cave dive. This time we didn't encounter any issues with the visibility and made it to Stage Rock. The current was strong, but the DPVs were able to handle the resistance. We had a great time zooming through the cave passages moving about one hundred and twenty feet per minute. Our usual swim pace was fifty feet per minute when the current wasn't bad. The DPVs were proving to be useful tools. Not only could we use them to get farther inside of the cave, but we could use them to get to areas we wanted to visit. Instead of swimming to the Hall of the Mountain King to go see King's Canyon, we could scooter to the Hall, secure the DPVs to the guideline, and swim to the Canyon from there. The offshoot tunnels didn't have as much water flowing through them, so swimming was much easier. The DPVs allowed us to spend a lot more time farther back in the cave.

We did have to adjust the way we planned our dives. The rule of thirds no longer applied. If the DPVs failed, we would have to swim out. We needed to make sure we had enough air in our scuba tanks to do that. Even though the current helped us swim out faster, it did not push us at a pace of one hundred and twenty feet per minute. We had to plan on taking two to three times as long to exit as we did to penetrate the cave.

* * *

The weather turned cold, and we decided to avoid the water until the arctic front left Florida. That's right! It can get that cold in the Florida panhandle. The air temperature was in the high thirties to low forties during the day and dropping into the twenties at night. One night it was forecast to get down to nineteen degrees! Fahrenheit! We decided to look for access points to the Chipola River on one of those cold, blustery days. We wanted to start taking the canoe to some of the river caves not typically visited by tourist cave divers because access wasn't easy.

We were at the Peacock Road bridge to look for a nearby spring when we encountered a small black dog with white markings on her. We could count her ribs and see her teats hanging. She had recently had a litter. I parked the van and tried to approach her, but she growled. She was curious but cautious. She also appeared to be guarding a small hole she had dug out for herself to stay out of the cold breeze. We happened to have a bag of granola mix in the van and offered it to her. Jen folded down the sides of the bag to form a bowl and we placed it in front of the pup. As soon as we moved away, she eased forward and began eating the granola. While she was distracted with the food, I walked behind her to investigate her dugout.

Inside were two tiny puppies squirming around. Neither had opened its eyes. I wanted to reach down and grab them, but I didn't want to spook their mother while she was eating. I stood next to her babies and let mama finish the granola. When she was done, she turned around and walked directly toward me. I guess she figured out we were good people. I slowly held my hand out to let her smell it and cautiously pet her. I had won her over.

Jen opened the van door to get a towel to wrap the puppies in. The dog ran toward her and jumped in. She had claimed us. I carefully picked up her babies, wrapped them inside the towel, and laid them in the van next to her. There was no way we could leave those dogs in the elements when it was going to get so cold that night. We had just gone from a three-dog family to a six-dog family.

We learned that the puppies had been born within hours of us finding them when their eyes finally began opening ten days later. Once their eyes were opened, we couldn't keep the puppies contained. They crawled all over the house exploring as much as they could. They were little explorers like their new people. It was cuteness overload and Jen and I fell in love with them. We couldn't bear to part with them. We named the mother Maddie, short for Maddachalk, the name of the spring located only three hundred yards from where we found them. The puppies were named Jackson and Madison, after two of the Blue Springs we had been diving in. We never called them that, though. Instead, we called them Little Dude and Baby Girl.

* * *

A couple of weeks after we found Maddie and her pups, we headed to Mexico for our second cave diving trip. We used sidemounted tanks rather than backmounted tanks during our dives. We revisited a couple of the caves we had been to the year before and did a guided dive to see a different cave. That was our last trip to the mainland. We started to plan a return trip a little more than a year later after Jen graduated from nursing school, but the Mexican mainland was on its cycle of increased crime. Every few years there's an uptick in crime there. It wasn't just crimes against tourists. These were crimes targeting cave divers. When that happens, it's best to wait until reports of crime decrease.

One of the reports we read was of equipment stolen from a truck parked at a cenote. The attendant that was watching the truck was assaulted and had serious injuries. That cenote, one we had been to during our first trip, was closed to diving for several months after that. We also heard a report of cave divers arriving in Mexico, checking into their resort, and going out to dinner. They left their dive equipment in the trunk of the rental car during dinner and when they returned to the resort and opened the trunk, it was gone. They had lost thousands of dollars of dive equipment and were unable to dive during that trip. It was probably an inside job. That didn't change the fact that they had lost so much, including the ability to do what they came to do – cave dive. We decided we would put off our third trip to Mexico for a year or two.

Before we started to make plans to return to Mexico, I came across an open invitation for a trip to dive the caves in Cozumel, Mexico. I jumped at the opportunity. The caves in Cozumel had the reputation of being advanced, difficult caves to dive. They were also known to be very unique. I couldn't pass it up. You can read about the first trip as well as all of the others in my *Beneath the Jungle of Cozumel* series.

20

Avalanche Alley lives up to its name

I began doing a lot more solo diving after our return from Mexico. Jen was busy in her second semester of nursing school and didn't have as much time off. I pushed my comfort levels and started diving solo with my DPV. The current in Jackson Blue was still strong and I had no desire to swim against it. I did conservative dives at first, extending the distance of my penetration little by little. I was eventually scootering to the fourth intersection. I brought Al with me on every dive, feeling better knowing I could depend on it should there be an issue. Counting the air in Al, I was surfacing with three fourths of the air I started my dives with.

I got more courageous, or maybe more daring, and scootered beyond the fourth line intersection. I made it to Stage Rock and parked the DPV so I could swim beyond it to learn the cave at a slower pace. One of the general rules of cave diving with a DPV is to only scooter where you've been swimming. The point of that rule was to allow you to learn the cave passage slowly rather than zooming through it the first time. It was important to become familiar with the passage, so you knew where to expect those random line intersections.

You don't want to scooter where you have never been. You must familiarize yourself with the passage first. What if it suddenly gets smaller? What if there's a sharp turn? What if the ceiling dips around a corner? The time to learn those things wasn't as you were flying through the cave at a speed at which it would take a few seconds to stop. So I

ROB NETO

took things slowly. I did progressive penetration and learned what the cave looked like beyond Stage Rock. I was scootering more than half a mile into the cave and swimming beyond that. And I was doing it alone. As I became familiar with the cave, I pushed my penetration distance, eventually going beyond Stage Rock to the three-thousand-foot line marker before turning around. A DPV failure at maximum penetration would take close to an hour to swim back to the opening. That thought remained in the back of my mind. I occasionally asked myself what the hell am I doing back here.

One day I pushed it a little past the three-thousand-foot line marker. I didn't park the DPV but rather continued to scooter through the passage. For the first time, I saw a line intersection formed by the gold line and a white line. At first, I thought it was a jump spool, but I knew there was no one else in the cave. Closer inspection revealed it was a permanent intersection. I had never seen such a line intersection in Florida. Prior to that dive I had only seen the four gold line intersections in Jackson Blue and two gold line intersections in Little River cave. All of those were alternate passages to the same location. That wasn't the case with this white line. This line led to a different section of the cave. It didn't loop back into the main passage. I felt like I had been transported to a cave in Mexico where line intersections were not only common, but frequent.

The line intersection seemed like a good place to turn around. I chastised myself for scootering where I hadn't swum before. It was a foolish thing to do, but I quickly learned my lesson when I saw the unexpected line intersection. I had been pushing things too quickly and it could have gotten me into trouble. I slowed my scootering pace after that. Rather than moving through the passage at one hundred and twenty feet per minute, I slowed down to about eighty feet per minute. It was faster than swimming, but slow enough to be able to react. The line intersection would have been easy to miss if I hadn't been paying attention. I needed to slow my progression.

I scootered to the line intersection a few more times, secured the

153

DPV to the line, and proceeded by the power of my fins. I wanted to learn the cave at a safer pace. Once I swam from the line intersection to the thirty-five-hundred-foot marker, I scootered past the intersection to the new location. That was the limit of the DPV. It took thirty-two minutes to scooter thirty-five hundred feet against the strong current.

The distance a DPV can travel is limited by battery endurance. The DPVs Jen and I purchased had a run time of seventy minutes with a good battery. The older the battery, the shorter the runtime. The general rule is to use eighty percent of the battery during a dive. That meant I could be on the trigger for fifty-six minutes. Any more than that and I risked draining the battery before making it back to the opening. I risked having to swim part of the way out.

I wasn't overly concerned. While it was taking me thirty-two minutes to get to the line intersection, I was getting back to the Deco Room in about twenty-two minutes. I was cutting it close, but I had a small buffer. Even if the battery drained with a few hundred feet to go before reaching the opening, the current would push me out at a faster swimming pace. I had more than enough air in my scuba tanks to swim out from maximum penetration if I had to. Al made sure of that. I still had some sense left in my brain.

Our buddy, Mark, purchased a new DPV and we began scootering together. For our first dive, we penetrated to the thirty-six-hundred-foot line marker before Mark turned the dive because he was getting cold. A couple of days later, Mark and I planned a dive to the end of the gold line. Yeah, I know. I hadn't swum to it yet. But the end of the line was too enticing to pass up. I had a friend willing to go with me, so I had to try it just this once. The dive would bring us one thousand feet farther than either of us had been before. I knew neither of my Makos would get me that far and back out, so I borrowed a DPV with longer range. Mark borrowed a second DPV to bring with us in case one of the DPVs malfunctioned. The end of the line was forty-six hundred feet in. That would be a long way to swim out, even with the current helping us. It would have taken ninety minutes. That also meant a lot more decompression obligation. Neither of us wanted to swim that far or be on a decompression stop that long.

We didn't make it to the end of the line. Mark had issues with the second DPV wobbling around and not staying in the proper position. He signaled me to turn around at the second line intersection. It was a sign. We were focusing on trying to get farther in the cave and had increased the risk of our dives because of an objective. That was not a good thing. That wasn't what DPVs should be used for. I reevaluated what I was doing and decided to stop trying to go so far during every dive. I pushed back the complacency that had taken me over and regained my sense. I began using the DPVs to get to areas that I wanted to explore rather than to go farther into the cave.

The first area we explored was King's Canyon. Mark hadn't been in it since we first took him there. He knew what to expect this time and was mentally prepared for it. We scootered to the offshoot passage connecting the main passage to King's Canyon, secured our DPVs to the line, and swam the rest of the way. As soon as I arrived at King's Canyon, I felt a rush of awe come over me. It had been a while since I had been there, and I had forgotten how beautiful it was. I swam slowly and took it all in.

When we arrived at the end of the line in King's Canyon, I looked around the corner and saw the gold line twenty-five feet away. I instantly recognized the passage we were in. I had been through it dozens of times. I signaled Mark to hold his position as I swam to the gold line. Once there, I grabbed the line and signaled Mark again. He also recognized the passage and swam across to join me. We drifted toward our DPVs, which were parked three hundred feet downstream.

I unclipped my DPV from the guideline and backed away to give Mark room to retrieve his. I faced Mark to maintain a visual on him. I was also facing into the cave with my back toward the exit. It took Mark a few minutes to get himself situated. During that time, the current pushed me backwards into an area of the Hall of the Mountain King that I hadn't noticed before. It was located to the right when exiting the cave and extended about thirty feet in. There was no guideline in this part of the room, and the gold line was not visible. It was on the opposite side of the passage and behind a section of the ceiling that dipped down.

I ended up in this small alcove about forty feet from the line, no longer able to see it. The current pushed Mark into the alcove with me. There was a small moment of panic as disorientation set in. I looked around, searching for the guideline. I don't know if Mark was aware of our loss of visual on the line because he was still working on getting himself situated. As I scanned the room, I recognized the mounds in the Hall of the Mountain King about thirty feet behind Mark. I pointed the nose of my DPV toward them and hit the trigger. The DPV pulled me past Mark toward the center of the Hall of the Mountain King. A few seconds later I saw the gold line once again. Crisis averted.

It was a short-lived incident, and neither of us was negatively affected by it, but it was a valuable lesson. It taught me I had to maintain better situational awareness and better line awareness. It could have been a very bad situation, especially when using the DPV. The alcove we were pushed into had a thick layer of sediment on the floor. If we had been pushed into the sediment, a large silt cloud would have formed around us. There was nowhere in that alcove where we could secure a safety line if it had come to that. Finding the gold line would not have been easy.

Once I was reoriented to the gold line, I signaled Mark. By that time, he was situated and ready to go. He moved closer to the gold line, and I asked him to hold his position. I went into the alcove where I had just been pushed, this time intentionally. I wanted to see the area without the state of panic at the edge of my mind. It was just an alcove at the end of the Hall of the Mountain King that had been carved out by the water current. The main passage was to the left but not directly visible or accessible from there.

The alcove was in line with the Hall of the Mountain King and in the direct path of the current. The main passage curved to the left and down. The alcove had a large silty slope likely caused by centuries of the water current pushing the silt from deeper in the cave. It was a large dirt mound more than twenty feet high sloping up to about ten feet below the ceiling. The area was about fifteen feet wide from wall to wall. The possibility of a small passage that led elsewhere buried beneath the mound entered my mind.

I returned to the gold line where Mark was waiting, and we continued out of the cave. An important lesson had been learned. I would pay more attention to my position, especially relative to where the line was. It was unnerving to be in a dark, silty area of the cave with no reference to the line and I had no desire to find myself in such a situation again.

Mark and I continued to meet at Jackson Blue to dive. The next time we ventured out of the main passage was just beyond Stage Rock. We scootered to Stage Rock, secured the DPVs to the line next to our stage tanks, and swam another hundred feet where I set a jump line to a white line I had found on the right side. This line led to a passage named Avalanche Alley, an interesting and concerning name. Why would anyone name a passage in a cave avalanche? I would find out several years later during another dive.

During that dive years later, I was scootering alone in Jackson Blue, came to the end of the Trash Room, and turned left at the bend we call the Elbow. Less than one hundred feet later, before I reached Stage Rock, I found myself in a large silt cloud. The silt engulfed the passage from floor to ceiling and wall to wall. I had to release the DPV trigger and make contact with the line. The visibility was so bad I couldn't see a foot in front of me. I should have turned around and exited the cave, but my curiosity was piqued, so I kept going. I wanted to find out what caused the silt cloud. When I got to the area where the offshoot passage to Avalanche Alley was located, the visibility cleared. I looked back and saw the silt billowing out from Avalanche Alley.

I continued farther into the cave and about twenty minutes later turned around to exit. I expected the silt to be gone and the visibility restored. I didn't expect it to be perfect, but I did expect improvement. I was wrong! When I got to the Avalanche Alley offshoot, the silt was still pouring out from the area and looked worse than earlier. I released the DPV trigger and made contact with the line again. I had to swim more than two hundred feet before the visibility cleared. It wasn't because the silt had stopped moving through the passage, but rather because the current pushed the silt straight past the Elbow where I turned right to follow the gold line out of the cave.

I was the only one at Jackson Blue that morning. No one else had signed in before me and there were no vehicles in the park. The only explanation I could come up with for this event was that Avalanche Alley lived up to its name. There was a collapse that created a silt cloud large enough that it poured out into the main passage, destroying the visibility.

I eventually went back to Avalanche Alley to investigate but couldn't find what had fallen. I wasn't thoroughly familiar with that area of the cave at the time and was not likely to recognize changes. I am convinced that there was a collapse. The amount of silt I witnessed could only be caused by divers or a collapse, and there were no divers. Maybe a piece of the ceiling fell. This was the first time I became aware of cave collapses being a possibility in present times.

I thought a lot about the cave topography after this. I've mentioned the Rock Garden and the first and second breakdowns. There's also a third breakdown, although we don't call it that, which starts right before the second gold line intersection. These areas are called breakdowns because the rocks, or rather boulders, that comprise them used to be part of the ceiling. The rocks on the floor of the Rock Garden came from the ceiling in that room. If you look at what is now the floor and ceiling, you can see how the puzzle pieces fit together. It's unnerving when you think about it.

Those collapses happened long before anyone began diving Jackson Blue. There are fossilized sand dollars and crinoids on the surface of the rocks, so we know it happened eons ago. It makes sense that it continues to happen. Although thankfully, not all that frequently. Collapses are more likely to happen when divers frequent a cave. Doron Nof, a friend of mine who has since passed, was an oceanographer and studied these phenomena. He came up with a theory for the cave collapses that were actively happening. I'll go into more detail on his theory and a much bigger collapse later in the series.

Several weeks passed since Jen had the opportunity to dive, but the opportunity finally came. We visited Twin so we could do a nice, easy dive in a low flow cave. We also had another purpose. We were extending the beginning of the gold line from where it was two hundred feet from the opening out to a few inches inside of the cave. I had been volunteered to organize the annual convention being held in Marianna for one of the cave diving organizations. It turned out to be a large event. We expected to have close to two hundred and fifty cave divers coming together in Jackson County over the weekend.

Thankfully, not all of them would be cave diving, but we expected that the caves would be overrun with divers. In order to make things safer, I installed a temporary line from the opening of Jackson Blue to the gold line so we wouldn't have multiple guidelines running through the cavern. Because Twin Cave was only accessible by boat, I decided it would be better to extend the gold line there and leave it like that. I never saw the point in the beginning of the line being two hundred feet from the opening. It didn't make sense. Even the lines at Peacock I started only a few feet in.

A couple of days later, we checked out Gator Hole, another cave on Merritt's Mill Pond. That's the name known by cave divers. I differentiate it because some of the springs and caves have different names depending on who you talk to. Locals tend to call them by one name and cave divers call them by another. The two caves on the east bank of Merritt's Mill Pond are called Gator Hole and Hole in the Wall. Cave divers call the cave across from the Hunter Fish Camp Road boat ramp Gator Hole. The cave that's located about a mile and a half upstream near a wooden dock is called Hole in the Wall. Locals reverse that. Gator Hole is the one by the dock and Hole in the Wall is the one across from the boat ramp.

What the locals call them makes more sense because the one across from the boat ramp is literally a hole in the wall of a small bluff. The top half of the cave is open to air and is large enough to fit a kayak inside. You can kayak or snorkel into the opening and penetrate about one hundred feet. If you feel brave, you can dive underwater beneath the ceiling and pop back up into another air-filled room that continues for another hundred feet or so. The opening to the underwater portion of the cave is in the area where you have to duck under the ceiling.

We paddled across the pond from the boat ramp and explored the first portion of the cave where we had access to the surface, including beyond the bend where the duck under was located. On the way back, I found the guideline leading into the underwater section of the cave and secured my primary line to it. Jen wasn't having any of the small cave so she waited in the cavern while Mark and I went into the cave. We only penetrated about one hundred feet before Mark decided he wasn't having it either. It was too small for his comfort level. I accompanied him back to where Jen was waiting and then returned by myself to look around a little more. The passage continued getting smaller, forcing me to belly down in the sand. You must be in sidemount configuration to be able to fit inside of Gator Hole. Even then, it's a tight fit.

My progression into becoming a resident cave diver was going well. I was diving Jackson Blue on a regular basis and becoming very familiar with it. The DPV was providing me with opportunities I wouldn't otherwise have. It was also creating issues. I don't know if I was getting too comfortable with cave diving or if it was just my time to experience problems during my dives. My skills in dealing with the DPV were put to the test. It hadn't taken long for the first few problems to finally rear their ugly heads.

21

Pass the scalpel, please

I continued diving Jackson Blue with Mark and building my experience with my DPV. On one particular dive, we planned to go to the traffic light and turn around. We wanted more time on the trigger and more time maneuvering the DPVs. We were getting to know our DPVs better so that we could eventually do longer and more complex dives. It was a good thing we did this.

The floor of the cave in front of the traffic light is bare. There are some small pieces of limestone and gravel, but there's no fine silt. It resembles a patio. On the way out from the traffic light, the white *patio* narrows into a path about three to four feet wide that leads out into a large room with mounds of sediment. The path was created by centuries of strong current pushing sand and gravel over its surface. It's very distinctive and leads to a restriction named the Rabbit Hole that's about three feet in diameter and located at the bottom of a slope about twenty feet from the third line intersection.

There's a lot of water coming out of the Rabbit Hole. *A lot.* The passage on the other side is a decent size and a significant amount of the water moving through the cave is directed through that restriction. Even faster, more powerful DPVs struggled to make headway through the restriction when the current was strong. From the traffic light until about a foot before the Rabbit Hole, the floor was free of fine sediment. The current pushed it out and created the slope that followed. All that was on the floor for about two feet in diameter around the Rabbit Hole

161

was sand and fine gravel.

During this dive, Mark and I reached the traffic light and turned around as planned. I aimed the beam of my dive light at the white path seventy-five feet away. The gold line runs along the path and then slopes up to the ceiling where it's difficult to see. I'd been through the passage enough times, I felt comfortable following the white path rather than the guideline. I knew the guideline would reappear when I went around the bend and the Rabbit Hole came into sight. At the time of this dive, the DPV I was using had two handles and triggers. I intended to remove the handle on the left side because I never used it. This was a common modification done on these old style DPVs. The handle was still attached because I hadn't had the time to perform the triggerectomy. Or rather, I hadn't made time to do it.

The tunnel just before the Rabbit Hole was less than three feet tall and didn't provide much clearance. As I approached the restriction, I rotated the DPV, as I always did, so I could push it to the right and make the left turn to follow the white path. I kept the DPV rotated as I continued toward the Rabbit Hole. This positioned the left handle and trigger down toward the floor. As the nose of my DPV entered the restriction, I felt a bump. I had misjudged the clearance and the handle on the left side, the one I intended to remove, gently brushed through the pile of gravel and sand that had settled on the floor in the restriction.

I adjusted the position of the DPV, pulling it up and off of the floor before I got to the much finer mud slope that began right after the Rabbit Hole. Disturbing that would have caused a big mess and Mark would have been left with no visibility to see the Rabbit Hole or the slope after it. I also didn't want to leave any marks on the floor of the cave. I made it through the Rabbit Hole with Mark close behind. We continued scootering through the cave passage, heading toward the opening. A few minutes later, we had gone through the Hall of the Mountain King and were back at the breakdown near the second line intersection. Both paths at that line intersection required moving through restrictions. We usually went through the larger one on the left.

At the time, I wasn't completely comfortable scootering through restrictions. I released the trigger so I could slow down and coast through at a more reasonable pace. Nothing happened when I relaxed my hand. I didn't slow down. The propellers didn't stop spinning. I continued to head toward the restriction at full speed.

DPVs aren't like boat motors. They don't spin down to a stop. When you release the trigger, the propellers stop moving. Or rather, they were supposed to stop moving. I squeezed and released the trigger several times, but the propellers kept spinning. I was going to have to go through the restriction at full speed. It didn't help that the current was pushing me as well. I was moving more than one hundred and fifty feet per minute. I ducked my head and aimed for the center of the restriction, hoping that I wouldn't hit the cave. I had decided I didn't like wearing a helmet, so my head was unprotected.

I managed to get through the restriction without smacking my head. Somehow, I didn't touch any part of the cave. I glided through there like I had been scootering for years. The skill I had acquired was partly responsible, but it was mostly luck. I squeezed and released the trigger several more times, still to no avail. I wasn't getting a response. The DPV continued to pull me through the cave at what I considered a not so safe speed. I focused on steering and avoiding the cave walls and ceiling. Flashbacks to Jen's near concussion incident flew through my mind.

I grabbed the handle on the left side and squeezed that trigger. It didn't move. The trigger was stuck in the handle. I tried to look at it as I was speeding through the cave passage more than one hundred and fifty feet per minute while I continued to focus on steering the runaway DPV. The trigger was fully depressed. I grabbed it between my fingers and tried to pull it out, but it wouldn't budge. I stopped trying to unjam the trigger and focused all of my attention on steering through the passage. I had three restrictions to maneuver through before I exited the cave. I managed to get through the restrictions at both ends of the second breakdown, buying myself about two minutes to figure

163

something out before I reached the restriction at the first breakdown. After that, I would have less than a minute until I was at the bottom of the chimney fissure where I had to do something. I couldn't ascend from eighty-five feet to forty-five feet deep while moving so quickly. The risk of getting the bends was too great.

The trigger was stuck. Nothing I did was getting it to release. I had one other option besides running the DPV into a wall and leaving it there until the battery died. I risked cracking the nose and flooding the DPV if I did that. My final option was to change the pitch of the propellers to slow down the DPV.

Most DPVs designed to be used inside of underwater caves have a propeller pitch adjustment. Nine is the greatest pitch and will move the most water, causing the DPV to go faster. One sets the propellers at the lowest pitch. A DPV set at pitch one will pull a scuba diver in full cave gear slower than a diver who is swimming. On the DPV I was using, a pitch setting of one barely had enough power to pull me. If I could drop the pitch to one, I could overpower the propeller movement and swim out with the DPV. If that didn't work, I would run it into a wall and leave it behind to retrieve after the battery died.

In order to adjust the hub, we release the trigger to stop the propeller from spinning, then rotate it. I couldn't stop the propeller movement with a jammed trigger. Fortunately, DPVs were designed with such an incident in mind. I knew about an emergency method of decreasing the pitch with the propeller still moving. I had practiced this method on the surface, but I had never done it in the water. That time had arrived.

I prepared myself for the task at hand. I had to bump the hub of the DPV propeller with my palm with enough force to stop the outer hub from spinning while the propeller continued to spin. This sounded easy in theory. In reality, palm bumping a fast-spinning propeller while moving through a cave passage at one hundred and fifty feet per minute and continuing to steer the DPV was not so easy. I had to protect my fingertips. They were going to get awfully close to the spinning propeller. I thought about how I was taught to feed horses by hand so they wouldn't bite my fingers off. I imagined holding an apple on my palm and faced it toward the hub.

Thankfully, the propellers on my DPV were not metal. A slip of the finger would definitely result in an amputation if that were the case. However, they were made from high impact resistant plastic. The edges were thin and sharp. They wouldn't cut you if you grabbed them while they were not in motion, but they could do some serious damage if you placed a finger in their path. I knew someone who had done that. He didn't lose his finger, but he had to get sutures.

I kept my hand as flat as I could. Actually, it was curved back a little to get my fingers farther from the blades. I brought it back so I could have momentum when I forced it toward the hub. I punched the hub, smacking it with my palm. The DPV instantly slowed down. It worked! I pulled my hand back and checked my fingers. They were all accounted for. I smacked the hub a couple more times for good measure to make sure it was at the lowest pitch setting.

A couple of seconds later, I arrived at the bottom of the chimney fissure after having traveled fifteen hundred feet through the cave behind a runaway DPV. The DPV was moving slowly enough that it was no longer pulling me. I guided its nose toward a flat spot on the wall and gently set it there, holding it in place while I took a moment to settle my nerves. With the stability of the DPV pushing against the wall, I was able to closely examine the handle on the left side. It was much easier to do while I wasn't moving so fast and dodging protrusions from the walls and ceiling. I finally saw what the issue was.

There were several pieces of gravel that had hitched a ride from the Rabbit Hole restriction. They were jammed in tightly holding the trigger depressed. Instead of trying to manipulate the trigger, I pulled on the wire that connected the trigger to the mechanism inside of the motor housing and jiggled the entire outer mechanism. The debris finally fell away, and the propeller stopped spinning. I could exit the last two hundred and fifty feet without having to fight the DPV.

It was quite an experience. I managed to make it out of the cave unhurt. Mark didn't even know there was an issue. He was surprised at how fast I maneuvered through the restrictions and thought I was hotdogging it. I let him know I absolutely was not. When I got home later that day, I immediately pulled out my tools and performed the much more urgent triggerectomy. I wasn't going to allow a repeat performance.

In retrospect, I should have initiated the palm bump much sooner than I had. I had considered it, but I was focused on maneuvering the DPV. I was also concerned that if I wasn't able to get the trigger loose, I would be stuck with a DPV that wasn't pitched high enough to pull me. I would have had to swim out of the cave from fifteen hundred feet. I had enough air to do that, but I preferred to scooter that distance. Another valuable lesson was learned.

The next day Mark and I returned to Jackson Blue, my DPV fully recovered from the triggerectomy, and this time we scootered to Stage Rock. Once there, we secured the DPVs to the guideline and went for a swim toward Avalanche Alley. This was our first visit to the area. There were several line intersections along that first offshoot line. The first couple of intersections led back to the main passage. The third and fourth lines led to Crinoid Glory and to an area named the Middle Grounds. We turned onto the third line so we could explore Crinoid Glory.

As with many caves in the Florida panhandle, Jackson Blue is full of fossils. They can be seen in the Rock Garden all the way through to the Terminal Room beyond the end of the gold line. Florida used to be underwater and part of the gulf. The caves in the Florida panhandle, particularly in Jackson County, were formed thirty-eight million years ago. When the water levels dropped, remains of marine life stayed in the caves and eventually became fossilized. The most common fossils seen are large sand dollar shells embedded in the walls, floor, and ceiling. The Rock Garden contains dozens of sand dollars, many sticking out of the limestone boulders. There are also sea urchin shells, crinoid fossils, and even shark's teeth. I've found a couple of small shark's teeth in the Deco Room. The abundance of fossils in Crinoid Glory was what gave it its name.

We don't find as many fossils in the other Merritt's Mill Pond caves. It's not that they aren't there. We just can't see them. There are so many fossils found in Jackson Blue because of the strong current. The fast water movement cleared the sediment from the floor and unearthed the fossils that were buried beneath. If Hole in the Wall or Twin caves had strong currents, the fossils in those passages would also likely be unearthed. I have found a few fossils in their passages, but I'm guessing there are hundreds, if not thousands, buried beneath the sediment.

Mark and I swam through Crinoid Glory, taking in its beauty. The passage we swam through was twenty feet tall and forty to fifty feet wide. We found fossils embedded in the walls and on the floor at their bases. The current wasn't very noticeable in Crinoid Glory because it runs parallel to the main passage. I'm sure there were more fossils buried beneath the silt-covered floor.

Several weeks later, Jen and I finally got a chance to dive together. It was Jen's first time scootering to Stage Rock. She hadn't been back there since before the current had made it impossible to swim to. We had a good dive and returned the next day. That dive didn't go as well. As we were scootering into the Rock Garden, I felt my DPV getting heavy. The nose dropped and pulled me toward the floor. It wasn't supposed to do that. Underwater DPVs are typically neutrally buoyant. They are supposed to hover horizontally in the water when you let go of them. My DPV had been neutrally buoyant during all of my previous dives. Something was wrong.

I released the trigger and the DPV sank. It was too heavy to hold up. Something was definitely not right. Fortunately, this happened before we made it to the beginning of the gold line. I turned around and signaled Jen, directing the DPV back out of the cave. I had a feeling I knew the problem and I wanted to get to the surface as quickly as possible. I also wanted to keep the nose angled down. My DPV was taking on water.

I made it to the surface and lifted the DPV, which was a few pounds heavier, out of the water with the nose down. The motor was located at the other end of the DPV body with the battery placed directly in front of it leaving a void near the front. I was trying to keep the water in that space. I unclipped the nose piece from the scooter and spilled a quart of water from the body. My heart sank. I placed the DPV on the grass drip drying while I unclipped my scuba tanks so I could exit the water and secure the flooded DPV inside of our van. I would deal with it later. Jen and I revised our plans and decided to practice towing each other with the remaining DPV. We practiced in the Rock Garden and in the large room at the bottom of the chimney fissure for about an hour. Our original plan had been scrapped, but we salvaged the day and had a productive dive.

22

Cave of the giant catfish

We hadn't lived in Florida for quite a year when I went into my first unlined passage in an underwater cave. It happened to be in Jackson Blue Unlined passages have either never been found and explored by previous cave divers or they weren't deemed worthy of having a line left in them. For this passage, it was probably the latter because it wasn't a large passage, and I can't say for sure that no one had ever been in it. I didn't deem it worthy of leaving my line in it so chances were no one else would either. Many cave divers dream of finding their first virgin cave passage. I was no exception. I didn't expect to find any such thing in the caves I was diving because they were well-known caves that had been explored two decades earlier. That didn't keep me from looking.

I penetrated the tunnel about one hundred and thirty feet before the passage became too small for me to continue. I knew the distance because I counted the knots I had tied every ten feet onto my guideline. I turned around and reeled my line back up through zero visibility. The sediment on the floor was mostly comprised of clay and I had stirred it up as I moved through the small passage. I hadn't touched the floor of the tunnel. It was just so small that movement within its confines pushed the water around enough to disturb the silt. It was no different than when I fanned my hand over the cave graffiti I had found in Peacock Springs.

When I returned to the main passage where Jen was waiting, the sediment I had disturbed caught up with me. Apparently, the small tunnel looped back into the main passage at some point farther in and the current was pushing it through. I retrieved my line from where it was secured to the gold line and the silt cloud enveloped me. I began swimming toward the exit and noticed that the visibility in the main passage was quickly deteriorating. About one hundred feet of the main passage was no longer clear. I was shocked. I had no idea I could cause such a disturbance. The diminished visibility in the small tunnel I came from was expected. I didn't expect it to move into the main passage, at least not as rapidly as it did. Thankfully the current was strong enough to clear out the silt from the passage quickly. Another lesson was learned.

* * *

I was given an opportunity to dive a not so popular cave that did have potential for unexplored, virgin cave passage. Promise Sink is a part of a series of sinkholes known as Leon Sinks, which are located in the Apalachicola National Forest south of Tallahassee. It's one of nine sinkholes that lead to an underground river system beneath the forest. Most of the cave is shallow, which accounts for the multitude of access points along its path. The ground collapsed centuries ago so we weren't concerned about it happening again. That may not have been smart.

The Apalachicola National Forest restricts the use of motorized vehicles to certain areas within its boundaries. Promise Sink is located in one of those areas and about a mile hike from the closest parking area. This made it difficult to gain access to dive it because of the logistics of getting the heavy scuba equipment to the site. Fortunately, the sinkhole is located near the edge of the forest boundary adjacent to private property, and a gentleman known as Wild Bill owned one of those properties. Wild Bill's property happened to be located about three hundred yards from Promise Sink, and he was kind enough to allow cave divers the use of his property to park our vehicles. There was a trail leading from his place right to the sinkhole. I was fortunate enough to be able to do several dives in Promise Sink before the national forest service placed signs around the sinkhole stating no diving allowed. They were on to us.

All of the sinkholes in Leon Sinks are the result of ground collapses over the hidden river below. Promise Sink was no exception and had an upstream and a downstream side to it. Unlike Hole in the Wall cave, these labels actually coincided with the direction of the water flow through the cave. The downstream side was on the far end of our approach from Wild Bill's. It was also the deeper side. Depths of greater than two hundred feet could be reached in that passage. The upstream side, located on the opposite end of the oblong sinkhole, was shallower and led to the other sinkholes in the system.

We went into the downstream side during our first dive in Promise Sink. The cave was very dark. I'm not referring to the lack of lights. The walls in this cave were black and the water was hazy, causing our light beams to be swallowed into the void. The light beams disappeared only a couple of dozen feet away. Wherever I pointed my beam, I saw black. I had to focus on the guideline to maintain awareness of my location. When I reached ninety-five feet of depth, there was a gap in the line, so I set a short jump line. The second line continued deeper into the earth and brought me to one hundred and fifty feet before I stopped and began my ascent. I didn't have helium in my scuba tanks and began to experience narcosis. Any deeper and I might have lost control of my faculties.

As I ascended, I joined Jen and two friends. They had remained at about eighty feet of depth checking out a third guideline that was placed around the perimeter of the large room. We continued our ascent together and surfaced. We had only used our stage tanks during the first dive and still had full sidemount tanks for the second dive. We took a short surface interval because the upstream side averages a depth of thirty feet and would allow us to continue to off gas the nitrogen we had absorbed during the first dive. We swam upstream for an hour, about three thousand feet from Promise Sink, passing several sinkholes

– Go Between, Fern, Cream, Woods, Trench, and Venture – along the way. The shallow depth and number of windows to the surface made it feel like we were diving in Mexico. The only things missing were the speleothems. About half of the sinkholes contained continuous guidelines. In the other half, the guideline was buried deep beneath the debris, and we had to reline them.

Not only was the guideline buried beneath the silt in the sinkholes, but we also encountered several sections inside the cave where it was buried, indicating that no one had been in there for many years. We might have been the first divers in that cave since the original explorers. We pulled up on the guideline in several areas to make sure it was still there and intact. We turned around when the cave passage started to get deeper. It wasn't quite as deep as the downstream side, but we reached seventy feet, and it continued its downward slope. The appearance of the cave was much like the downstream side. The walls were dark, and the floor was covered with a thick layer of sediment. The passage was not as large, so our lights didn't get swallowed by the darkness. It was a beautiful cave, and I felt fortunate that I had the opportunity to dive it.

* * *

A couple of days later, Jen and I visited another new cave known by some locals as the cave of the giant catfish. There used to be an article online that described these monster fish, but it seems to have been taken down. I had already been in dark, murky water not knowing if an alligator was waiting for me below the surface, so the threat of giant monster catfish that could swallow me whole, wasn't a deterrence. The other names for the spring were Maddachalk and Peacock Springs. The land along the bank where this spring is located has been owned by the Peacock family for decades, giving it that name. The bridge three hundred yards away, where we found Maddie and her little babies, was also named after the Peacock family. US Fish and Wildlife refers to it as Maddachalk Spring. Cave divers adopted that name.

There isn't easy access to the river from the bridge. There's a steep hill with several steps, but no flat area to stage dive equipment and no way to easily launch a canoe. We decided to enter the water at a boat ramp about two miles upriver from where the spring is located and paddle to it. We were just scouting so we didn't have our dive equipment with us. The current assisted our travel down the river, and we arrived at the bridge fairly quickly. We hadn't seen signs of the spring along the way. We weren't sure if we missed it or if it was well hidden.

We eventually learned that unless the river level was low enough to allow the water to clear, the opening couldn't be seen. The only way to find it was to descend into the tannic river water, hoping there wasn't an alligator waiting below, or a giant man-eating catfish, and feel for the temperature difference of the water flowing out of the cave. The spring water is always sixty-nine degrees. The river water varies based on the season.

We turned around and paddled back upriver looking more closely for signs of the spring opening. We spotted a cave line arrow nailed to a tree on the west bank of the river about ten feet above the water line. The spring had to be nearby, so we steered the canoe toward shore to look for more signs of it. The river water was too tannic to see anything, but it had to be there.

We paddled back to the boat launch to load our dive equipment so we could do a proper search. Along the way we passed several kids paddling canoes and kayaks downstream. Kayaking and canoeing is a popular pastime in the Florida panhandle, and it wasn't uncommon to see this. Jen and I were moving at a pretty brisk pace despite moving against the current. We were anxious to get our dive equipment so we could search for the cave. One of the kids in a canoe noticed our small wake and yelled at his friend sitting in the front, "Paddle harder! Those people are moving faster than us and they're going upriver!"

We returned to the line arrow tree with our equipment, ready to get into the water and find the opening to Maddachalk cave. We stepped out onto the shallow riverbank and quickly geared up. I tied my primary

173

reel line to the bottom of the tree with the line arrow and descended into the tannin-stained river water. I felt my way along the bank, a little concerned that there would be an alligator or catfish lurking below. The water was dark and murky, and I could barely make out the beam from my dive light. If I came upon an alligator, it wouldn't be a long encounter.

Fortunately, there were no alligators. I didn't find any giant catfish either. About five minutes after I disappeared beneath the surface, I felt a drop in temperature and the water began to clear. I sprinted forward and saw the opening. It was magnificent! The clear water pushed the tannic river water aside and created a pocket about ten feet wide and six feet out from the riverbank. The surface was only six feet above the top of the cave opening. I tied the line from my reel to a large rock in the clear water and ascended back along the line to get Jen.

With Jen close behind me, we followed the line to the reel, and I retrieved it to continue into the cave. About twenty-five feet in and to the right, I found the beginning of the permanent guideline. The line was the standard white cave line that we used on our reels and spools. There was no gold line in this cave at the time. There weren't enough offshoot tunnels to justify it. I secured my line to the permanent guideline, and we continued into the cave. While not small by any means, the cave was not as big as what we were accustomed to in Merritt's Mill Pond and Peacock Springs. The section near the opening was the largest area, measuring about seven or eight feet tall and ten to twelve feet wide. The farther we went into the cave, the smaller it got.

The passage was large enough for someone to dive it with backmounted tanks, but it was more comfortable with sidemounted tanks. It allowed for more room and less drag against the current with scuba tanks mounted on the sides. We encountered some larger areas along the way, but most of the passage was not very big. We hadn't been in the cave for very long when we saw our first giant catfish for which the cave was famous. I was swimming through the passage following the guideline when I saw movement directly beneath me. The floor stepped down at this point and the movement came from a lower step. It must have been four feet long and close to ten inches in diameter. It wasn't quite as large as I had expected. With all of the hype, I thought I would encounter a catfish that could swallow me whole. It was still the biggest catfish I had seen in person.

The catfish was hanging out perpendicular to the tunnel less than a foot below me. I jumped a little when I saw it and felt my heart rate increase. The fish didn't scare me. I just hadn't expected it to be there. The fish didn't twitch. It didn't seem bothered by my presence. I wasn't sure it knew we were there. I signaled to Jen to look below as she passed the area. Not that she could have missed seeing it, but I didn't want her to get spooked. We saw three more catfish in the next couple of hundred feet. The other three varied in size from just a few inches shorter than the first one we had seen to one that was approaching five feet in length. They were swimming in an area to the right of the tunnel and none behaved aggressively. They were just hanging out in their commune several hundred feet inside of the cave.

As we continued to follow the guideline, the intensity of the current increased and slowed us down. Maddachalk isn't a first magnitude spring. However, the small size of the passage meant the water current moving through it was something to contend with. It felt almost as strong as the current in Jackson Blue. We turned around forty-one minutes into the dive and made it back to the opening in sixteen minutes. Granted, we were moving slowly and learning the cave on the way in. We were taking it all in and enjoying the sites. We were also fighting against the current. On the way out, we didn't fin at all. We let the current push us out and used our fins to maneuver.

Maddachalk has interesting topography. The depth changes regularly, varying from fifteen feet to forty feet of depth. The sections that remain at a constant depth are short and few. It felt like we were on a roller coaster ride. We had a great time on the dive and Maddachalk became a favorite of ours. We paddled back up the river at a leisurely pace and spent time exploring spring runs we had seen on the way to

Maddachalk. One of the spring runs led to a couple of sinkholes that were located just a few feet from the riverbank. Neither looked large enough to be able to fit inside. It was a spring, but unfortunately it wasn't a cave we could dive. The other spring run we saw was really long but also very shallow. We walked through it for close to forty-five minutes before deciding to turn around and save that exploration for another day. According to a map of the area, the spring was about five miles from the river, so getting dive equipment to it would prove challenging.

* * *

The day after diving Maddachalk, Jen and I returned to Hole in the Wall, loading the canoe a little heavier this time with a couple of stage tanks that we planned to use in the Upstream passage added to the pile. The freeboard decreased another inch. We were close to our limit of equipment and divers. One more tank would probably sink the canoe. We were going to have to get a larger boat.

The upstream guideline in Hole in the Wall wasn't easy to find. While the downstream guideline is tied to the top of a small mound almost directly ahead when descending the chimney, the upstream guideline is to the right and secured near the ceiling of the low tunnel and blends in with the limestone wall behind it. The tunnel isn't easily visible during the descent. By the time we got to a depth where we could see it, we were almost at the floor.

I eventually found the tunnel and the guideline. After securing our primary line to it, we swam into the low dark tunnel. By low, I don't mean Maddachalk low. This tunnel was about eight feet tall from floor to ceiling and twice as wide. However, compared to the downstream passage, it was low. The tunnel ended about two hundred and fifty feet later at the bottom of the largest room I had seen in an underwater cave up until that point. Well, it was the largest room I *could* see. The room on the downstream side of Promise Sink may have been bigger, but I couldn't see the walls to know for certain. The room in the upstream passage of Hole in the Wall was eighty-five feet deep at the floor and twenty-five feet at the ceiling – sixty feet tall! I turned my head and looked up in awe at how far away the ceiling was.

We followed the forty-five-degree slope of the gold line, arriving at a formation called the Bridge, located near the top of the room, at thirty-five feet deep. The Bridge is a forty-foot-tall wall about fifteen feet thick that divides the room. It has a narrow corridor located in the top center, resembling a large notch. On the other side of the wall was an even larger area. It was just as tall but bigger around. The room was absolutely incredible.

We swam over the Bridge, followed the gold line down toward the floor, and passed through an arch into the next room where we turned around. We had reached turn pressure in our stage tanks. It was even more impressive when we crested the Bridge and saw the section of the room we had first passed through. I swam along the ceiling until I was above the turn in the gold line where it disappeared into the low tunnel leading back to the chimney while Jen remained next to the guideline. The visibility was clear enough for us to see each other even sixty feet apart. I descended to the guideline, and we continued toward the chimney.

I retrieved our reel from the upstream gold line and relocated it to the downstream line. We secured our stage tanks at the bottom of the chimney and continued into the downstream section. Conditions suddenly became strange. The bottom two-thirds of the cave passage was milky. There was a definitive line between the clear water and the murky water at seventy feet of depth. It was reminiscent of the haloclines seen in Mexican caves, but with the warm, clear layer on top rather than on the bottom. Hole in the Wall didn't have any saltwater in it, though. We tried to stay shallower than seventy feet where the water was sixty-nine degrees Fahrenheit and clear. Below seventy feet, it was four degrees colder and only five feet of visibility.

This was a first for us. The upstream section had been clear from floor to ceiling. There was no milkiness or temperature difference. I was intrigued and curious to know why the downstream side was the way it was. The last time we were diving in the downstream passage, conditions were perfect. I wouldn't be able to investigate this any further for a couple of months. That was our last cave dive for the summer. Unfortunately, we had to return to Arizona.

23

Your life will depend on me

We didn't move back to Arizona. It was a temporary trip to tie up loose ends. When we moved to Florida the previous summer, it was with short notice. We left our house in Tucson with unfinished projects despite our best efforts to complete them and get it ready to sell. We were taking advantage of time Jen had off from nursing school to drive to Arizona and finish those projects. We began the long drive back to Florida a little more than six weeks after arriving in Arizona. At least this time we were in the same vehicle and could take turns driving. We arrived in Florida, happy to be home, and happy to be near our beloved caves.

We took a couple of days to recuperate before heading to Jackson Blue for a much-needed cave dive. It had been too long since we had been in the water. The seven weeks we were away was the longest we had been out of the water since we got our first scuba diving certification. Living in Florida had spoiled me. I was able to dive much more often than when we lived in Arizona. I was cave diving almost as often as I wanted to.

Jen and I did a nice easy dive to reacquaint ourselves with the gold line circuit. It was our go to dive for practice and testing new equipment. It was a good way to knock the rust off. We wanted to make sure our skills hadn't suffered from the long period during which we were dry docked. Almost a week later, we returned to Jackson Blue. For some reason, I chose to dive with backmounted scuba tanks after almost a year of diving nothing but sidemount configuration. I don't know what I was thinking.

Truth be told, I did know. When my transition from tourist to resident cave diver was complete, I decided I wanted to become a cave diving instructor. I researched the requirements and learned I would have to complete my internships using backmounted tanks. Sidemount diving wasn't popular at the time. Most days, Jen and I were the only ones at the dive sites in that configuration. I also didn't know any instructors teaching in sidemount. I was fairly certain they wouldn't let me intern with sidemounted scuba tanks. I wasn't thrilled with it, but I wanted to teach people how to cave dive.

My first dive with backmounted tanks in Jackson Blue after a year of only using sidemounted tanks was less than stellar. I felt unstable in the water. The tanks on my back kept trying to flip me over so that they were underneath me and I was facing the ceiling. I felt wobbly and I was swimming slower than normal. I calculated my swim pace using the one-hundred-foot line markers and discovered I was swimming about thirty-five feet per minute, two thirds of my normal swim pace! When Jen and I reached the second line intersection, the pressure in my tanks dictated that it was time to turn around and exit. The current wasn't all that strong, and I should have been able to get farther. I had been diving with smaller scuba tanks in sidemount and could easily get several hundred feet beyond the second line intersection before reaching turn pressure. Something was not right!

A few days later, I returned to Jackson Blue, this time with sidemounted tanks. The sidemounted scuba tanks held three-fourths of the amount of air that the backmounted tanks used during my previous dive. That was a significant difference. I decided to retrace the path Jen and I took so I could compare the two. The only differences were the tanks I was using and where they were mounted. I reached the second line intersection with plenty of air remaining in my scuba tanks. In fact, I breathed one-fourth less air than I had with the backmounted tanks. The difference was unbelievable. If I hadn't done it myself, I wouldn't have believed it. I was also back to my normal fifty foot per minute swim pace.

I wanted to know why there was such a big difference. I couldn't have such poor performance while interning with instructor trainers. After a few more dives, I knew the answer. The backmounted tanks created more drag as I moved through the water. This made me uncomfortable enough that I struggled and breathed faster to compensate. I had to rebuild my experience using backmounted tanks if I was going to be comfortable enough to complete the required internships. I wasn't happy about it, but there was a light at the end of the tunnel. I wanted to get to that light.

I returned to Jackson Blue with smaller backmounted tanks. I used the same size tanks as what I had used during my previous sidemount dive and felt much better. The smaller tanks made a difference. I wasn't as comfortable using the backmounted tanks as I had been using the sidemounted tanks, but I was confident I could get back to the level of skill I had achieved diving sidemount.

A couple of weeks later I drove to High Springs to begin my cave diving instructor internship. I arrived a couple of days before the students so I could dive with my sponsor and complete the didactic portion of the program. After that, we spent four days diving the Ginnie Springs cavern, Devil's cave, and Peacock I. It had been almost three years since my first visit into an underwater cave, and I considered myself to still be a rookie cave diver. I had also only been living in Florida for a year and had completed less than two hundred cave dives. I wasn't sure I was ready to start teaching other divers how to safely cave dive. I didn't know if I was ready to take on the responsibility of ensuring the survival of the divers I would take into these dark environments with no direct access to the surface. Was I ready to be able to anticipate their mistakes and make sure they didn't do anything to get themselves or anyone else killed? Was I ready for their lives to depend on me?

Any kind of scuba diving instruction brings with it a certain amount of risk. As instructors, we teach people how to breathe underwater and how to deal with issues that happen beneath the surface, hopefully without panicking. I had already been an entry level instructor for three years and taught well over one hundred students during that time. Most of my students didn't have *any* training before coming to me. They had never been underwater with an apparatus that allowed air to be breathed in that environment. At least with cave diving students, I knew they had the foundation. They had experience being underwater. The only difference was that they no longer had direct access to the surface.

For some people, that was enough to cause panic. Fortunately, most divers knew their limits and wouldn't pursue cave diving instruction if the thought of being in an overhead environment made them anxious. That's not true of all scuba divers. I've had students that panicked once inside a cavern. I've had students that did fine in the cavern but panicked when we moved beyond the daylight zone. I got them back to the surface and told them that they should pursue other activities. Most of them agreed. Fortunately, the first students I had as an intern were very comfortable in the water and in an overhead environment. Panic wasn't a concern. I was also only doing an internship. My instructor trainer was ultimately responsible for the safety of everyone. He was responsible for their lives.

I had to do six internships to qualify for my cave diving instructor certification. Three internships were completed at the cavern and introductory cave diving levels and three were at the full cave diving level. After each set of internships, there was a written test, a teaching presentation, and a diving test. I was prepared to spend several months completing the internships for the first level before I qualified for the testing. Then I would be allowed to bring my own students into the caves without supervision. That was the next phase of the process. I had to teach six classes at the cavern and introductory cave diving levels before I qualified to continue to the next level of instructor. I expected this to take a while. I was a new cave diving instructor, after all, and while I had built a reputation as a recreational scuba instructor, cave diving was on an entirely different level. I didn't expect students to break down my door to learn from me.

* * *

I finally got a bigger boat. I purchased a Jon boat so that I wouldn't have to continue to overload the canoe and potentially sink it. A few days after returning from High Springs, I took the new Jon boat onto Merritt's Mill Pond for the first time. We loaded the boat and took off up the pond toward Hole in the Wall cave. I coasted in next to the small dock and secured the boat, grateful for the dock. The Jon boat was big enough to hold us, but it was narrow and not very stable. The original Hole in the Wall dock, while not very large, made it easier to gear up.

We went downstream during the first dive, remaining in the main passage. Conditions in the cave were much better than they had been during my last dive there. The murky layer in the bottom two thirds of the passage was no longer present. The water temperature was the same throughout. During our second dive, we headed upstream for my second visit to that passage, and we made it to the end of the gold line. That sounds like a greater accomplishment than it was. The gold line ends fourteen hundred feet from the opening.

The upstream gold line isn't at the end of the passage. It transitions to white cave line in a location named Alford's Room that continues into a tunnel resembling a borehole. We followed the line along an ascending slope about twelve hundred feet in, just after a line intersection with a white line coming from an offshoot tunnel to our right. The offshoot tunnel led to an area named the Century Tunnel. It was also the continuation of the main passage. I knew this from studying the map and looked forward to exploring it.

I spent time solo diving over the next couple of weeks, accessing Jackson Blue from my Jon boat rather than by land. I tied the boat to a tree in a shallow area and geared up while standing in waist deep water. I no longer had to carry my tanks from my van to the water. It also felt

183

good to be out on the pond in a boat, motoring along in between the cypress trees. It was peaceful and relaxing. It was something I could get used to.

I was doing progressive penetration into Jackson Blue, going a little farther each time so I could learn the cave. During one dive I scootered to the four-thousand-foot line marker, the farthest I had gotten. Beyond the thirty-five-hundred-foot line marker, the ceiling gets lower and the sediment on the floor gets thicker. The gold line is also routed just under the ceiling rather than near the floor, making it difficult to see. It took me thirty-seven minutes to scooter to four thousand feet and twenty-eight minutes to get back out to the opening. The current was still strong.

I had pushed the limits. I had been on the trigger for sixty-five minutes. That was a lot longer than the recommended fifty-six-minutes for that DPV. I knew what I was doing and expected to have to swim out the last few hundred feet. I was prepared for it. Fortunately, that didn't happen. The DPV battery was still going strong when I exited the cave. I was happy, but I knew I had taken a risk. In fact, my DPV started to leak near the end of that dive. Fortunately, it didn't happen until I was almost out of the cave. I didn't scooter that far in with that DPV again.

I knew those DPVs were prone to leaking. I read as much information as I could about them to try to fix the issue. They were the most popular DPV for cave diving in the nineties and there was a lot of information. I implemented the solutions that were recommended. I could keep the DPV dry for a few dives before I had to reseal it. While the DPV was drying out, I was back to swimming for a few days. During that time, I decided to dive somewhere other than Jackson Blue rather than fight the current. Hole in the Wall or Twin caves, were viable options, but I wanted to experience different caves. I took the Jon boat onto the Chipola River for the first time. Jen was buried in schoolwork and clinicals, so that left me solo. I was about to go diving alone in a remote, unfamiliar cave that was only accessible by boat.

24

Solo diving

Other than my venture into Black Spring, my solo diving excursions had been limited to Jackson Blue. I only went into Black Spring solo because Jen wasn't having any of that dive and we had worked so hard to get to it. I was having fun learning the caves on Merritt's Mill Pond, but the desire to see other caves was compelling me to branch out. The dive we did in Maddachalk sparked something within me. I had to see more river caves, even if it meant going solo.

The cave that kept calling to me was Bozel Spring, located on the Chipola River about a mile and a quarter upriver from the boat ramp in Florida Caverns State Park. The spring was said to be one of the most beautiful in the area from the surface, so it was a popular kayak and canoe route. I had also heard good things about the passages hidden beneath the surface. I wasn't about to paddle up the river in the canoe full of scuba equipment. There were alligators in the water along that stretch of the Chipola River, and I didn't feel protected in a small canoe floating on tannin-stained water where you couldn't see anything beneath you. You're probably thinking back to my tannic water entries into Black and Maddachalk springs. Those were different. I knew there were caves where I was headed. The payoff was worth the risk. There was another reason I didn't want to take the canoe.

Before owning the Jon boat, Jen and I had paddled up the Chipola River to visit Bozel Spring. We were just scouting, so we didn't bring our scuba equipment. As we were floating near the bank, we felt something bump the bottom of the canoe. Something had risen up from the depths below us. We didn't know what it was, but it was big. Fortunately, we weren't tipped over. A few seconds after the encounter, we spotted an alligator swimming toward the other bank. She wasn't small. The outcome could have been really bad had she caused the canoe to capsize.

I loaded the Jon boat, satisfied that it would be nearly impossible for an alligator to tip it over, and headed to Bozel. The spring run was about thirty feet wide and pumping clear water into the tannic brown river. It was shallow with lots of large-leafed vegetation covering the rocky bottom. It was as beautiful as I had remembered it. I turned into the spring run and slowly cruised along its four-hundred-foot stretch. A few minutes later, I found myself in one of the most peaceful settings I've been in, floating over the deep, rich bluish-green pool of water surrounded by cypress trees. There was an old abandoned red house a few hundred feet away on the other side of a fence that added to the charm. I sat in my boat taking it all in. I was in paradise.

After a few moments of pure enjoyment, I suited up and donned my scuba equipment, anxious to see the cave. I had heard so much about Bozel and couldn't wait to see it for myself. The opening was a small hole at the bottom center of the basin and required a head down entry into strong current. About twenty feet deep, the passage narrowed and forced me to turn sideways to fit with tanks mounted at my sides. It would almost be easier to dive in backmount except there was a restriction farther in that wouldn't allow passage with backmounted tanks. The fissure bottomed out at forty feet, then twenty-five feet later, began to slope up to twenty feet of depth. A short distance later, a wall appeared with a line running vertically along the side of the passage.

When I arrived at the wall, I looked up and saw a space between it and the ceiling over my head. It was wide but only had about two feet of clearance front to back. I wondered if the wall in front of me had once been attached to the ceiling. I glanced up, hoping the limestone that was directly above was securely affixed to whatever was holding it in place. I pushed the thought aside and ascended through the narrow slit. When I made it to the top of the wall, I saw a narrow bedding plane. The ceiling hadn't fallen far, offering only about two and a half feet of clearance. The current seemed stronger as I pulled myself through. Once at the other end of the room, I saw daylight streaming down.

The Bozel Spring group is a series of four openings to the surface. The first opening, the one I entered, is the main one, and I had just arrived at the second opening. This opening could be accessed through a sinkhole located about ten feet from the spring basin where my Jon boat was secured. There was a path between the spring basin and the sinkhole that was on private property. The sinkhole contained three additional openings to Bozel. I had just swum a distance of about one hundred and fifty feet to what was only forty feet apart by land. I continued past this opening and a few feet farther saw more rays of light penetrating the darkness – vent number three. I passed beneath it and continued to follow the guideline. A short while later, it made a sharp turn to the left into a fissure.

The fissure was a narrow slit between two walls that required me to turn sideways. I would have been able to fit in backmounted tanks, but only for part of the distance. There was a restriction at the other end, leading to the next room, that was too narrow for backmounted tanks. I met a diver who had gone to Bozel with backmounted tanks. He went with a mutual friend who was diving with sidemounted tanks. When they arrived at that restriction, the sidemount diver slipped through without issue. The backmount diver made it about three fourths of the way before his scuba tanks became wedged between the walls. He tried a couple of different angles but couldn't get through.

The sidemount diver turned around and signaled the backmount diver to get as close to the floor as he could. He obliged and moved another foot before getting wedged by his tanks again. The sidemount diver grabbed the manifold between the valves of the backmounted tanks and pulled with a lot of force. The backmount diver slipped through that last foot of the restriction.

187

As he was telling me this story, the backmount diver mentioned it was the worst dive he had done. He didn't enjoy the rest of the dive and barely remembered what the cave looked like beyond that point. Throughout the whole dive, all he could think about was how he was going to get back through the restriction to get out of the cave. His concerns were valid. Just because he could slide through going in one direction didn't mean he would be able to slide through going in the other. In addition to that, he was dependent on the sidemount diver to pull him through. If something happened to the sidemount diver, the backmount diver didn't think he would get through without taking the tanks off of his back. Fortunately, nothing happened. They returned to the restriction. The sidemount diver went first and pulled the backmount diver through. The backmount diver did not dive Bozel in backmounted tanks after that. That first dive was far too unnerving. This was the ultimate trust me dive because he was completely dependent on someone else to get out of the cave.

What the backmount diver didn't know during that dive was that the fourth opening of the Bozel spring group was just after that restriction. Had he looked up after being pulled through, he would have seen daylight streaming in from directly above. That opening was large enough for him to fit through with backmounted tanks. He was too stressed to notice it though.

I turned sideways and pulled myself through the next fifteen feet until I popped out on the other side. Because I was in a sideways orientation, I noticed the daylight streaming in from above. It wasn't a large opening, but it was big enough to pass through either in backmount or sidemount. I noted the location should it ever need to be used in an emergency. I rotated back to a prone position and continued to swim and pull myself through the cave. The tunnel was narrow, and the current was still strong. I saw several catfish in this narrow corridor. They weren't as large as the ones in Maddachalk, but they were a decent size. I named this short section Catfish Alley.

After Catfish Alley, the room got bigger, and the line continued through a small crack in the floor leading to a deeper level. I swam through and found myself in the largest room in Bozel. It was about twenty feet wide and ten feet tall at that point and continued as far as my light beam penetrated. I saw sediment on the floor of the cave for the first time. Up until that point, the passages were small, and the current cleared most of the sediment away. The larger room allowed the water current to decrease in intensity, so the sediment remained.

I was hovering over what appeared to be a hilltop. It sloped down on both sides, dropping about twenty-five to thirty feet. Fifty feet later, the floor continued to slope deeper below a wall that extended down from the ceiling about twenty feet. The slope leveled out more than fifty feet beneath the hilltop. I named this room the Stadium. I was sixty feet deep and the floor at the bottom was more than one hundred and ten feet deep. The walls were at least seventy feet apart. It was truly a grand hall.

About fifty feet after reaching the leveled-out floor, I encountered a four-way line intersection. The main line continued straight, and another line crossed it perpendicularly. I looked to my right and left and saw the lines disappear into low duck unders. I went straight, coming to another vertical climb a couple of hundred feet later, and ascended to ninety-five feet of depth. Bozel was beginning to feel like a roller coaster. I swam along a winding tunnel, passing two more line intersections. The farther I penetrated, the more sediment I saw on the floor. The passage was getting wider and distributing the water flow across the room.

Because I was alone in an unfamiliar cave, I held to more conservative dive planning and was diving the rule of fourths. Doing so allowed me to have a lot of air should an emergency occur. I turned around when I had breathed one-fourth of my air and let the current carry me out. Bozel had become my favorite cave. The dive also gave me more confidence. I had just done a solo dive in a new cave and survived. As long as I followed conservative dive plans, I didn't see a reason not to dive solo. I was either getting more confident, or more reckless. This seemed to be an ongoing theme.

A few days later I returned to Jackson Blue to visit Crinoid Glory again. I wanted to spend more time learning the area. No one was available to dive, so I was alone again. The only limitations were the ones I placed on myself. I planned my air usage using cave DPV rules and brought along Al as a buddy. I spent more than half an hour exploring the passages of Crinoid Glory. I found more line intersections, ventured into a couple of the offshoot tunnels, and exited the area even more confused than I had been. Crinoid Glory was a maze and the map didn't do it justice. There were passages that were not depicted on it. I knew it would take several dives to learn my way around.

My exploration was done for several days. I was returning to High Springs to continue my cave diving instructor internship. I was about to meet with a different instructor trainer and see a vastly different teaching style. It would prove to be an interesting experience.

25

Out of air…twice!

The next internship was more eye-opening than interesting. It was carried out differently than the first one. The cave instructor had GUE leanings. Global Underwater Explorers is a technical and cave diving training organization with stricter standards than most other training agencies. The organization allows one configuration of dive equipment and one way of teaching and diving. If you want to dive under their standards, you dive their way. Keeping to one configuration and one set of standards results in divers around the world being able to almost seamlessly pair with any other diver who has received the same training. When GUE trained divers dive with others for the first time, they know exactly what to expect…in theory. Training and equipment standards can be created, but the human factor still creates a variance that is not as easy to control. I've personally witnessed this.

The instructor I was interning with was GUE trained, but he wasn't a GUE cave diving instructor. He taught under the standards of other training organizations. His GUE leanings were apparent, though. There were things I liked about this experience and things I didn't like. The standards he was teaching under allowed him to condense the cavern and introductory cave diving classes into three days at the instructor's discretion rather than the typical four days. This was a three-day class. Going into this internship, I already knew I didn't agree with this.

Cave diving is serious business. The cavern diving and introductory cave diving classes were the foundation for everything that followed.

The cavern diving class introduced a majority of the skills that would be used throughout the eight to ten days of training. The introductory cave diving course added a couple of new skills that were specific to going beyond the cavern zone. By the time a diver was ready to move onto the full cave diving course, the only thing added was dive planning using the rule of thirds rather than the rule of sixths and navigation away from the main guideline. The cave diving class was supposed to give the instructor an opportunity to help students refine skills and ensure they could handle issues. I thought that shaving a day off was a disservice to the students.

Another issue I had with this internship experience was that the student was using a single backmounted scuba tank for the course rather than two tanks. Use of a single tank is allowed by standards at the cavern and introductory cave diving levels. I just don't agree with it. I believe that if a diver is going to go beyond the cavern zone of an underwater cave, there should be redundancy. The student had an H valve on her tank – two independent valves so two independent first stage regulators could be used. The o-ring on the valve where it screwed into the scuba tank was the only thing that was not redundant. That wasn't my main concern. I've only seen three extruded o-rings in twenty plus years of scuba diving. While that would be a bad thing in a cave, it wasn't something that couldn't be dealt with.

The bigger concern was that there was a lot less air for the diver in case of an emergency. If that o-ring extruded, there wasn't a second scuba tank of air to rely on. Add to that the fact that the standard allowed students using single tanks for their introductory cave diving classes to use the rule of thirds rather than the rule of sixths and you're asking for trouble. When the standards were written, the intent was to limit the penetration distance into the cave at the introductory cave diving level. A diver using two tanks and the rule of sixths was using the same amount of air to penetrate the cave as a diver using one tank and the rule of thirds. I looked at it from a different perspective.

The introductory cave diver using one tank doesn't have as much air reserved for emergency use. A diver using two scuba tanks and limited to the rule of sixths has two-thirds of the starting air held in reserve for emergencies. A diver using one scuba tank, using the rule of thirds, has only one-third of the starting air held in reserve. It didn't make sense to reduce the amount of emergency air available.

Introductory cave divers are inexperienced. It takes them longer to deal with issues than someone with more training and experience. If an introductory cave diver encounters a situation in the cave that will delay the exit, there should be more air reserved to deal with it. The introductory cave diver will be slower to react. Anxiety levels will be raised. Breathing rates will increase. I believed that more air should have been reserved to deal with situations regardless of the number of scuba tanks being used. Penetration distance should not have been the major consideration. Did that mean that the rule of sixths was the best option? I didn't think so. I thought it was too conservative. The rule of fourths would have been a good compromise. The standards haven't changed despite my efforts to get them changed, and they likely never will.

The student's boyfriend, who was a certified cave diver, was tagging along in the class. After talking to her and seeing how she performed in the water, I had the impression that she was pursuing the introductory cave diving certification because her boyfriend was a cave diver, not because she had a desire to pursue it on her own. She wanted to be able to experience the caves with him. I had a similar situation years later with one of my own students. The boyfriend was a cave diver, and the girlfriend wanted to dive the cenotes in Mexico with him. She also used a single backmounted scuba tank. I accepted her as a student, but I encouraged her to transition to double scuba tanks. More importantly, we did not plan dives using the rule of thirds. I limited her to the rule of fourths and told her she had to stick to that rule even after she completed the class. That was the only way I would accept her as a student if she insisted on using a single tank. I don't think she ever did any cave dives outside of class. The trip to Mexico never happened and she didn't return to Florida. She was the only student that I ever taught using a single tank. It bothered me too much to allow it again.

Not only was the student in the internship class using a single scuba tank, but, as I mentioned, the class was also held over a three-day period. Most of the first day was spent in the classroom with only one dive completed that day. The instructor counted it as two. To be fair, we did surface for a five-minute debriefing of the first part of the dive and a briefing for the second part. The next day we completed the cavern diver portion of the training with another dive that was also counted as two by inserting a short surface interval for debriefing and briefing. I was learning more about what I didn't want to do as an instructor than what I could do. I knew I didn't want to conduct short back-to-back dives like that. It wasn't beneficial to the student.

We moved from Ginnie Springs to Devil's cave to begin the introductory cave diving training after lunch. The morning dive(s) had been so short that I had plenty of air left in my tanks to do the afternoon dive, so I didn't even refill them. The afternoon dive didn't last very long. Class was done for the day. Things were about to get much more interesting.

My instructor trainer was contacted by a friend of his who drove down from the northeast for a week of cave diving. The friend arrived that day and we saw him before heading into the water for our first introductory level cave dive. Plans were made to dive later that evening after we completed the training dives. This friend was a husky guy who had a set of backmounted double scuba tanks with a cage around the valves. This was most likely to be seen in the northeast among wreck divers. It was rare to see in caves. The cage was a frame used to prevent damage to the valves if they came in contact with the ceiling but still allowed the diver to reach the valves to close them in the event of an air leak. It was an equipment solution to a skills problem. A diver shouldn't be making contact with the ceiling in a shipwreck or a cave.

I was concerned about this configuration, but I kept an open mind. Besides, I wasn't going to turn down an opportunity to go cave diving. I had a full set of sidemount scuba tanks in my van for such an occasion.

The husky friend was already breathing heavily from the struggle of putting his drysuit on and carrying the tanks to the water. It was less than one hundred feet, but it winded him. The cage added weight to the backmounted tanks, but he also had an additional twenty pounds of weight secured between the tanks. He was a big guy, more husky than overweight, although it was obvious he enjoyed the occasional beer or three. I didn't think he needed so much weight. I had been teaching scuba diving for three years and had never had a student that required as much weight to get neutrally buoyant in the water as this guy had on his tanks. He wasn't my student, though, so other than a whisper to my instructor trainer, I said nothing.

The northeast wreck diver regained control of his breathing after a few minutes of standing in the water and we briefed the dive. We were doing a leisurely dive along the main passage of the cave. Nothing complex. Nothing too taxing. My instructor trainer led the way, his friend followed, and I took the rear position. I watched my instructor trainer gracefully move into the Ear and through the Gallery toward the Lips. His friend did not follow directly behind him. Instead, he positioned himself in the middle of the passage, directly in the path of the strongest current. I had to stop and let him gain distance so that I could remain behind him.

We made it to the Lips in about twice the amount of time that it should have taken. Granted, I didn't make it to the Lips my first time in Devil's cave, but I was a brand-new cave diver doing my very first introductory cave dive at that time. And Jen had turned the dive before she reached turn pressure. This guy was a fully trained and certified cave diver who had done dives in Devil's cave. A few minutes later, we arrived at the Keyhole. The friend put his hand out with his thumb up, signaling us to turn around and exit. He pointed at his pressure gauge and indicated he was at turn pressure. We were only twelve minutes into the dive. The current had kicked his butt.

The most important rule of cave diving is that any diver can call any dive at any time for any reason. I was disappointed. Gearing up takes

195

time. I had breathed some air from full tanks. Here we were turning the dive twelve minutes in. We would be on the surface less than twenty minutes after we submerged. I turned around. A rule is a rule.

I've heard of divers that didn't adhere to that rule. Our cave diving instructor told us about one particular diver that would continue into the cave until he was ready to turn around regardless of what his dive buddies signaled. He didn't care what the reason for turning around was. If he wasn't ready to turn around, he wasn't going to turn around, dive buddies be damned. I don't imagine he had many repeat dive buddies.

As I was turning, my instructor trainer signaled me to go on and continue my dive and he would exit with his friend. I was surprised because GUE doesn't condone solo diving. There weren't any training agencies that did. I asked if he was sure and he confirmed. My dive was saved. I didn't have to exit after a twelve-minute penetration. I felt bad for my instructor trainer, but I turned back and continued through the Keyhole restriction.

I had a fantastic dive. It was my first time diving Devil's cave solo. I adjusted my turn pressure, stayed in the main passage, and penetrated beyond the Maple Leaf formation, a rocky outcropping hanging from the ceiling that has a shape similar to a maple leaf. I turned around at the set of double line arrows about twelve hundred feet from the opening that marked the Hillier Tunnel offshoot, named after the cave diver that found that passage.

The next day, we met at Peacock Springs State Park for the third day of class. My instructor trainer pulled me aside and told me his friend turned the dive because he was working too hard against the current and had tired himself out. Then he told me when they exited the cave into the spring run, he had to pull his friend to the stairs because he had worn himself out so much he didn't have the energy to swim against the current to the steps fifty feet away. When they surfaced, the friend yelled, "We have to go back and get Rob!" He thought they had abandoned me in the cave and that I was in trouble. It took some doing, but my instructor trainer finally convinced his friend that I was fine and didn't require assistance. I felt bad for the guy, but it was funny that he thought he was going to save me when he couldn't even save himself. He would have breathed all of the air in his scuba tanks long before he reached me.

After having a good laugh at the northeast wreck diver's expense, we returned our focus to the day ahead of us. I was looking forward to diving Peacock Springs again. I took over the class for our first dive. We did an air share drill with simulated zero visibility. The student breathed from my tanks during the exercise, and I shut off both of our lights. We swam a few hundred feet in the dark. My instructor trainer and the student's boyfriend followed us with their lights out. This was my first time having direct responsibility for a student and here we were exiting with no visibility. I quickly learned to use my other senses.

During the second dive, my instructor trainer was back in the instructor role. We swam the Olsen Tunnel and penetrated several hundred feet until the student had breathed one third of the air in her scuba tank. We turned around and began our exit. The boyfriend and I were hanging back and watching. When we reached the line leading up to Pothole Sink, my instructor trainer signaled to the student that he was out of air. She donated her second stage regulator and switched to her backup regulator, both attached to her single tank, and the lights went out. We would be simulating a zero-visibility exit again.

I had exited in the dark so many times by this point that I found it relaxing. I formed a circle around the guideline with my thumb and forefinger, closed my eyes, and slowly swam out. My breathing rate slowed as I followed the student and instructor trainer while maintaining my distance by feeling the vibration of their movement on the line. I didn't want to run into them and disrupt the drill. Every fifteen seconds or so I opened my eyes to see if the drill had been cut and the lights turned back on. The boyfriend remained behind me. We did a bump and go exit. I swam along the line for about ten seconds, stopped, and waited for him to catch up and bump into me. He then waited while I moved forward. We continued the bump and go exit, waiting for the drill to be over.

I was waiting for the boyfriend to bump into me when I sensed a commotion on the guideline ahead. The line began to shake wildly so I tightened my grasp to keep it from popping out of the circle I had formed. I noticed a faint stream of light penetrating the darkness ahead indicating we had just arrived at the edge of the cavern zone. Maybe the student was trying to retrieve the reel. That would not be good. First, they were simulating a zero visibility out of air exit, and second, she had three divers behind her that still needed to use the line to exit.

The primary reel is retrieved during the exit from a cave dive except during certain situations. If one of the divers is out of air or there is no visibility, the reel remains in place. It takes too much time and causes too much confusion in those situations. Both conditions were met. Sometimes students try to retrieve the primary reel anyway. They forget that it's supposed to remain in place during an air share or zero visibility situation.

The light I saw didn't illuminate the area much. It wasn't enough to see anything except shadows. After about thirty seconds of commotion with no resolution, I turned my dive light on. Something wasn't right. If the instructor trainer wanted to reprimand me, so be it. I would deal with the consequences after the dive. With the passage illuminated, I saw the student and my instructor trainer juggling second stage regulators between them. There were also regulators dangling from the student's tank and resting on the sediment covered floor. The student and the instructor trainer were both breathing from his tanks.

I found out during the dive debriefing that the student and instructor trainer had breathed the student's single scuba tank empty. They had run out of air for real! This happened while they were breathing from the same single tank, sixty feet deep, and seventy feet from the opening where we could surface. The one-third of air that was reserved for emergencies hadn't been enough to get them safely out of the cave from five hundred feet. The drill hadn't started at our maximum penetration.

Fortunately, my instructor trainer was able to get working regulators into both of their mouths. This was a valuable lesson for all, especially for me. It served to reinforce my belief that the use of the rule of thirds with single scuba tanks during introductory cave dives was not safe. If it hadn't been a drill, they would have both drowned seventy feet from the opening.

I've mentioned that I tried to get this standard changed but couldn't get anyone onboard with the idea. They were satisfied with the standards as they were. They cited that there were no fatalities resulting from that rule. What they didn't know about were the near misses that occurred. It was difficult enough to keep a record of the fatalities. No one was keeping a record of near misses. No one was reporting near misses. The idea behind only allowing one sixth of the air in double tanks so penetration into the cave could be limited was faulty logic. They thought that by only allowing one sixth of the starting pressure for penetration, the intro cave diver wouldn't get far into the cave. That student and instructor almost died after beginning an air sharing drill five hundred feet from the opening.

As a full cave diver, I've never used a full one third of the air in my scuba tanks when diving a cave. I don't believe it provides enough of a safety buffer in case of an incident. The training dive we had just completed was a perfect example. We turned around when the student had breathed one-third of the air in her scuba tank. Ideally, that should have been enough to get her and my instructor trainer both breathing from that tank out to the surface from maximum penetration. Except situations are rarely ideal.

Her breathing rate increased because of the anxiety produced by sharing air and being in a simulated silt-out. She was breathing almost twice as fast as she normally did. I expected this, especially for a new, inexperienced diver. This was how cave diving fatalities occurred. I hoped that she learned a valuable lesson from the experience.

I only breathe about one fourth of the air in my scuba tanks before turning around to exit. That allows me to reserve half of the air in my scuba tanks for emergencies, making the dive safer. It requires me to turn two to three hundred psi sooner than I would if I was using the rule of thirds. I have done thousands of cave dives, and I still follow this rule.

Another lesson I learned was to listen to your students underwater. After this incident, I always paid close attention to the breathing pattern of my students. With the lights on and good visibility, I could see the bubbles escaping from their second stage regulators as they exhaled. During zero-visibility exercises, bubbles aren't visible, but the exhalations can still be heard. I knew when my students were calm and relaxed or starting to panic just by how often the exhalation sounds occurred. I've cut drills because I could hear my students breathing too fast and I knew they were beginning to panic. Panic underwater is never a good thing. It's worse if you can't see what's going on. It needs to be stopped before it gets out of control.

When we surfaced, I could tell my instructor trainer was embarrassed. To his credit, he made it a teaching point to both me and the student. He was also quick enough when it happened to realize what was going on. He dealt with it and got one of his own regulators to the student before she drowned. A fatality in a cave is never a good thing. A fatality during training is really bad. I doubted my instructor trainer ever did a similar drill after that without first checking the pressure gauge on the student's tank. Maybe he didn't even teach students using single scuba tanks at the introductory cave diving level. His only source of income was teaching scuba diving, though, so that wasn't as likely. When you're trying to keep the lights on, you'll do what's necessary to keep the money coming in. He did everything by the book and didn't violate any standards, but the book isn't conservative enough in my opinion. I've always abided by much higher standards than required. I was also in a unique situation where I never had to compromise safety because I had a job that wasn't dependent on scuba diving students so I could pay my bills.

26

Diving with a legend and the Grand Traverse

Two weeks after the out of air internship, I returned to Peacock Springs to complete my final cavern and introductory cave diving internship. I was working with Paul Heinerth, one of the cave diving legends. Paul did quite a bit of exploration in his younger days and was involved in a lot of the big projects of the 1980s and 1990s. He was also one of the early pioneers among the Florida sidemount divers and had done hundreds, if not thousands, of dives using sidemounted tanks. I was nervous about diving with Paul but felt honored that I had the opportunity to intern with him. I was ready to learn as much as I could.

Paul was laid back, both on the surface and in the water, and my anxiety quicky dissipated. It was amazing to watch him move through the water with grace, as if he belonged there. His buoyancy was perfect as he positioned himself above the students and remained motionless, fins crossed behind him. That was the level of diving I aspired to attain. I wanted to feel as comfortable and at home in the water as Paul looked. That's not to say I wasn't comfortable in the water. I had done nearly six hundred dives since getting my first certification. About half of those were cave dives. I felt at home in the caves, but I still struggled at times and felt I could improve. So I watched Paul and tried to learn as much as I could about diving as well as about teaching cave diving.

Paul was like a fish in the water and his teaching style was relaxed. He taught to standards and covered the essentials. I was more of a stickler for the details. That said more about my personality than Paul's teaching. Paul had no issues with me interjecting my thoughts. He asked if I had any input during the briefings and debriefings and encouraged me to participate. The main thing I stressed was air management, always adding something about managing the air in our tanks. My most recent experience was still fresh in my mind.

During this internship, I saw Cow Spring for the first time. Cow was owned by one of the cave diving training organizations (the one I was working to become an instructor with), and only members of the organization were granted access. There is an upstream side and a downstream side. The upstream side is where the "DIC" graffiti was carved into the clay bank. Training was only allowed in the downstream side, which is a shallow, dark, silty cave that penetrates about four hundred feet before getting too small. It's a mild siphon, but nothing that requires any alteration in air management. Even students will reach the end of the passage before they have to turn due to air pressure.

We did the lost line and out of air drills in downstream Cow Spring. During the lost line drill, the student's ability to see was removed. This was done either with a blacked-out mask or lights turned off. The student was then moved away from the guideline and given ten minutes to find it. With my other internships, a blacked-out mask was used. Paul turned the lights off and put us all in the dark. I was thrown off by this at first, and I wondered how Paul kept track of the students if he couldn't see them. Less than thirty seconds later, my eyes adjusted, and I saw the illumination from their dive computers and clearly heard their breathing patterns. There was no need for lights. We knew where the students were and could hear whether they were beginning to panic. My ability to use my other senses was being honed.

We returned to the spring basin and Paul signaled me to follow him while the students surfaced. He wanted to show me the entrance to the upstream section. I was grateful. The basin isn't large, but the opening was tucked away in a corner and difficult to see. If not for the current coming out of there, it would be nearly impossible to find. Even after I returned on my own to dive the upstream section, I had difficulty finding it. That's a story for another time.

* * *

I was teaching an advanced open water class with a student the previous weekend. We had already done three dives and had two more to complete the certification. My student met me at Troy Springs the day after I completed my third internship so we could finish the class. Troy Springs is a deep pit located in Troy Springs State Park, not far from Peacock. Cave diving is not allowed there. I don't know if the cave is large enough to penetrate or if they consider it a higher risk. Perhaps, they just want to keep it available for open water divers only.

There's an opening in one of the walls, but it's rather small. I was there with a student so I couldn't check it out even if I wanted to. I glanced in but didn't have a light that I could use to illuminate the dark crack. Because cave diving isn't allowed, neither are dive lights. Troy Spring also has an old paddle boat shipwreck in the spring run between the pit and the river. Only the ribs of the deck remain visible above the sediment. There are several slats of wood over a large area but nothing more to it. It's the only spring run wreck dive that I'm aware of. We completed a couple of dives in Troy Spring. My student earned his certification, and I was finally able to see the spring underwater.

* * *

I had been spending a lot of time at Peacock during my internships and became interested in doing a dive called the Grand Traverse. This dive entails entering the cave at Orange Grove or Peacock I and swimming through the winding passages below the park, crossing under the road twice before exiting from the other opening. I had already swum most of the route during previous dives. We entered the Orange Grove opening, swam beneath Challenge Sink and Olsen Sink, and continued out to the Peacock I opening, a total of forty-six hundred and seventy-one feet. Much like doing a circuit, a traverse required a setup dive and sometimes even a cleanup dive to retrieve any reels and spools that may have been left in the cave.

We entered Peacock I to do a setup dive and swam along the Olsen line, arriving at Olsen Sink, where I set a line from one of my jump spools to bridge the gap between the lines on either side of the sinkhole. We continued beyond Olsen Sink along the Challenge line through one of the prettiest cave passages I had seen. The first few hundred feet of tunnel meandered back and forth in a lazy river fashion. The water had carved beautiful shapes into the walls. The sediment on the floor was pristine. It was evident that this area of the cave wasn't visited very frequently. It was an amazing experience.

We eventually passed the intersection with the Peanut Restriction line, and several hundred feet later we turned around. The distance markers on the line indicated we were two hundred feet from Challenge Sink. We left our personalized line markers on the guideline and turned to swim the way we had come knowing we would be able to complete the Traverse. Orange Grove to Challenge Sink was deeper, but it was only eighteen hundred feet in distance. We had to swim two thousand feet to reach our line markers. We had already swum almost twenty-seven hundred feet from Peacock I.

The greater depth of Orange Grove to Challenge Sink had to be considered when planning the dive. While I was confident we could do it, just because we had travelled twenty-seven hundred feet on the first dive didn't mean we would make it to our markers two thousand feet from our new entry point before reaching turn pressure. We placed markers at the turnaround point to indicate where we had stopped. If we reached the markers from the other side using the same size or larger scuba tanks, we knew we had enough air in them to continue safely out of the cave through the other opening. If we didn't make it to our line markers before we reached turn pressure, we would turn around.

Depth dictates how much air we need to fill our lungs. If a balloon is filled with air on the surface and taken to thirty-three feet of depth, it will be half the size that it was on the surface. To get it back to the original size, it needs to be filled with the amount of air equal to what it was originally filled with. It will have twice the amount of air in it. As you ascend, the air must be released otherwise the balloon will double in size and may pop. Peacock I averages fifty feet of depth while Orange Grove averages eighty feet of depth. On the Peacock side, the balloon must contain two and a half times the amount of air as on the surface. On the Orange Grove side, it must contain three and a half times the amount of air.

Our lungs are similar to balloons. More air is needed to fill them at eighty feet than at fifty feet. We weren't likely to be able to swim twenty-seven hundred feet coming from the Orange Grove side using the same scuba tanks. My calculations indicated that we could make it to two thousand feet though. That afternoon, we stepped into Orange Grove Sink and descended below the surface. We lucked out. A cave diving instructor that I knew had left his primary reel in place from the basin to the beginning of the gold line. I had seen him teaching a class earlier in the day, and when he left, he mentioned he was leaving his primary reel in the cave overnight. This was a common practice when teaching, so I knew that line was going to remain in place until the following day. It meant I didn't have to run my own primary reel line, and we wouldn't have to do a cleanup dive.

We swam toward Challenge Sink and as we passed the area where Debra Reeves had her primary light failure, I looked at the lines and thought about that incident. I could see how easy it would have been to confuse the lines before gold line was implemented as a safety measure. I looked down the tunnel where she and her boyfriend had first gone after her primary light failure. This was where he realized they were in the wrong place and tried to get Debra to turn around. I wondered how he was doing and if he ever got over that incident. Had he continued to cave dive after that? Had it ever gotten easier?

We moved past the intersection and continued to Challenge Sink. As I approached the end of the gold line, I noticed the beginning of the gold line leading to Olsen Sink only a few feet away. I could stretch my arms between the two and touch both ends. Our line markers were on the next line only two hundred feet away. I checked my pressure gauges and saw that I had plenty of air to make it to the line markers and we could complete the traverse. Rather than continuing to the other line, we surfaced for a brief moment to discuss the plans for the rest of the dive. I suggested that we didn't install a jump line between the two gold lines below us. The lines were close enough to touch both at the same time, and we were only two hundred feet from our midpoint. Once we made it to the markers, we would continue forward if there was an emergency. If we chose to turn back, we could surface and exit from Challenge, as difficult as that would be.

When doing a traverse, a third dive is typically required to retrieve the lines we leave in the cave. There was already a primary reel in place at Orange Grove that didn't belong to me, so we wouldn't have to retrieve that. If we didn't leave a jump spool in place at Challenge Sink, we wouldn't have to swim eighteen hundred feet one way to retrieve that either. There was some risk to what I proposed, but it was minimal. We descended below the surface, and I retrieved the line marker I had left on the line for the purpose of differentiating the two passages. We continued toward our markers two hundred feet away.

Four minutes later, we arrived at the line markers. The hard part of the dive was over. We had made it to the midpoint of our air consumption and still hadn't reached turn pressure. We continued swimming along the line, passing through my favorite passage once again. This time, I took a few minutes to stop and look around. I had plenty of air and could afford to take my time. I retrieved the jump spool I had left at Olsen Sink and continued swimming toward Peacock I. We had just swum from one side of the park to the other, passing three sinkholes, and crossing under the road twice. We had completed the Grand Traverse.

27

It feels like I'm swimming in piss!

I mentioned river caves a few chapters back. In reality, most caves are river caves. Even the caves in Merritt's Mill Pond are river caves. The water springing from them meanders along the pond, over the dam, and continues as Spring Creek until it spills out into the Chipola River. There are access points to caves, such as Orange Grove Sink, that do not directly connect to a river, but the Peacock Springs Cave System, which it is a part of, does empty into the Suwanee River.

There's a distinction among cave divers between tourist caves and river caves that goes deeper than location. Tourist caves are the more popular locations that most cave divers visit. They include Jackson Blue, Devil's Spring, Little River, and so on. Some of those caves are located in or adjacent to rivers, such as Devil's Spring and Little River. The designation of a river cave goes to locations such as Maddachalk and Bozel.

Devil's Spring and Little River are considered tourist caves because visitors can drive directly to them and park near the water. There are parking lots at both, as well as picnic tables to set up equipment. Devil's Spring even has tank racks for cave divers. True river caves can only be accessed by boat. The exception to this is Hole in the Wall and Twin caves, which are only boat accessible, but still considered tourist caves because rental boats are readily available. They get a higher amount of diver traffic than most other boat accessible caves due to this. Because most river caves aren't as easily accessible, they aren't frequently visited by cave divers. They require more effort to get to. Most people tend to go for the easier option.

River caves are known for having the potential for exploration. Because they aren't as easily accessible, they aren't as likely to have been fully explored. Bozel is the perfect example of such a cave. When I first began diving Bozel, the explored passage in the cave was only twenty-five hundred and forty feet in length. Less than half a mile of surveyed and mapped tunnels. A couple of friends and I eventually changed that. I'll go into detail about the exploration we did there in a subsequent book in *The Hidden Rivers of Florida* series.

I had fallen in love with Bozel and returned at my first opportunity. The Chipola River level was higher than it had been the last two times I went diving there. Jackson County had received quite a bit of rain, and it was enough to make the river rise. What I didn't know prior to this dive was just how much the level of the river affected the conditions in Bozel. The visibility wasn't its usual cracking unlimited distance that I had experienced during my previous dives. It was hazy and my lights only penetrated about twenty-five feet. Considering that most of the cave wasn't very large, the exception being the Stadium, twenty-five feet was not bad. I had hoped for better, though.

We made it to the third line intersection, the same place I had turned around the first time. That seemed to be as far as the air in my tanks would get me. I still didn't know exactly how far into the cave I was getting. My usual swimming pace was fifty feet per minute. Thirty minutes would have meant fifteen hundred feet. I knew that wasn't the case. The current was too strong to allow that, and the passages were too winding to make a quick forward progression possible. When I eventually surveyed the cave, I discovered that the third line intersection was just over seven hundred feet from the opening. My swim pace in Bozel was only twenty-five feet per minute! Half of what it normally was. Interestingly enough, Bozel is not a first magnitude spring. It goes to show that size does matter.

Unfortunately, the rain kept coming, and the river level continued to rise. I watched the river gauge daily, hoping the level would drop. Just when I thought the river level would be low enough to make conditions in Bozel favorable for diving, it rained again, and the river would rise. This pattern continued and kept me away from Bozel for six months.

While I was waiting to dive Bozel, I was invited to dive Springboard, a cave that required permission to access the land surrounding it. Springboard is located on Spring Lake, the same body of water where Black Spring is located. If we hadn't obtained land access, it would have taken half a day to get to Springboard by boat, maybe longer. I was thankful that we had land access and jumped at the opportunity to dive the cave. We arrived at the spring on a brisk December morning. The air temperature during the preceding few weeks had been cold, so the water in the Springboard basin was in the high fifties. At that location, the spring is a siphon so there was no sixty-nine-degree spring water feeding the basin. All of that water was flowing out of one of the other seven springs in Spring Lake and getting cooled by the brisk air temperatures. I stepped into the basin anxious to get far enough into the cave to find the sixty-nine-degree spring water and warm up.

In addition to the cold water temperature, the visibility wasn't good. It was less than ten feet and hazy. I could barely make out the other divers as we submerged. I had to maintain contact with the guideline so that I knew where to go. It was impossible to tell when we had passed through the opening into the cave. Springboard wasn't nearly as bad as Black Spring. It was more of a grayish-blue tone. I had my doubts about whether it was worth diving a cave in such conditions. I visited underwater caves to see them and enjoy the beauty within the tunnels beneath the ground. If I couldn't see the walls, I wouldn't be able to see how beautifully shaped they were. The only thing going for it at that time was that we didn't have to worry about alligators. It was too cold for them. I went into the cave, hopeful that conditions would improve.

About ten minutes into the dive, the visibility was still diminished. I had been told it would clear, and I remained hopeful. However, I wasn't seeing it (pun intended). We arrived at a line intersection, and I still couldn't see more than a few feet in front of me. We followed the line to the left and encountered a restriction about the size of the Rabbit Hole in Jackson Blue. I saw just enough of it to gauge its size. The visibility appeared to be getting worse. Maybe it was the diver in front of me disturbing the silt. I followed anyway.

I popped through the restriction and found myself in a large room that I could finally see. The visibility had improved and not just a little. It was immensely better. The ten feet of hazy visibility was left behind on the other side of the restriction. The visibility on the side we were on was nearly perfect. The water temperature was also warmer. We were back in sixty-nine-degree spring water. Dr. Richard Pyle popped into my head. If you've read *Beneath the Jungle of Cozumel: Connecting the Crowns*, you'll recognize the following story.

* * *

The temperature change reminded me of a video I had seen about a year before that dive. The video was taken by Dr. Richard Pyle, an ichthyologist. He was gathering specimens in the South Pacific off the coast of Christmas Island. He and his assistant were diving rebreathers because they were doing deeper and longer dives. They were diving to depths in the four-hundred-foot range, so they had helium in their scuba tanks. They also had full face masks on so they could communicate with each other. The helium they were breathing made them sound like Alvin and his chipmunk brothers when they spoke. Pyle and his assistant descended into the warm waters surrounding Christmas Island. The surface temperatures were in the mid-eighties, so they were wearing shorts and T-shirts. At some point during their descent, they passed through a thermocline. The water temperature had just dropped significantly.

I've experienced thermoclines. The first time was in Lake Pleasant located northwest of Phoenix, Arizona. It wasn't a distinct thermocline in the lake. It was more of a gradual change. As you got deeper, the water got colder. We had as much as a twenty-degree Fahrenheit difference in that lake. The first time we experienced a distinct thermocline was off of the coast of Mexico in the Sea of Cortez. We were in San Carlos, Mexico with a group of clients, and we headed out to do a couple of dives on the north end of San Pedro Island, an uninhabited, rocky outcropping several miles off the coast that was known for its sea lion population. We were descending along the sloped wall when Jen and I saw the water shimmering below us. As we approached the shimmer, we felt an instant drop in the temperature. The water in this pocket was several degrees colder. Fortunately for us, this was only a thermocline pocket. We kept descending, leaving the shimmering water behind, and returning to the warm eighty-two-degree waters we were expecting. We saw a few more thermocline pockets during that dive and did our best to avoid going through them. The temperature difference had been a bit of a shock. The thermocline pockets were indeed a unique experience; one we've never encountered since.

Another experience with a thermocline was when we were diving on a couple of shipwrecks off the coast of Nags Head, North Carolina, including one of the famed U-boats that was sunk near the coast during World War II. Rather than a thermocline pocket, this was an actual thermocline layer. The Gulf Stream and Labrador Current both converge along the coast of North Carolina. The Gulf Stream, coming from the south, contains warmer water. The Labrador Current comes from the north and is much colder. Oftentimes, the temperature difference is twenty-five degrees colder than the Gulf Stream. Usually the Gulf Stream is shallower than the Labrador Current. That was the case during these dives.

Foolishly, Jen and I hadn't bothered to bring our drysuits with us. I had called the dive center prior to traveling to the area and was reassured that the water temperature was in the eighties, so we only brought 3mm wetsuits with us. The water was eighty-two degrees...on the surface! The Labrador Current temperature was fifty-five degrees! I toughed it out the first day but nearly froze. Jen toughed it out long enough to drop down to the U-boat, then ascended just above the thermocline back into the Gulf Stream. She patiently waited there, watching me as I explored the submarine. The next day we rented 7mm wetsuits from the dive center. I wondered if the employee I spoke with was clueless or if he got commission on rentals.

Back to the Christmas Island story – When Pyle and his assistant descended through the thermocline into the colder layer, Pyle immediately began to comment on how cold it was. Pyle started by simply saying, "It's cold down here." This was in that helium induced chipmunk voice that one gets when they suck in the contents of a helium-filled balloon and start to immediately speak. Before long Pyle was emphasizing just how cold it was with some choice expletives. Yet rather than stopping and ascending back into the warm water, he continued the mission and descended even deeper into the cold water! The temperature of the water he was in was fifty-five degrees. He was wearing nothing but swim trunks and a T-shirt! The video only lasted seven minutes, but the dive lasted well over an hour. Pyle and his assistant were in the fifty-five-degree water for a much longer period of time than seven minutes.

Once they had collected the specimens they encountered, they began their ascent. This is how I know the dive was much longer than seven minutes. First, helium requires a slow ascent and decompression stops to prevent decompression illness, otherwise known as the bends. When breathing a helium mix while diving, the possibility of getting the bends during the decompression part of the dive is much higher than when breathing an air mixture without helium. The bends are more likely to occur when breathing air after a diver has surfaced. With helium, on the other hand, the bends can occur while the diver is still underwater and ascending. That's never a good situation.

Another issue that necessitated a prolonged ascent was the specimens they collected. Specimens found at those depths must be allowed to equalize as they are brought to shallower depths. If they aren't equalized, they will essentially explode, ending their usefulness to an ichthyologist like Dr. Pyle. They had to stop before they ascended to two hundred feet of depth to allow the specimens to equalize and then again for one to two minutes every ten feet. It took them well over twenty minutes to ascend above the thermocline.

When they finally reached the thermocline and passed back into the tropical eighty-six-degree water, Pyle immediately let out a sigh of relief and commented to his assistant, "It feels like I'm swimming in piss!" Again, this was in his best Alvin Chipmunk impersonation. Pyle let out sighs of relief almost continuously and repeated this phrase several times. To this day whenever I move from a colder layer of water into a warmer layer, that sentence pops into my head. And even with only a two-degree difference, it certainly does feel like I'm swimming in piss!

* * *

Back to the Springboard dive. The temperature difference wasn't as extreme as what Dr. Pyle experienced, but it was significant enough for me to feel it. Dr. Pyle's phrase immediately jumped into my mind. I continued through the new passage, feeling warmer and happier. I felt like I was swimming in piss. Maybe I was. There were two divers with pee valves in their drysuits directly in front of me.

We arrived at another line intersection a short distance later where our options were to go straight or to the right. We went to the right and found ourselves in a large fissure about twenty feet wide, twenty-five feet tall, and a couple of hundred feet long. It had a slight resemblance to King's Canyon, only much bigger and not quite as pretty. There was no need to rotate sideways to get through it. I swam near the ceiling of the passage on the way in. We reached the end of the fissure and there was no way to continue forward. The passage ended so we turned. I looked around attempting to find a missed lead. The water that carved this magnificent tunnel had to go somewhere. I wasn't ready for it to end. I saw nothing.

I descended along the back wall while continuing to look for an opening. There was nothing but solid limestone. On the way out of the fissure, I swam near the floor hoping to find something below a lower shelf on one of the walls. There was a space about three feet high that stretched back several feet. I searched for a missed lead in that crawl space to no avail. I didn't have much time to explore. There were four other divers in our team, and they were swimming back to the line intersection. I hurried to catch up with them as they arrived at the line intersection, and we turned to follow the other line. This led us into a small, winding passage that continued farther into the cave, seemingly forever. This was named the Distance Tunnel. We penetrated about nineteen hundred feet based on the amount of time we swam. There was very little current in the cave to slow us down. We eventually turned around. There were two divers behind me. And behind them was a wall of silt.

28

A bottle of booze and a bone or two

The wall of silt surprised me. I thought the visibility might be diminished from our bubbles percolating on the ceiling, but I didn't expect a complete blackout. The silt filled the entire passage, and nothing was visible beyond it. We had been swimming through the Distance Tunnel for twenty-five minutes and I wondered if the silt encompassed the entire length of it. Whenever I'm in a small silty passage, I look back every thirty seconds or so to make sure my technique hasn't gotten sloppy and the sediment on the floor isn't being stirred up. I did this several times as we swam through the passage. The water remained clear. I hadn't looked far enough behind me, though. I was concerned with my own skill and ability and hadn't thought about the two divers that were bringing up the rear of the team. They had been cave diving a few years longer than I had and I assumed their skill levels were at least equivalent to mine. We all know what happens when we assume something.

As I followed them through the tunnel, I watched the silt cloud get thicker. The divers now in front of me were using rebreathers and their rigs made them foot heavy. They swam with their bodies at an angle that had them in a foot down orientation that disturbed the sediment on the floor. I saw nothing but hazy fins the entire thirteen hundred feet out. There were areas of the Distance Tunnel that got slightly bigger and the visibility cleared momentarily, but most of the tunnel was silted out. I maintained contact with the line until we arrived in the large

215

room. We finally had a few minutes of clear visibility before we had to go through the restriction back to the murky cold water that would allow us to reach the surface. When I arrived at the beginning of the line in the spring basin, I had no idea I was out of the cave. The visibility was so bad that daylight wasn't penetrating through the surface only ten feet above.

A few days later, I was diving alone again. Diving with four other divers, three who I hadn't been diving with before, had tested my patience. I returned to the Chipola River and headed to Maunds Spring, another cave I hadn't been to yet. The river cave bug had bitten me hard. I was hoping that Maunds hadn't been affected by the river level like Bozel.

Maunds Spring is located at the end of a small, beautiful spring run about two hundred feet from the Chipola River. The spring basin is small, measuring about twenty-five feet in diameter. The opening to the cave is a narrow slit in the bottom of the basin just to the right of center as you enter from the run. It appears a little menacing at first. You can't see the opening to the cave. All you see is a long narrow fracture in the floor of the basin.

After several minutes of enjoying the beauty surrounding the spring, I descended below the surface into the crack, securing my primary line to a tree branch located just above the opening. As I moved through the fissure, I felt a rush of water blowing past me. This wasn't a first magnitude spring, but the current was strong. I knew I was about to encounter a small opening. About forty feet below the surface, that's exactly what I found. It was a small restriction choked down by debris that had fallen from the forest. Leaves and branches filled the opening so all I could see was a small black void. I unclipped one of my sidemount tanks and pushed it ahead of me displacing the debris. And then my world turned black.

I probably should have backed out at this point. I had no idea what was ahead. I hadn't spoken to anyone who was familiar with the cave. I had my guideline, though, and it was secured to a tree just below the surface. I knew I could find my way out even if I couldn't see my way out, so I continued moving forward. When my head finally broke through the muck and was inside of the opening, visibility was partially restored. I saw the permanent guideline secured to the ceiling on my right. If anyone had kayaked to the spring run at that moment, all they would have seen was a pair of legs sticking out of the opening forty feet below the surface. On second thought, they probably wouldn't have seen anything but debris swirling around deep inside of the crack.

I wrapped the line from my primary reel around the guideline while remaining in position plugging the cave opening. With my line secured, I pulled myself into the cave. This resulted in the opening being unplugged and the current resumed its full force exit. I followed a steep slope down through the first room to a depth of sixty feet where I found a sandy floor and another restriction. This one wasn't filled with debris. It also resembled the Jackson Blue Rabbit Hole except the top of it was lower. My chest brushed against the floor with my back sliding just below the ceiling. The hard limestone floor was covered by a thin layer of gravel rather than silt, so my movement through the restriction didn't disturb the visibility. About five feet later, I found myself in a room that was much larger than the previous one.

The current didn't feel as strong. The restrictions were the apparent cause of the intensity I had experienced. It appeared that I would have a nice easy swim going forth. As I moved farther into the cave, a wine bottle came into view. It was propped on the floor as if it was a welcoming gift from the cave. A small fish rested on the bottom assuming the role of maître d'. All that was missing were wine glasses...and wine. The bottle was uncorked and filled with water. I didn't know if the wine bottle had fallen into the cave during a river flood or if another cave diver had brought it in and left it there as a greeting to those who managed to pass through the restrictions. The bottle remains there all of these years later.

I swam past the bottle and a couple of minutes later arrived in an area of the cave in which the floor was covered by a strange material that resembled puffy blow-in insulation. It was a yellowish color and looked like clouds settled on the floor of the cave, disappearing in a small passage to the left. What appeared to be the main passage of the cave was to the right, so I went that way. I would save the insulation room for another dive. I placed a line marker before the line intersection to mark my exit and continued my penetration. A few minutes later I arrived at a second line intersection. After placing another line marker, I continued to swim through the larger of the passages, passing three more intersections before turning around.

The main passage was a decent size, measuring fifteen to twenty feet wide and ten to fifteen feet from floor to ceiling. About every fifty to one hundred feet were fissures perpendicular to the direction of the main passage. I didn't see any lines leading into the fissures, which didn't appear to go more than a few feet into the walls anyway. It was a strange sight that I had yet to encounter in a cave. I ventured into a couple of the fissures to learn that they were dead-ends. The perpendicular fissures and the insulation type material were unique attributes.

When I returned to the opening, the debris that plugged it, had returned and filled it completely. I couldn't see daylight streaming in from where I had come through. My only clue to where the opening could be located was the line from my primary reel. I grabbed the reel, removed it from the permanent guideline, and pushed myself into the dark debris, spooling the line back onto the reel as I went. I felt the ceiling of the opening and felt my body pass through. I found the wall on the opposite side of the fissure crack, but only by feel. I was still in the dark. I ascended along the wall. I knew I was getting shallower because I could see my exhalation bubbles rising around my head. I was also reeling in my line. It was still pitch black, and I began to wonder whether there had been a collapse.

I continued my ascent and when I was twenty feet deep, I finally got a glimpse of light. The debris had been disturbed so much during my exit that the current was pushing it up and filling the fissure crack.

* * *

As I mentioned, rainfall had an effect on the river caves. Bozel remained blown out for months. The river level rose enough to blow out Maunds, as well. Fortunately, the caves on Merritt's Mill Pond were largely unaffected. The Jon boat began to spend a lot more time on the pond. I started diving Hole in the Wall regularly. Conditions continued to get worse as the winter wore on. The layer of cold, hazy water below seventy feet of depth returned to the downstream side. The upstream side was largely unaffected. Or so I thought. On one dive, Jen and I swam upstream to the white line intersection I had seen on a previous dive. The line leads to the Century Tunnel, so named because the average depth was one hundred feet, and the tunnel continues for a few thousand feet until ending at a champagne bottle.

If you're a cave diver, you've probably heard of the champagne bottle in Hole in the Wall. For those of you that haven't heard of it, this is the famed champagne bottle placed in the cave by Sheck Exley in the 1980s as a reminder of the efforts it took to get there. It remains in the cave at the end of the line almost one mile from the opening. It would be a while before I would see it.

When Jen and I turned to follow the line into the Century Tunnel, we encountered zero visibility. It wasn't just diminished. We couldn't see a thing. There was a milky white substance in the water that reflected my dive light beam back at me. When I turned back to look for Jen, I couldn't see the beam from her dive light. We continued forward anyway, hoping the visibility would clear. About one hundred feet later, I decided to turn around. Not only couldn't I see the cave wall directly to my right, the wall my hand would occasionally bump against, but I could barely see the glow from my own dive light. The light beam was diffused by the milky substance and made things worse. When I turned around, Jen and I bumped heads.

With Hole in the Wall going the way of the river caves, I decided to

219

return to Twin Cave. Conditions were much better there. Up until this point, I had only been through the Subway Tunnel and the gold line circuit. I had yet to venture off of the gold line into the offshoot tunnels. It was time to change that. I swam to the opposing arrows indicating the midway point of the gold line circuit and set a jump line to a white line on the right so I could check out the other end of the Training Room. The guideline in this passage was positioned just above the sediment and sections of it were buried. I carefully pulled the line up out of the silt to make sure it was intact. Every pull caused a small bit of dusting, but it wasn't enough to disturb the visibility.

A hundred feet after swimming into the Training Room, the wall to my right opened into an alcove containing a large boulder situated in the center and looking out of place. There was another tunnel to the right of the boulder. I continued past the alcove another few hundred feet, coming to an area where the ceiling sloped down, and the floor sloped up. There was about two feet of clearance between them, so I carefully moved into the space. I was glad I had followed the guideline instead of swimming along the perimeter of the mound because I found a line intersection hidden at the top. One line went straight, and the other led into a fissure to my left. The fissure looked inviting, but the line ahead appeared to be the main line. I continued over the mound and arrived at a duck under.

I glided through the low space into one of the most incredible rooms I've seen in a cave. I've said this before, but this one was really amazing. I was ninety feet deep at the bottom of the room and the ceiling was twenty feet deep at its highest point. I swam around the perimeter in a corkscrew path toward the ceiling while taking it all in. I couldn't believe how big and beautiful it was. It was one of the most amazing experiences I've had. Even now, years later, it's still one of my favorite places to visit.

A few weeks later I returned to Twin Cave with my DPV and used it to scooter the Subway Tunnel to the top of the first fissure. I left the DPV and my stage tank clipped to a metal plate that was secured to the wall to provide cave divers with a place to leave stage tanks without damaging the floor. There were no good locations to leave a stage tank in the Subway Tunnel without disturbing the sediment on the floor so someone decided it would be better to drive a bolt into the wall to hold the plate rather than do more damage to the floor of the cave by regularly leaving stage tanks there. I have mixed feelings about it. It probably was the lesser of the two evils.

Long sections of the floor in Twin cave have been disturbed and damaged over years of abuse by careless divers. The marks in the sediment appear to have been caused by cave diving students in sidemounted scuba tanks with pressure gauges that were sticking straight up. There are trenches in the floor about shoulder width apart that extend for hundreds of feet. My guess is that an instructor conducted zero visibility air sharing drills where they shouldn't have been conducted. The gold line was originally routed only a few inches above the floor in that section. The trenches ran parallel to where the line used to be located. The line has since been repositioned, but the damage was done.

After clipping my DPV and stage tank to the plate, I swam to the tall fissure room and continued to the end of the line. I had been so mesmerized by the fissure the last time that I hadn't left myself enough air to continue farther into the cave. I continued another couple of hundred feet beyond the room and arrived in a small room named the Terminal Room. It was a nice swim, but after seeing the Terminal Fissure it was anticlimactic. The Terminal Fissure, the name I had given the large room, was the attraction. On the way out, I stopped to enjoy its beauty once again.

While the river caves local to me were blown out, there were other river caves that weren't. I headed about an hour away from home with the Jon boat to Holmes Creek to look for Bone Cave or Hidden Springs. The name of this cave depended on who you were speaking to. It was named Hidden Springs by locals because the opening was located on the floor of Holmes Creek and not visible from the surface unless the water level was really low. Holmes County had to be experiencing severe drought conditions for Hidden Spring to be visible, so its location had to be known if you wanted to dive it. I was with a friend who had been there before. I've been there several times since and have seen the entrance from the surface only once.

We entered the dark, murky water hoping we wouldn't encounter any alligators hanging out in the depths. We even threw some large branches and rocks in the direction of the opening, hoping to scare any that might be lurking below. We descended below the surface, and the visibility remained poor. I knew there had to be an alligator waiting for some unsuspecting divers to swim into the cave, so I made sure my friend led the way. That didn't offer me any protection from behind, however. At least, when bringing up the rear, I wouldn't see a gator coming in for the attack. We swam toward the suspected location of the opening and watched the visibility begin to clear. Fortunately, we didn't see any alligators. That didn't mean there weren't any nearby.

Once at the opening, we continued into the cave against the current, finding the guideline about fifty feet inside. We followed the guideline and arrived at a line intersection a short distance later. We went to the right and as I came around the corner, I saw the reason Hidden Spring had been named Bone Cave by cave divers. Embedded in the wall three feet above the floor, measuring about four feet long, was the spine of a dugong.

A dugong is a relative of the manatee. They are often both referred to as sea cows. They are large, gentle animals that feed on vegetation found in rivers, as well as in the ocean. When the waters in the gulf turned cold, manatees and dugongs moved inland to the warmer waters of the spring fed rivers in Florida. There are locations in Florida where hundreds of manatees can be found congregating in the warm spring waters during the winter months. The Florida panhandle was not known for this. The springs were too far inland. Dugong had lived in these waters at some point in our history, though.

There are distinctive differences between manatees and dugongs.

Manatees have flat, paddle-shaped tails while dugongs have fluked tails much like whales. Manatees have excellent eyesight and can live as long as forty years. Dugongs have poor eyesight and can live up to seventy years. Manatees are abundant around Florida with as many as five hundred congregating in the St. Johns River in the winter. Dugongs are typically found in Africa and Australia. There hadn't been a dugong in Florida in ages. It was likely that the spine on the wall of Bone Cave came from an extinct cousin of the dugong family. While dugongs are no longer found in Florida, their fossils have been found throughout the state. They were believed to exist in Florida seven to fourteen million years ago.

I stared at the fossil in amazement. Not only was the fossil several million years old, but it was embedded in the limestone wall two feet in front of me. I wondered what the story was behind it. How had the spine come to be embedded in the wall of this cave and were ribs embedded behind them? I wondered if there had been ribs on the floor of the cave that were scavenged. After a few minutes of reflection, we continued into the cave, following the guideline for about twenty minutes before turning to head out.

The passage was small and silty. I followed close behind my friend and watched his exhalation bubbles cause silt to percolate off of the ceiling. There was also a touch of silt being stirred up from the bottom caused by our movement through the water. When we turned around, we were faced with zero visibility. Initially, we did a bump and go exit, but I quickly figured out that I could feel the movement of my dive buddy on the line behind me so I kept going, stopping occasionally to make sure I could still feel movement in the line. We proceeded out of the cave in this fashion until we neared the opening. Visibility was still diminished, but at least I was able to see my dive light once again. I looked forward to returning to Bone Cave at some point in the near future and searching for more fossils.

29

The life of a crack dealer

It was finally official. I was issued my cavern and intro cave diving instructor certifications, and my first class was scheduled with a couple of students to whom I had taught cavern diving. It went well, and I issued my first intro cave diver certifications. I had officially become a crack dealer. That became the ongoing joke. The crack I was dealing wasn't the white powdery substance that alters your ability to make important life decisions, or any decisions for that matter. It was the openings in the ground that led to the hidden rivers of Florida. It was the cracks through the earth that took us to beautiful places carved by water moving through them over the course of millions of years. I was addicted to those cracks, and I was doing my best to get others addicted as well. It was a much safer crack than the white powdery substance featured on *Narcos*, but I'll argue that it's much more expensive.

The next step in the process went quickly. Before I knew it, I had taught and certified six students as cavern and introductory cave divers and received the green light from my sponsor to continue my internships. I sought opportunities to intern, avoiding the instructors I had previously interned with because I wanted to experience different teaching styles. While I waited for classes to schedule my internships, I continued building my experience. On one dive, I ended up at the end of the gold line in Jackson Blue. Finally, a little less than a year and a half after moving to Florida, I saw my first end of the line. Well, gold line anyway. Beyond the end of the line was white line and another

224

room.

The Mako DPVs Jen and I had were decent. They pulled us through the caves against the current much faster than we could swim, but their range was limited. I researched the DPVs on the market and borrowed different models to test drive. If I was going to be spending that kind of money, I wanted to know what I was getting. I had been to the four-thousand-foot line marker in Jackson Blue and wanted to go beyond it. The gold line in Jackson Blue ends forty-six hundred feet from the opening and continues for another few hundred feet into the Jackson Blue Terminal Room.

Mark and I finally scootered beyond the end of the gold line. A couple of minutes later, we stopped at a breakdown area just short of the Terminal Room. I released the trigger and began to ascend through a restriction when Mark signaled that he was ready to turn around. I was more than halfway through the restriction, so I continued until I was in a large enough space to turn. I would see the Terminal Room during another dive. I had to go into a head down orientation to get back through the restriction, and when I did that, my left foot came out of the foot pocket of the dry suit. Thankfully, my fin remained strapped onto the drysuit boot. I tried to pull the boot back onto my foot, but I couldn't get enough leverage. I would have to bend my knee so I could grab the material around my ankle to get it back on, and the passage we were in didn't offer much clearance. I was concerned that I might disturb the sediment on the floor and create a silt cloud. I hit the DPV trigger hoping to make it to a larger area where I could fix my suit. My left fin flapped in the current behind me as I scootered toward the exit.

I was anything but comfortable as my DPV pulled me through the next twelve hundred feet of passage. When I hit the trigger to exit, my body rotated to the right. I thought the loose foot pocket was responsible for the odd orientation. I tried to rotate back but couldn't maintain a prone position. I stopped and tried to pull the boot onto my foot a couple of times without success. I moved my stage tank to my left to try to counter the positive buoyancy without effect. I continued to scooter out until I finally arrived in a taller section of the passage where I had room to pull the boot on without disturbing the mud on the floor. Unfortunately, that didn't correct the rotation issue. My body continued its clockwise rotation as I scootered toward the exit. Mark asked me if I was okay and I signaled yes and kept going. There was no point in continuing to struggle with it the entire way out. I accepted that my body was going to remain in that position, and the left wall would be my floor. I'm sure Mark was behind me thinking it quite strange that I was scootering through the cave sideways. Maybe he thought I just wanted a different perspective of the cave. I eventually learned that the DPV I was using was known for rotating its users sideways. It would have been nice to know that before the dive.

A few weeks later, we returned to Jackson Blue to visit King's Canyon. When we got to the end of the line in the Canyon and crossed back to the gold line, Mark and I took a moment to go beyond the third line intersection to visit the memorial plaque of a friend that had died nearby. Richard Mork had been diving in Jackson Blue about four months prior. I first met him during one of my trips before moving to Florida. He also lived out of state and visited Marianna every few months to go cave diving. After I moved to Florida, I saw him during most of his trips. We spoke often but hadn't had a chance to dive together.

Richard had been certified on a rebreather not long before I met him and was building experience on it. Rebreathers are devices that require very little air to function. They contain a canister that holds sofnolime absorbent. Exhaled air passes through the canister and makes contact with the absorbent initiating a chemical reaction with carbon dioxide. The remaining air continues to the other side of the breathing circuit and reenters the lungs with a breathable level of oxygen. Rebreathers are limited by the absorbent, with most lasting up to four hours. Once the four hours have passed, the absorbent is considered to be fully bound to carbon dioxide and unable to continue binding. The benefit of rebreathers is that much smaller tanks can be used.

Richard was diving with a friend when he passed. The details as I heard them are as follows. They scooted into the cave and had a DPV malfunction before reaching the beginning of the gold line. The two decided to secure the DPVs to the guideline and swim. Richard was using his rebreather, and his dive buddy was using backmounted scuba tanks. The current was strong that day, but they managed to get to the third line intersection nineteen hundred feet from the opening. The current coming out of the Rabbit Hole was significantly stronger than in the rest of the cave. As Richard struggled against the current, his respiratory rate increased. Rebreathers work most efficiently with slow steady breaths. Richard's increased breathing rate likely resulted in the carbon dioxide moving through the scrubber not having enough time to bind with the absorbent and continuing to the other side of the circuit. Richard began to breathe air containing an unsafe level of carbon dioxide and lost consciousness. At least that's what we think happened.

Richard's dive buddy watched him lose consciousness, grabbed him, and ascended to the ceiling where he tried to revive him. He put his regulator in Richard's mouth in hopes that he would regain consciousness. Richard drowned in the cave nineteen hundred feet from the opening. A few months later, a plaque was placed near the location where he died. Mark and I were seeing it for the first time.

Richard wasn't the first person to die in Jackson Blue. There had been another fatality in there a few months after I moved to Florida. I didn't personally know that diver, but I did know of him. I was told that he wasn't trained to dive in caves. He had never even taken a cavern diver class. He went diving in Jackson Blue on a regular basis though. It was well known that he was doing that, but no one tried to stop him. He was getting his tanks filled and going to Jackson Blue in his boat. He had done more than sixty dives in the cave before he lost his life in it. There wasn't much anyone could do to stop him other than not fill his tanks. There were no laws preventing him from diving in a cave. He couldn't get access to the park to dive it at the time. Only certified

227

cavern and cave divers could sign in at the sheriff's office. There was nothing stopping him from going there on his boat.

Sadly, he was diving with a certified cave diver, someone who knew better, the day that he died. The two went into a small offshoot tunnel in Jackson Blue located at the top of the second breakdown. The ceiling gets low and there's a section that is impossible to pass with backmounted scuba tanks. He and his buddy didn't know this. To complicate things even more, the floor of the tunnel had a lot of sediment covering it. According to the certified cave diver that made it out of the cave alive, the uncertified diver led the way into the tunnel and destroyed the visibility almost instantly. He continued swimming farther into the tunnel, probably not wanting to backtrack into the silt cloud he had created. He had no training in using the guideline in zero visibility.

Had he been trained to cave dive, he would have known what to do and could have turned around to swim back to the main passage. Instead, he continued pulling himself through the restriction. It was too small for him to fit. His buddy, the trained cave diver, not being able to see anything, turned around, and exited the cave to call for help. The uncertified diver's body was found in the passage where he had last been seen, stuck to the ceiling with his tanks on the floor beneath him. It appeared he had removed the tanks to push them through the restriction. Unfortunately, when he removed the scuba tanks, he also removed all of the weight that was keeping him neutrally buoyant. His positively buoyant body rose to the ceiling, and he lost hold of his regulator. He drowned stuck to the ceiling not far above scuba tanks that were full of air.

30

An unfortunate victim of circumstance

A long time had passed since I was last at Peacock Springs State Park. It was time to rectify that. One of the cave diving training organizations was hosting a critter counting workshop and I signed up. Population counts of troglobites, creatures that live inside caves, were being done regularly at Peacock Springs. The albino salamander and crayfish I had seen in Twin and Hole in the Wall were classified as troglobites. Peacock Springs has mostly amphipods within its confines, while the caves on Merritt's Mill Pond in Marianna have all three. The project coordinator was interested in getting more volunteers and expanding the program. I wanted to do critter counts in the three main caves on Merritt's Mill Pond. I was especially interested in the troglobite compound I had encountered in Hole in the Wall.

Critter counts created a record of the populations. The program coordinator collected the information and sent it to the Florida water management division. The objective was to see if above ground activities were affecting below ground life. If the population numbers changed drastically, we could try to learn what was causing the changes.

Two divers are required to conduct critter counts. The first diver swims and breathes from scuba tanks. No rebreathers for these dives. The exhalation bubbles rise to the ceiling and disturb any critters hanging above. The second diver follows about twenty feet behind, looking for critters and keeping count of them on an underwater slate. These counts must be done regularly at the same time each month for consistency. The coordinator was doing regular critter counts in Peacock Springs, but there was no one doing the same in the Marianna caves. I started working on it. I managed to do several critter counts, but I couldn't maintain the necessary consistency. Jen was busy with school, and I had difficulty finding a second diver to join me on the dives. I finally abandoned the project.

After the critter count workshop, which consisted of a short lecture, a dive in Peacock I, and a debriefing, I headed to Telford Spring, a cave near Peacock Springs State Park. Telford is at the end of a short spring run that feeds the Suwanee River. The land surrounding it is privately owned so legal access is only possible from the river. Fortunately, there was a public boat ramp about two hundred feet downriver from the spring run.

I brought my DPV and scootered up the river. Telford Spring is not only a beautiful cave, but it also has an interesting story. Many years ago, a cave diver was diving in Telford and never resurfaced. He was reported missing, and divers searched the cave for his body but were unable to find him. After several expeditions, the search was called off. It wasn't known if the diver had perished in the cave or if he had made himself disappear.

Telford is a maze of tunnels. There are several four-way intersections. Many of the tunnels loop back to the main passage, but some keep going. It can be a confusing cave, and divers are cautioned about this. About five years after the missing diver report, a cave diver was swimming through one of the passages when he saw what appeared to be another diver. There were no lights, just the outline of a person wearing scuba tanks. The cave diver slowly approached, noticing that in addition to no lights, there were also no bubbles rising to the ceiling. Then he noticed that the diver didn't have a regulator in his mouth. The diver was dead. He marked the location and quickly exited the cave.

The body was recovered, and it was discovered to be the body of the diver that had disappeared five years earlier. He must have gotten lost in the cave and breathed through the air in his tanks, eventually drowning in the location he was found. Because the cave is so complex, no one had ventured into that area during the search dives or in the following years.

I went into the cave knowing this story of the ghost of Telford Spring but fortunately didn't know of any missing divers being reported since. I was fairly confident that I wouldn't find any bodies. There was a lot of variety to Telford Spring. It was a dark and silty cave and the gold line was stained brown by the tannins that backed up into the cave when the river level rose. I passed through bedding plains and fissures and several four-way intersections. I could see how easy it would be to get confused and lost. I did not want to suffer the same fate as that other diver, so I made sure to use line markers at every intersection.

Telford Spring connects to another spring nearby named Luraville Spring. The two openings are about a mile apart straight-line distance. Much like Peacock Springs, a traverse can be done from Telford to Luraville. I know of one person that has been successful in doing it. There have probably been others, but access to Luraville Spring was eventually restricted.

A few weeks after the workshop, I went on a dive in Hole in the Wall with another cave diver. We scootered downstream and headed into an offshoot tunnel that my dive buddy wanted to look at. We arrived at the junction and found a lead to a tunnel that didn't have a guideline in it. My dive buddy led the way and left three hundred and fifty feet of line in the newly discovered passage. This was my first time in an unexplored, virgin cave passage. I wasn't the first one in it and didn't place the line, but I was there. I finally experienced the joy of being in a passage that had never been discovered. This was a turning point in my cave diving.

It ruined me. I was hooked. I wanted more. I wanted to search for and find more tunnels that no one had ever found. Unfortunately, it would be five months before I was able to find my own virgin passage. And that time, I was the one who went in first.

* * *

While I was diving and teaching, I picked up a few additional instructor certifications. The first one I pursued was sidemount instructor. I had been mentoring students who desired to transition to sidemount diving, and I wanted to be able to offer an official class with certification. This was not an easy instructor rating to get. There was only one training agency that offered a sidemount diving course at the time. They had created an advanced cave sidemount course and added a bare bones basic sidemount course. It seemed like an afterthought. There were very few instructors certified to teach the basic sidemount course. There were even fewer instructor trainers.

I found an instructor trainer located about four hours away who could certify me. He rarely did any dives in sidemount. I was certain I had more experience diving with sidemounted tanks than he had, as well as more experience mentoring new sidemount divers. But he had the authority to make me a sidemount diving instructor and there were no other options.

I traveled to Blue Grotto Spring, a sinkhole that was developed into a popular training site in north central Florida. Blue Grotto has a decent size basin that allows students to swim around in a wide circle and practice skills. There's a small area that's in the overhead with a steeply sloped ceiling making it much safer than a typical underwater cavern zone. At the bottom of the basin are two tunnels that lead to deeper, darker depths of a cave. The tunnels slope down to a depth of just over one hundred feet and join together, creating a small cave circuit.

The sidemount diving instructor trainer was training a rebreather diver and I was tagging along to demonstrate that I had the appropriate level of skills proficiency required to teach the sidemount diving course. I didn't have to teach anything, and the didactic portion of the class lasted about ten minutes. We didn't discuss much. I had to demonstrate good buoyancy and trim in the water. I also had to unclip one tank and hold it in front of me and then do the same with both tanks. While I did that, I had to maintain my buoyancy and trim. I would be a sidemount diving instructor after that dive.

During the ten-minute session, we reviewed basic information about sidemount diving and the instructor trainer was satisfied with my self-taught knowledge. He briefed the dive, and I immediately regretted having brought my larger steel tanks as they would not be easy to hold out in front. It was too late to do anything. My other scuba tanks were four hours away.

We suited up and I looked at my instructor trainer, who happened to be a portly fellow. When he put his drysuit on and slipped the neck seal over his head, I switched into nurse mode. I looked at him and instantly knew he was a heart attack waiting to happen. His face turned crimson red, and veins popped to the surface in protest. I imagined his blood pressure would likely break the gauge on a sphygmomanometer. The thought of him passing out in the water flashed through my mind. The surface of the water was two dozen steps down a steep hill. It would not be easy to pull him out of the water onto the dock, never mind having to drag him up the steps.

Fortunately, we got through the dive without any medical events. I got my sidemount diving instructor rating and we discussed working on my technical diving instructor ratings. He told me to get in touch with him the following week to schedule a date. I wasn't sure I wanted to do decompression dives with him after seeing his physical response to putting his drysuit on, but, again, my choices were limited. A few days later, he called me and told me he was out of commission for a few months. He had a heart catheterization the day before and there were multiple blocked vessels. His cardiac doctor recommended heart surgery…soon. I wasn't surprised. When you've been a nurse for a while, these things are easy to clinically identify. I was happy he was getting his health attended to, but back to square one for continuing my decompression instructor training. That was more than fifteen years ago and last I heard, he's still alive. That surgery saved his life.

Over the next few months, I expanded my experience by diving in more new-to-me caves. The first one was Indian Springs, located south of Tallahassee in Crawfordville. Indian Springs was located on the property of a boy scout camp and had an agreement between the owners and cave divers to allow diving there with a sanctioned guide.

Unfortunately, the boy scout camp has since closed and the property was sold to a private company, so the agreement is no longer in place. Before it was sold, one of the cave diving organizations held a workshop on location and I was able to do my first of three dives there. Indian Springs has a sad history in terms of cave diving. At the time, it was the site of the only cave diving fatality that was determined to not be caused by the diver breaking one of the rules of cave diving. These rules are:

Dive within your training limits
Always have a continuous guideline to the surface
Use proper air management to plan and conduct your dives
Use the appropriate air mixture for your planned depth
Maintain your equipment and lights in good condition
Make certain you are healthy and feeling good

If you've read my book, *Into the Darkness Beyond*, you know this story, but it bears repeating. The entrance to Indian Springs cave begins ten to fifteen feet below the surface, depending on the water level. It's fairly close to the coast so the tide affects the water level in the spring basin. Parker Turner, one of the early Florida underwater cave explorers, and his dive buddy, Bill Gavin, the inventor of one of the first modern DPVs used in caves, were exploring Indian Springs looking for new passages.

Turner and Gavin dropped below the surface, immediately got into a horizontal position, and assessed their equipment. All seemed in order. They turned toward the opening of the cave and squeezed the triggers on their DPVs as they descended to twenty feet of depth, just below the ceiling of the cavern. They passed from the safety of the surface above into the dark confines of the overhead environment. About twenty feet in, the coarse sand floor quickly dropped away down a sharp slope that ended about ninety feet deep. From there the floor kept getting deeper but not at as steep of a slope.

They reached the bottom, went through a quick mental checklist of their equipment and the dive plan, and continued to scooter deeper into the cave. The plan was to check out leads in the Wakulla Room, a large room at three hundred feet of depth that they had found on a previous dive.

After spending about twenty-five minutes in the Wakulla Room and finding nothing, Turner and Gavin began to make their way toward the exit. When they were about fifteen hundred feet from the opening, Turner signaled to Gavin that his DPV was getting sluggish. Turner clipped his tow line to Gavin and Gavin increased the speed on his DPV continuing toward the exit. About ten minutes later they arrived at a point in the line where another line tied into it, forming an intersection. They turned left to continue heading toward the exit.

Immediately after turning left, the visibility began to deteriorate. There were silt clouds hovering over the floor. The farther they went, the bigger the silt clouds got and the worse the visibility, until they couldn't see more than a foot in front of them. Gavin released the trigger and he and Turner made contact with the line to swim the short distance remaining.

Except soon after, they discovered the line they were following in the near zero visibility conditions was buried under the coarse sand. They began pulling the line up, trying to get it out from under the sand, until they reached a point where it was too deep to pull up. At that location, the sand rose all the way to the ceiling. They were trapped.

For the next forty-five minutes Turner and Gavin frantically searched for a way out of the cave as their limited breathing gas supply dwindled away. At one point, Gavin deployed a safety spool, secured the cave line on it to an unburied portion of the main line and began spoking out to look for an alternate exit. When he returned several minutes later Turner was gone.

Gavin continued to search, breathing the last of his stage tanks empty. He went back to breathing from his backmounted double tanks with only three hundred psi of breathing gas remaining. Gavin made one last effort at finding an exit when he came across another line intersection, one which he didn't remember being there before.

He followed the new line not knowing where he was heading but having no other option.

Eventually, Gavin found himself in a larger area, looked up, and saw the permanent line above him. With only a few breaths remaining in his tanks, he picked up his pace to try to get to his staged decompression tank, which was waiting for him at one hundred feet of depth. If the tank had been any farther, he might not have made it out of the cave alive.

Bill Gavin then had to endure four long hours of decompression stops knowing his teammate and good friend, Parker Turner, had not made it out of the cave.

There were other divers on the surface providing support for Turner and Gavin who reported seeing the water in the basin drop by about a foot and the water current rushing into the cave. They didn't know if this caused the avalanche or if the avalanche caused it. Regardless, the exit was blocked. It appears Turner found a small tunnel through the sand, removed his backmounted tanks, and pushed them through in front of him. His efforts resulted in the small opening becoming large enough for Gavin to be able to fit without removing his tanks.

Unfortunately, Turner ran out of breathing gas before he made it to his decompression tank just thirty feet away from where his body was found stuck to the ceiling, his empty double tanks hanging from the main line below him. It was most likely because of Turner's actions that Bill Gavin was able to get out alive and there wasn't a double fatality that day. For many years, Parker Turner held the dubious distinction of being the only cave diver fatality that was not attributed to a violation of one of the cave diving rules.

It was a sad event. The only way it could have been avoided was if they hadn't been diving in the cave on that day. One theory suggests that it may have been the exhaust bubbles from their exhalations that contributed to the sand avalanche that occurred that day. As the bubbles hit the ceiling and ascended up the slope toward the surface outside of the cave opening, some found their way into cracks in the limestone and caused large pieces to dislodge and crash to the floor.

That event in turn caused the sand slide that trapped Turner and Gavin inside of the cave. We'll never know exactly what happened to precipitate the sand slide. We do know that Turner was not violating any of the rules established to keep cave divers safe and alive. He was doing everything by the book. He was just the unfortunate victim of circumstance.

As I descended below the surface and made my way toward the opening of the cave hidden beneath the grounds of the camp, I thought about Parker and how he died. I swam into the opening and saw the floor drop down a steep slope a few dozen feet ahead. I could see how easy it would be for a sand slide to occur. I looked around for evidence of the event that occurred nearly twenty years earlier. Of course, I didn't see anything. It had been far too long. There hadn't been a similar event since. I hoped one wasn't overdue.

I quickly and carefully moved through the cavern, not wanting to trigger an avalanche, and found myself at the top of the slope. I looked into the dark abyss below us and began my descent, arriving at the bottom about ninety feet deep. The passage was a decent size. The mound of sand that had trapped Turner and Gavin was long gone. We swam for about twelve minutes until we reached a line intersection. I thought back to Turner and Gavin's dive. We were hovering in the location where they first encountered diminished visibility. The avalanche had caused the sediment to spread more than six hundred feet through the passage. We turned right to go upstream toward the Wakulla Room and continued for about six minutes before arriving at a location named the Big Elbow.

At this point, the passage formed a sharp turn to the right. We were still a long way from the Wakulla Room, not even having reached the halfway point. We didn't have enough scuba tanks to make it that far. We never intended to try. We turned around and headed back to the intersection, continuing past it into another branch of the cave. We passed through a large room named the Hall of the Green Giant. It was possibly named this because someone imagined the Green Giant could have easily made a home there with plenty of room to spare. They obviously hadn't seen the next room we were heading to when they named the first one.

The next room was named the Grand Canyon. It was a name well deserved. I remained twenty feet beneath the ceiling at a depth of one hundred and ten feet. One of the other divers with us swam just above the guideline which was routed along the floor of the cave. He was more than one hundred and sixty feet deep. The room was close to seventy feet tall. The walls were also a good distance apart. We swam along the wall to our left and I could barely make out the wall to our right. There were times when all I could see to my right was a black void. I aimed my light beam at it, but nothing changed. The wall had to be more than sixty feet away. The room was truly magnificent. I could have spent an entire dive just exploring the Grand Canyon.

We turned around after arriving at a large formation named the Great Pyramid. You can probably guess why it was named that. This formation stood tall in the middle of the passage. As large as it was, it seemed small compared to the room we were in. The current assisted us with our egress, and we made it back to the line intersection quite rapidly, turning to exit. Thoughts of Gavin and Parker first experiencing a disturbance in the visibility swam back into my head. This was where they released their DPV triggers and made contact with the guideline.

I was thankful to find the visibility in the same condition as it had been when we began the dive. We arrived at the bottom of the slope, once again, thankful to find the passage wide open with no sand mounds to hinder our exit. We began our long ascent to the surface. We had survived a dive in Indian Spring.

31

One of the prettiest springs I've ever seen

Rainstorms continued to blow into North Florida from the Gulf keeping the river level too high to dive the caves along its banks. I was anxious to return to Bozel, but that wasn't happening anytime soon. Whenever the water gets above a certain level, the tannic river water backs into the spring run and into the cave, diminishing the visibility significantly. During those times, the caves in Merritt's Mill Pond were the only caves worth diving. The pond was created by a dam more than one hundred years earlier that kept the caves from flooding. The river could back up only as far as the dam. That meant the pond and the caves before the dam were almost always clear.

Except Hole in the Wall. For some reason, as I previously mentioned, Hole in the Wall gets hazy and cloudy in October and remains that way through May. The layer below seventy feet gets very cloudy, and the water temperature drops by several degrees. Eventually, the entire passage is consumed by the haziness and cold water. I've only seen it not do this a few times over the years.

Rain in Jackson County also affects the intensity of the current in Jackson Blue, with more rain resulting in stronger current. Our dives in Jackson Blue were getting difficult. Jen and I did a dive with our DPVs to Stage Rock and I had to pull myself through the Rabbit Hole. The DPV didn't have enough thrust to get me through. Jen chose to go the other route after the third line intersection. Even though it was the same distance between the third intersection and the fourth, it took her two additional minutes to make it to the traffic light.

The rain finally eased off as the summer months approached. The river level dropped enough for good visibility to return to Bozel. I was ecstatic! I didn't waste any time loading the boat and heading up the river. It had been far too long since my last dive in Bozel. Jen was with me on this dive. She started to feel the effects of nitrogen narcosis as we descended through the Stadium. She had to stop and ascend back to the top of the mound where she signaled me to continue while she waited and explored the Stadium. This would soon become a common practice during exploration dives. Jen didn't mind waiting where she felt comfortable while I explored possible leads or continued into the cave. I tried to stay away no longer than ten minutes, five minutes in and five out.

Jen graduated from the nursing program and was available to dive more often. We frequently visited the three main caves in Merritt's Mill Pond, as well as other locations. One spring we went to was Cypress Spring, located in Vernon, Florida. Cypress is said to be one of the most beautiful springs in Florida, and possibly the world. I agree with that assessment. The spring is surrounded by privately owned property making the only access by boat. Fortunately, there's a launch less than a ten-minute boat ride from the spring run, twenty minutes if you're paddling a canoe or kayak. It's a popular location for kayakers and canoers, so we went during the week when we were less likely to encounter others.

We launched the boat and made our way down the tannic river looking for the clear water coming from the spring run. I was told it would be obvious and there was no way we could miss it. About six minutes after we launched the boat, we saw the run to our left. It was easily twenty-five feet across. I maneuvered the boat out of the river and followed the clear water. We could see the bottom of the spring run only a few feet below. There were places shallow enough that I had to maneuver my way around shoals to avoid hitting the outboard motor on them. We continued up the run for a couple of hundred feet before we finally saw the spring basin. It was amazing.

The basin is about one hundred and forty feet wide and surrounded by cypress trees that are rooted both in and out of the water along the banks. There's a small beach area to the west located on private property and a fence several feet back from the water. Surprisingly, there weren't any no trespassing signs posted.

We slowly motored around the edge of the basin before moving directly to the center over the deepest part. I couldn't see the cave opening. There were dark areas hidden in the shadows of ledges, but I couldn't be certain those led to a hidden passage. I maneuvered the boat to the east bank where there were some fallen tree trunks sticking above the surface and secured the boat to one of them where it was shallow enough to stand in the water. Jen and I suited up and began our dive. We brought single aluminum scuba tanks and planned to do something we called monkey diving – single tank sidemount diving.

We swam around the spring basin, poking our heads into every dark hole we could find looking for the cave opening. The bottom of the open area where I thought it might be located was twenty-five feet deep. There was a sandy oval patch measuring about thirty feet long and fifteen to twenty feet wide in the center. There were dark recesses around the west and south walls, but none of them led into the earth. I swam out of the central location and ascended over some boulders to the southeast. As I began to crest the boulders, I was pushed toward the surface by an invisible force. It was as if a hand had slammed its open palm against my chest and pushed me up. I found the opening. The current coming out of the cave was the strongest I had experienced.

I moved away before the current made me break the surface and assessed the situation. I wanted to go into the cave to check it out, but that current was very strong. I needed to devise a plan for my approach so that I wouldn't be fighting it all the way in. The opening was below the boulders rather than in the wall where I thought it would be. I planned my approach and moved toward the void in the floor, pulling myself in. When I was about halfway through, I saw the opening. It was to my right in the wall of the hole I was descending into. I pulled myself closer so I could have a look and settled on the floor just below the strongest part of the current. I took a moment to catch my breath and focused my light beam into the cave. It was much larger than I expected.

I pulled into the cave where the current finally eased beyond the bottleneck opening. It wasn't as intense, but I still had to hold onto the floor to keep from being blown out. I pulled myself farther in through the small passage as it continued sloping down to a depth of sixty-three feet. I could see where the current was coming from at the back of the room, but it was too small for me to continue farther, even with only one scuba tank strapped to my side. I would be returning with both of my sidemount tanks to explore it further.

The next day, Jen and I went to Vortex Spring to do our first cave dive there. We had been to Vortex with students many times, but other than a couple of visits to the Piano Room where the metal grate is located, we spent most of our time in the spring basin. The grate is located three hundred feet from the opening and was placed there in the early nineties to keep untrained divers from venturing into the deeper and smaller parts of the cave. The passage from the opening to the grate is a fair size and opens into the Piano Room. The cave continues through a restriction in the wall at the back right corner beyond the grate. It's just over one hundred feet deep in that section.

An air box large enough for two divers to pop their heads up into, three if you're okay getting cozy, was located on the opposite side of the room. Divers sometimes raise their heads into the air-filled box and remove their regulators for a few seconds to talk. This isn't recommended because the oxygen content may not be high enough to support life. When divers exhale into the box, they release carbon dioxide, causing the oxygen content to drop. We exhale sixteen percent oxygen with every breath. Breathing air with less than eighteen percent oxygen is considered hypoxic and affects mental faculties and, eventually, unconsciousness. Someone is said to go into the cave every morning to refresh the air in the boxes, but that only maintains a high enough oxygen level for so long. It's better to have the box in place, though, because it provides an additional safety measure for the untrained open water diver.

Even though new scuba divers are told they should not enter a cave without the proper training, many do. Their curiosity takes over, and they venture in. There's a sign at the opening with a drawing of a grim reaper and three dead scuba divers at the reaper's feet warning untrained divers to GO NO FARTHER! Hardly anyone heeds the warning. Fortunately, Vortex hasn't had many fatalities in the cave since the early nineties, mostly due to the grate.

One fatality that did supposedly occur was that of Ben McDaniel. I say supposedly because Ben's body was never recovered. This event was the inspiration for my debut thriller, *Beyond the Grate*. The metal grate that's located inside of the Vortex Spring cave has a padlock on it with the keys kept in the dive shop. They can be signed out by certified cave divers who want to dive in the cave. It's not a very popular cave diving site because not many cave divers are willing to lock themselves inside of a cave. Doing so could present problems. If an emergency should occur, having to stop and unlock the padlock could waste precious time that could be the difference between life and death.

There are ways around this. We didn't lock the padlock when we went into the cave. Instead, we dummy locked it to give it the appearance that it was secured. Anyone more than casually looking at it would know the difference. Hopefully, those not trained to be inside of a cave wouldn't venture beyond the grate. If someone did, we would likely encounter them on the way out because Vortex cave isn't an extensive system. We were more concerned about having a quick egress if we needed it. It was a good thing we didn't lock it because Jen almost died on this dive.

32

Near death experience

Jen and I were breathing Trimix, a mixture of oxygen, nitrogen, and helium, during our dive in Vortex Spring due to a depth of one hundred and sixty feet near the fourth restriction. We weren't planning to get that far, but we didn't know the exact profile of the cave. We arrived at Vortex, signed in, presented our cave diver certification cards, and received the key to the padlock that secured the grate. We were going to lock the padlock on one of the rebar posts but not lock the grate closed. It would appear to be locked while allowing us easy egress should we need it. The risk of someone coming through the grate was preferred to locking ourselves inside of the cave. Should something happen beyond the grate, having to stop and fumble with a lock would only make it worse. I was also concerned about the possibility of losing the key.

Vortex Spring has a six-inch diameter pipe running from the basin through the passage back to about one thousand feet from the opening. It's been used over the years to vacuum the silt that accumulates inside the cave. The silt gets transported through the pipe to the basin and directed downstream into the spring run. There's a belief that had it not been for these efforts, Vortex Spring may have clogged and turned into a dead spring.

There are a few springs in Florida that have stopped flowing. This usually occurs because of over-pumping by water bottling companies or erosion. Erosion was the issue at Vortex. If the sediment in Vortex wasn't vacuumed out of the cave, the result could be a decrease in water flow. This would make the passage too small to dive, but more importantly, it would make the spring basin and the creek downstream of it a stagnant pool overgrown with algae.

Jen and I descended into the chimney and swam toward the warning sign that displayed the image of the grim reaper. We swam past it and into the dark cave. About ten minutes after we submerged, we arrived in the Piano Room and saw the grate in the far-right corner. I retrieved the key from my pocket as we swam toward it and inserted it into the lock. I had to jiggle the key to get the tumblers to fall into place. It took about thirty seconds of jiggling and manipulating before the key finally turned and the lock opened. This reaffirmed our decision to dummy lock the grate while we were beyond it.

Jen passed through the grate first. I followed, pulling it closed behind us with the lock secured to one of the pieces of rebar. I swam past Jen and took the lead. About twenty feet later, around the corner, I arrived at the permanent guideline hidden out of view from the Piano Room. I secured my primary line to it, and Jen and I clipped our oxygen decompression scuba tanks to the line making sure they were also hidden from the view of any divers that might venture into the Piano Room and look through the grate. We didn't want them to get curious and try to follow us.

We slowly swam through the passage with the partially buried pipe to our right. We could see most of the pipe in some stretches, but only an inch or two of the top in others. We felt the current flowing past us, fighting to keep us out. We made it through the first restriction, which wasn't much of a restriction. Jen went through it without pause, so that said something as to its size. We continued through the second restriction, which again wasn't much of a restriction. Both of these were smaller but still passable with backmounted scuba tanks. When we were almost at the third restriction, it was time to turn around. We were at our turn pressure. We were only one hundred and twenty feet deep and didn't need Trimix after all.

245

The exit went a little faster with the assistance of the current. Jen and I were back at our oxygen decompression scuba tanks in no time. We swam around the corner and Jen pushed the grate open. Or rather she tried to push it open, but it only moved a few inches. She pushed harder without result. I wondered if someone had come in behind us and locked us in. I gently nudged Jen aside and moved beside her. That's when I noticed that the bottom of the grate was digging into the sand. When I had pulled it open and pulled it back closed, the sand on the floor shifted and buried the bottom rebar piece. I stuck my hand through the grate, swept the sand aside, and pushed the grate open. It resisted, but I was able to get it open wide enough to pass through.

Once we were both back in the Piano Room, I turned around and pushed the grate closed while retrieving the key from my pocket. As I was trying to insert the key into the padlock, it slipped from my grasp and fell to the floor. I picked it up and used more care handling it. This time it wasn't as difficult to turn the key. The clock was ticking. I was breathing the supply of air in my tanks, and our decompression obligation was getting longer. I quickly resecured the grate, pocketed the key, and turned to follow Jen while spooling the rest of the line back onto my primary reel.

About a minute later, Jen quickly turned toward me and signaled that she was out of air. My training kicked in and I immediately handed her the regulator that I was breathing from. I was shocked. I had a difficult time believing she had breathed through the air in both of her scuba tanks. I had lots of air remaining. I hadn't seen a rush of bubbles from her equipment, so she should have air as well. I switched to my other regulator wondering what was going on. We each had two independent scuba tanks. If she had breathed through the air in one tank, she should still have air in the other tank. It made no sense.

A couple of seconds after Jen took my regulator, she spit it out and tried to breathe from her other regulator. She kept signaling me that she was out of air. My mind was racing. I didn't know what to do. I knew the regulator I had given her was working, but I didn't know why she had stopped using it. I wondered if she had bad air in her tanks. I grabbed my other regulator and pushed it toward her. The hose was much shorter, but I knew it was working. She put it in her mouth, and I grabbed one of her regulators. I cautiously took a breath and was rewarded with a blast of air into my lungs. I didn't feel strange, but I had only taken one breath.

We were too far from the surface to get there quickly. Besides, we had decompression stops to complete. The airbox in the Piano Room was too far back and I didn't know if the air in it was safe. Then I remembered that there were several air pockets in this part of the cave. I had seen Nik, a local freediver, use the air pockets to get to the Piano Room with no scuba tanks during previous visits. I looked at the ceiling and was rewarded with the sight of an air pocket directly above that looked large enough to accommodate both of us. I grabbed Jen's arm and pulled her up toward it, shoving her head above the surface. A second later, I brought my own head up into the pocket, but not before looking at the pressure gauges on Jen's scuba tanks. I knew I was getting air from them, but I wanted visual confirmation. There was plenty of air in both. They had more than half of what we had begun with.

"What happened? What's going on?"

"I...don't...know...I...felt...a...pop...in...my...chest...I...can't ...get...a...breath...now."

Jen was gasping for air. She could only get one syllable out at a time. But at least her head was out of the water, and she was breathing air rather than drowning. I thought about the air we were breathing. The air pocket had been formed by our exhalations. It likely only had sixteen percent oxygen in it. We wouldn't maintain consciousness long if we continued breathing from it. I grabbed one of my regulators and blasted air into the pocket to refresh it and buy us time. If we were there for an extended period of time, I would open the valve on my oxygen scuba tank and blast one hundred percent oxygen into the air pocket. I checked our depth and saw that we were almost eighty feet deep. I couldn't blast too much oxygen into the air pocket because we were too deep to breathe a high concentration. If we breathed pure oxygen deeper than twenty feet, we risked having an oxygen toxicity seizure. Our options were limited and the risks high.

After a couple of minutes, Jen's breathing began to normalize. She took deeper breaths and no longer gasped for air.

"Whatever happened...seems to be...resolving. I lost...one of...my fins, though."

"Okay, are you okay to stay here for a minute?"

"Yes, I'll be...okay."

"Stay here. I'll look for your fin and put it on your foot."

I dropped below Jen and saw the lost fin laying on the floor next to the primary reel I had dropped. I grabbed the fin and placed it on Jen's foot, then grabbed my reel. I was back in the air pocket next to Jen in less than a minute.

"How are you doing?"

"Better...I think I...can swim...the rest of the way...out now."

I looked at my dive computer and then at Jen's.

"We have fourteen minutes of decompression. We have to stop at thirty feet for a couple of minutes, and then at twenty feet for twelve minutes."

"Okay...Let's go...I just want to...get back on the surface."

We situated our regulators. I had deployed the extra length of hose from the regulator on my right tank, so I shoved it back beneath the hose retainers. It was sloppy, but it would work for the short distance we had to travel. We placed our second stage regulators in our mouths and descended to the floor. I signaled to Jen asking if she was okay. She returned the okay signal but rocked her hand side to side, indicating she was only sort of okay. I watched the bubbles escaping her regulator. Her breathing was even, but it was faster than usual. I got next to her, and we swam toward the opening side by side, holding hands.

As soon as we moved through the restriction near the opening and saw daylight streaming into the cave, Jen started to pull away. I finned harder to keep up with her and grabbed the rope that led to the surface.

Jen tried to quickly ascend to the surface, but I held her at the bottom of the chimney. I moved in front of her and looked directly into her eyes. I could see her breathing rate had increased. She was still having difficulty. I squeezed her hand several times, trying to reassure her. I watched the panicked look in her eyes start to ease off. I raised my wrist, so it was in front of Jen's face to show her we still had to decompress. She signaled that she understood.

I placed Jen's hand on the rope so I could finish spooling the line onto my reel and remove it from the pin. I took her hand again and we slowly ascended, stopping at thirty feet of depth to complete a one-minute decompression stop. Once that minute was over, we ascended to twenty feet and began breathing from our oxygen scuba tanks. We were above the rim of the chimney so we moved to the side to a rocky area where we could rest on the floor without disturbing any silt. We had eleven minutes of decompression before we could ascend the last twenty feet to the surface. That was when I started to feel pain in my elbow and wrist.

I moved my arms, bending and straightening them and rotated my hands. The pain was definitely there. Normally, the bends wouldn't present itself during the dive, but we were breathing helium. It was possible to get bent while still underwater when breathing such a lightweight gas. To complicate things further, I had exerted myself multiple times when pushing Jen up into the air pocket, holding her as we swam toward the opening, and holding her down at the bottom of the chimney. Normally, if there were signs of decompression illness, the best thing to do was surface and go to a hyperbaric chamber, but the closest one was more than an hour away. One training organization taught in-water recompression. It wasn't universally recommended because of the potential of losing consciousness and drowning. I was willing to take the risk. I waited until our decompression obligation was almost done and reassessed myself. I still felt pain in my joints.

I pulled out my wetnotes and jotted a quick note telling Jen about my joint pain. I asked her if she thought she could withstand staying where we were another five or ten minutes. The longer I remained at twenty feet of depth breathing pure oxygen, the better my chances of a good outcome. Jen could have ascended the final twenty feet on her own, but I was concerned about her situation. She could reach the surface and lose consciousness. I didn't feel comfortable leaving her alone. I also didn't think Jen would leave me alone at twenty feet with joint pain. Her breathing had stabilized, so she indicated we could remain in the water longer. I continued to breathe oxygen while keeping a close eye on Jen and she kept a close eye on me. I had cleared my planned decompression obligation, so I was ready to ascend if I noticed any changes in her breathing pattern. We were quite the pair with her breathing situation and my joint pain.

Ten minutes later, we began the last leg of our ascent to the surface. The pain in my joints had subsided and I was hopeful that I had remained at depth long enough to overcome any lasting symptoms. I was aware that symptoms could resurface anytime in the next twenty-four hours. I would monitor myself closely.

We surfaced and I asked Jen how she felt. She was fine. She was back to speaking full sentences with ease. I continued breathing oxygen as we swam to the steps. It could only help. I had one prior incident with joint pain a couple of years earlier and breathed oxygen in the van while Jen drove us home. I probably should have gone to a hyperbaric chamber that time, too, but I was stubborn.

We exited the water, and I accompanied Jen to the van where I helped her pull down the top of her wetsuit to relieve the pressure on her torso. She sat down and sipped cold water while I retrieved our scuba tanks from where they lay on the platform. I had a truck cart so that made the trek up the grassy slope easier. I grabbed my stethoscope from the van and assessed Jen's lung sounds. They sounded normal. I didn't detect wheezing or fluid. Jen said she felt much better than she had. I asked her to describe what happened on the dive.

Jen had been fine. She didn't have any issues as we swam through the passage. Suddenly, she felt a sharp pop in her chest and couldn't get a breath. She tried purging her regulator to force air, but that didn't work. The air just went out of the exhaust ports. She thought maybe her regulator wasn't functioning properly, so she signaled to me that she was out of air, but my regulator didn't improve her situation. We juggled the regulators until she tried all four. None of them helped her get enough air into her lungs. If it wasn't for the air pocket being directly over our heads, she would have drowned. I was thankful that the incident had happened in that location and not beyond the grate. Had we locked it, the time spent unlocking it could have proved fatal.

I asked Jen if she wanted to go to the ER to be evaluated. We discussed the treatment options. We had both worked in ERs and were familiar with them. There wasn't much the ER could do. They would get an x-ray of Jen's lungs, but that wasn't likely to tell us anything. Her lung sounds were normal. The x-ray would most likely be normal. Even if it revealed something, it wouldn't change the treatment. We decided we could monitor the situation and go to the ER if she felt worse. I was optimistic. Fortunately, the symptoms didn't reappear.

After extensive research, Jen concluded that the most likely explanation was a diaphragm spasm, an involuntary contraction of the diaphragm muscle. When we breathe, the diaphragm contracts to draw air into the lungs and relaxes to push air out of the lungs. When the diaphragm spasms, it doesn't relax, so any air in the lungs remains there and makes it difficult, if not impossible, to draw in a breath. The symptoms matched what happened. Jen also discovered that another diver that we knew had a similar incident while breathing Trimix.

We didn't have a definitive explanation for what occurred, but we had a possible cause. The common factor of the Trimix between Jen and the other diver was especially suspicious. It wasn't enough to place the blame on helium. It was enough that Jen decided she would be very cautious if she did more dives requiring Trimix. We both preferred diving shallower caves anyway.

33

Small caves, big caves, shallow caves, deep caves

As my time in Florida moved toward the end of its second year, I became interested in the other caves of Merritt's Mill Pond. There were more than Jackson Blue, Hole in the Wall, Twin, and Shangri-la. One of those caves was Indian Washtub, likely named because of its shape. It's located near Twin along the west bank of the pond, probably where the bank of the spring run used to be before it was dammed. It's a rectangular depression in the floor of the pond and would have been the perfect place to bathe or wash clothes when Native Americans were the only inhabitants of the area.

I tried to get into Indian Washtub without success on one previous occasion after a dive in Twin cave. I descended into the tub looking for the opening and saw two potentials. One was to the south and the other to the north. The opening to the south was much too small for anyone to fit. I stuck my head and shoulders into it and caught a glimpse to the right before the silt cloud took over. I would have had to lose about one hundred pounds if I wanted to get beyond the restriction. Even then, my scuba tanks wouldn't fit. The opening to the north was bigger, but only slightly. I was able to fit my entire body into it but kept getting hung up on the protrusions from the walls. I knew it was possible to get through because someone had placed line in the cave. I wanted to get in there, but it wasn't happening while I was wearing a drysuit and using large scuba tanks. I would have to return with a wetsuit and smaller tanks.

Another cave I heard about has the appropriate name of Hidey Hole because it's extremely difficult to find. You have to know the general location and what to look for. Even then, it's not easy. The opening is at the bottom of the pond nowhere near the bank and is usually choked in with sand. There's a small divot in the floor that slopes down about a foot and a half. At the bottom of that slope is an even smaller opening. How large that opening is depends on how much water is flowing out of it. The first time I found the opening happened to be a good time because the current made it larger. I only had to dig out a little sand to make it big enough for me to pass through.

Even with the larger opening, I wasn't going into the cave in regular sidemount configuration. The opening was far too small. I already knew that was a possibility and had a scuba tank that was set up for no mount diving, which involves using only one scuba tank that's usually pushed in front rather than mounted on the side. To make it safer, there's an H valve on the tank which allows two independent regulators to be screwed into it. The valves are typically shaped like an H, hence the name.

I learned from my experience at Indian Washtub and when I searched for Hidey Hole, I wore a wetsuit. I also removed the buoyancy compensator wing from my harness so I could maintain a smaller profile. Jen and I arrived in the area and began our search. More than half an hour passed before Jen found it. When I saw it, I had doubts about gaining entry. I wondered how anyone had gotten into the cave. I even wondered if there was a cave on the other side of the small hole. I approached the opening and felt a current escaping its depths. I pushed my left hand, followed by my head, into the hole to see if there was enough room inside. I was surprised to find a room about eight feet long by five feet wide and three feet from floor to ceiling. I also saw cave line tied to the right wall.

I backed up to reassess the opening and plan my entry. I began to sweep the sand out of the divot, but most of it slid back into the hole. I removed a fin and used it to scoop the sand farther back. That worked, so I swept enough sand out of the way to form a hole large enough for me to squeeze through. I placed the fin back on my foot and pushed my scuba tank into the opening in front of me. I anchored my feet on the sandy bottom behind me and pushed with all of my might. It took about a minute, but I managed to wiggle my way through the opening and popped into the room. I rotated my body so I was facing the opening to make sure the sand I had dug out wasn't sliding back down the slope to plug me inside of the cave. I wondered what amount of anxiety Jen was experiencing after seeing me swallowed by the tiny hole.

Because I wasn't sure how Jen was feeling and I didn't want to make her wait long, I wasted no time and began swimming farther into the cave. I swam for about ten minutes and arrived at a formation that I called the bridge. It wasn't quite as grand as the bridge in Hole in the Wall. This cave was nowhere near that big. It was a small limestone bridge cutting perpendicularly across the tunnel. The space beneath it was barely large enough for my hand to fit. The passage continued to get smaller after the bridge. While I was curious about what was beyond the next corner, I didn't want to push my luck with only one tank and Jen waiting, so I turned around. Fortunately, the opening was still patent, mostly anyway. I swung the scuba tank back in front of me and pushed it through, moving the sand that had built up in front of it while I was exploring the cave.

I've been back to Hidey Hole on a few other occasions, but the water flowing out of it wasn't enough to present an opening large enough to penetrate. In other words, it was even smaller than the first time I found it. I tried digging it out but only managed to obliterate the visibility around the opening due to the lack of current to push away the sediment I stirred up. I lost sight of the hole and couldn't see where I was digging. I keep revisiting it hoping to one day make it back inside with a couple of smaller scuba tanks. Until then...

* * *

The time arrived for the cave instructor institute. I had been teaching cavern and intro cave for seven months and issuing certifications through a technical diving agency. I was excited to be testing for instructor with the cave diving agency. I returned to Peacock Springs and met with two instructor trainers, putting the count at five different instructors evaluating me throughout the program. We completed the classroom portion of the exam and headed to Peacock Springs State Park to do a couple of dives.

Talk about stressful! I hadn't been evaluated by an instructor in almost four years (not counting the sidemount diving instructor evaluation). The last time had been during my Professional Association of Diving Instructors (PADI) Instructor Examination when I was evaluated by only one examiner. I was being evaluated by two instructor trainers this time. Their sole purpose was to determine if I was good enough to safely teach cave diving. I was confident in my abilities, but that didn't ease the stress. One week later, I was conducting my first class with my new ratings.

Between classes, I continued to build my experience as a cave diver. I returned to the Tallahassee area to dive Promise Sink. I wanted to get back into that cave to continue exploring it. I planned on diving the downstream side because it was a great place to teach technical deep diving. Before I would teach there, I wanted to become familiar with it. No one was available to dive, so I went alone. I arrived at Wild Bill's, hauled my tanks to the sinkhole, suited up, and got into the water. The sinkhole looked a little spooky. I was alone in a forest near a body of water that led to dark underground rivers. I listened for the sound of a banjo playing in the distance. Fortunately, I didn't hear anything but the birds in the trees surrounding me. No one was around. Wild Bill's was the closest property, and he had left to run errands in town.

I descended below the surface and found the guideline leading into the cave. I followed it into the dark abyss, setting a jump line in the gap. I continued beyond the point where I had turned around the last time, and before I knew it, I was more than two hundred feet deep. I didn't feel a bit of narcosis thanks to the Trimix I was breathing. I stopped for a moment and hovered in the middle of the room enjoying the peacefulness. I heard nothing but the sounds of my exhalation bubbles. The cave was big and dark. The visibility was slightly hazy and I couldn't see the wall to my left or the floor below me. The ceiling was also too far for me to see. My only visual references were the wall to my right and the guideline next to it. I had no idea how big or deep the room was. There were multiple guidelines in the passage, a couple of them running parallel to each other. I saw the potential for confusion, so I cleaned up the lines, removing the second line that didn't appear to serve a purpose. If I did bring students to train in downstream Promise, I didn't want to leave anything to chance. Following the wrong line could turn into a fatal mistake.

About twenty-five minutes into the dive, with the lines cleaned up and the potential for confusion diminished, I turned around. The cave continued to get deeper, but I only reached a depth of two hundred and eleven feet. I still didn't know at what depth the floor was. I hadn't planned to go deeper and wasn't prepared to find out that day. I turned around and began my slow ascent out of the cave. I got to one hundred feet and began my decompression stops, breathing from a stage tank that contained thirty percent oxygen. It would help accelerate the decompression and get me to the surface sooner. When I reached seventy feet of depth, I switched to a scuba tank containing fifty percent oxygen and breathed that as I continued my slow ascent. I made my way toward the surface ten feet at a time, until I reached twenty feet of depth where I switched to breathing pure oxygen. It took me longer to ascend from one hundred feet to the surface than the time spent at depth.

The next day I drove back to Crawfordville to dive Guy Revell cave, located in the Guy Revell Nature Conservancy Area. The property had been in the Revell family for many generations before E. Guy Revell donated it to the Northwest Florida Water Management District. He didn't want to develop it and preferred it remain in its natural state.

There are six sinkholes on the property as well as several hiking trails. The Guy Revell sinkhole is located in a woodsy area off of a dirt road and, when I was there, looked like a brown pit of mud. It had a foul smell emanating from it. There was nothing appealing about it other than the promise of hidden cave passages.

I unloaded my scuba tanks and placed them in the water leaning against old wooden steps along the bank. Each step I took was a cautious one. The steps creaked and swayed. I was concerned that they might not hold my weight, never mind the added weight of the scuba tanks. It looked like they were about to disintegrate. Once I was suited up, I carefully walked down the steps until my feet were submerged. It was the middle of the summer, and the water was warm. I wondered if there was really a spring in the bottom of the pit. I stepped off the stairs into soft mud, causing bubbles to rush to the surface. Inside the bubbles came more of the stench I had detected when I first arrived. The thought of bacteria festering in the murky pit entered my mind. I shoved the thought aside. There was a cave hidden somewhere beneath the surface that I had to explore.

I clipped on my scuba tanks and felt myself sink deeper into the mud. I was in thigh high water, so the tanks maintained their heaviness. I secured the end of the line from my primary reel to one of the banisters of the steps hoping it would hold. I backed up until I was chest deep, placed the regulator in my mouth, and dropped below the surface. My world turned black. I had an idea where the opening of the cave should be. I swam in the darkness hoping it wasn't far. I also hoped that the water would cool down and the visibility would clear. I felt a slight drop in temperature as spring water flowed past me. I was close.

The visibility improved, but only slightly. I followed the cool water until I arrived at the permanent guideline. I thought I was in the cave, but I couldn't confirm it because I couldn't see more than a couple of feet in front of me. I secured the line from my reel to the guideline and followed it as the visibility continued to improve. I could see about ten feet in front of me, but it wasn't a clear ten feet. I finally saw a ceiling and knew I was in the cave.

The passage sloped down to one hundred and twenty feet of depth before branching into two tunnels. At least I thought it was two tunnels. I went to the right and did a large circuit around the room, only knowing this because I came back to the line intersection and saw my line marker. I could see the floor and the wall to my right, but nothing more. I didn't know if I was in a large room or a roundabout of sorts. Either way, it felt like it was a decent size area.

I found other line intersections along the way and followed one, continuing to get deeper, eventually reaching one hundred and thirty-nine feet of depth before I turned around. Unfortunately, the conditions never improved. I didn't see much of a point in remaining in the cave if I couldn't see it. I had a meeting with the devil planned for the next day anyway.

34

The Devil is a virgin

A friend of mine mentioned a cave he had heard of that was a little less than an hour's drive from my house. He wasn't living in Florida at the time, so he put it on me to investigate. It wasn't the easiest cave to find, requiring me to drive off of the paved road onto dirt roads with occasional patches of sand. There were a few times when I was concerned the van might get stuck. About ten minutes after turning off the paved road, I saw a small green sign with white lettering on it telling me that I was almost there. Devil's Hole was nearby. I followed the direction on the sign and the conditions got worse. The road was completely covered in sand. My concerns about the van getting stuck grew. A few minutes later, I arrived in a parking area.

There was no sinkhole in sight. There were no signs of water. I knew I was near the Econfina, but there was no direct path to it. I explored the area until I found a path that led around some trees behind which was hidden a small, round greenish-blue body of water. I looked down at the surface from where I stood at the top of a slope six feet above. The water was cloudy and green and held its secrets close. I tossed a rock into the water and lost sight of it only inches below the surface.

Devil's Hole was a smaller version of Guy Revell, green instead of brown, and without the odor. I had driven an hour, so I might as well get in the water and see if it cleared when I got deeper. Unlike Guy Revell, I had no idea where the opening to this cave might be located. Twenty minutes later, I was standing in the water with my scuba equipment, trying not to slip down the steep bottom. At least the bottom was solid. The water also wasn't as warm as it was at Guy Revell. That didn't mean this sinkhole wasn't also full of bacteria. It was just different bacteria.

I thought about the possibility of alligators hiding beneath the surface. The path that I walked down could have been formed by humans or gators. It didn't have the distinctive rut in the center created by a tail, so I told myself it was human. I looked around the sinkhole, anyway, hoping one of the prehistoric creatures wasn't lying in wait for me. I dropped below the surface and disappeared into the murky green pea soup.

I followed the slope toward the center of the sinkhole and when I was about fifteen feet deep, the visibility burst open. It was crystal clear. Devil's Hole wasn't at all like Guy Revell! I shined my light around. To my left were fallen trees. To my right, the bottom sloped down to what appeared to be an opening to a cave forty-five feet below the surface. It was so small that I could barely see it.

It wasn't as small as Hidey Hole and there was no sand to sweep out of the way. The current blasting out of it was too strong for any build up in front of it. I was going to have to push one of my scuba tanks ahead of me to get through, though. Even with doing that, the vertical clearance would be tight. I unclipped a tank and pushed it forward while pulling myself in after it. The current coming out of the cave was so strong that it pushed in my regulator purge and caused bubbles to rush out of the exhaust ports. Scuba regulators have a purge button on the front that activates a lever and opens the valve. It's used to blow out water before breathing from it. There's usually enough tension so that it doesn't arbitrarily depress and release air. The tension spring was no match for the current. I had to tuck my head to shield the purge button. I felt water rushing in around my mask as the current pushed against my face. The mask was dislodged and filled with water.

I finally got all the way through the opening and into the cave. I moved to the side, trying to find cover from the current, anchored myself so I could clip my tank back in place, and repositioned my mask. I thought once I was beyond the opening, the current wouldn't feel as strong. I was wrong. I was going to have to fight to gain every inch forward in this cave. I looked for strong handholds, not wanting to damage the cave, and began pulling myself in. I found the beginning of the permanent guideline flapping in the current. It had come loose from wherever it had been secured. I grabbed the line and found a protrusion to wrap it around. Once it was resecured, I wrapped the line from my primary reel around it.

A hundred feet later, I came across a broken line. There was a loose end below me and another loose end flapping up and down fifteen feet away. I anchored myself again, grabbed the end below me, and repaired the line break with a five-foot section from one of my jump spools. With the new continuous guideline, I pulled myself farther into the cave. I encountered a bend in the passage and had to move across to the other wall to shield myself from the current. In reality, there was nothing to shield me. I was looking for the less intense path to follow. I continued to pull myself into the cave, eventually arriving at a line intersection. I was eighty-one feet below the earth. I looked at my pressure gauges and saw that it was just about time to turn around. Fighting the current and doing two line repairs had caused me to quickly suck up my air.

When I turned around, the fast-moving water assisted my exit. I arrived at my primary reel in no time and braced myself against the wall while unwrapping it from the permanent guideline. I pushed one of my scuba tanks in front of me and popped out of the opening like a cork popping out of a champagne bottle. I was worn out but happy. It was a beautiful cave.

I returned a few days later to have another go at it armed with the knowledge I had gained during my first dive in the Devil's Hole. I planned on replacing the permanent guideline from the entrance to the line intersection where I had turned around. I didn't know how long the line had been there and didn't trust it completely, especially after finding it flapping around in two places. I descended into the sinkhole

261

more confidently this time, wasting no time getting into the cave. It took twenty-two minutes to get to the line intersection. Twenty-two minutes to penetrate two hundred and fifty feet into the cave. Eleven feet per minute. The current was ripping! It seemed like it was even stronger than it had been five days earlier. I turned around and gathered up the old line on my way out.

Four days later I returned to fight the Devil again, this time with another victim, I mean a friend. We entered the cave and pulled our way to the line intersection with plans to go beyond it. The section that followed was a bedding plane that was so low I had to squeeze my body between the floor and ceiling to get in and out of it. If this had been after the holidays, I probably wouldn't have fit. About a hundred and fifty feet later, I encountered another line intersection indicating a circuit. We decided it was a good place to turn around. We rode the current out and when we got to the opening, my friend was slammed into it backside first, plugging it with his back end. He remained plastered to the wall kicking his feet and waving his arms, trying to fight the current to remove himself from his precarious position. He was blocking our only way out of the cave!

I moved to the side, grabbed his arms, anchored my feet against the wall, and pulled as hard as I could. After about a minute, we finally managed to get him pulled away from the wall and back into a face down head forward orientation. He wasted no time grabbing one of his scuba tanks and pushing it in front of him, slipping through and out of the cave. He was done. He had enough. So had I.

Back in the basin, I looked for the downstream side of the cave. The water shooting out of the upstream side had to be going somewhere. I followed the water flow, feeling where it disappeared into a cluster of trees that had fallen into the sinkhole. The passage was too small for anyone to fit. Even if I wanted to, there was no way I would be able to gain entry. Not that I would have tried to enter the downstream side of the cave. I didn't trust myself to be able to fight the current to get back out. I would have liked to find another sinkhole downstream of Devil's

Hole, though.

I took a break from the Devil for a few weeks to focus on the Merritt's Mill Pond caves. I needed some time in low flow caves. One of the passages I visited was Skiles Passage in Twin, named after the cave explorer that found it, Wes Skiles. He was the same person that Peacock Springs State Park was named after. Skiles Passage was the only offshoot passage in the Subway Tunnel before the fissure cracks. According to the map, it ran parallel to the Subway Tunnel with the opposite end opening into the Training Room. It was also twice as deep.

About five hundred feet after leaving the Subway Tunnel, I arrived in a tall fissure room. It wasn't quite as big as the Terminal Fissure, but it was just as tall. The bottom of the fissure was at about ninety feet of depth, and the ceiling was at twenty. After exploring the shallower depths of the fissure, I followed the line down to the floor and through a small restriction. It was a little reminiscent of the opening to Hidey Hole. It wasn't as small, but it was low and silty. The sediment was fine and thick. I stayed as far from it as I could, but my movement through the restriction disturbed it. The restriction was engulfed by a silt cloud that followed me a few feet into the passage beyond. Thankfully, the passage was bigger on the other side. I was in Skiles Passage.

I continued, knowing I had about eight hundred feet to go before I reached the Training Room. I had to move slowly so I wouldn't disturb the sediment. About fifteen minutes later, I encountered a line intersection and continued straight. Two minutes after that, I was hovering behind a large boulder sitting in the middle of an alcove. I recognized it from my first venture into the Training Room.

I turned around and swam back to the line intersection so I could explore the other passage. I expected it to bring me toward the gold line. About one hundred feet later, I was at the end of the line and saw the gold line flush against the opposite wall ten feet away. I immediately recognized where I was. I swam across and turned right to head toward the fissure that would bring me to the end of the Subway Tunnel. I was a little relieved that I didn't have to swim back through the silt cloud I had created when I first entered Skiles Passage.

After several dives in the caves of Merritt's Mill Pond, I decided to return to Devil's Hole. There was something about that cave that kept calling me back. Not many people were diving it, if anyone was, and I wanted to survey it. I also wanted to look for potential leads to virgin passages. I arrived at the second line intersection and this time followed the other line. Just as I suspected, it looped back and formed a circuit with the first line I had explored. I found a lead just past the second line intersection, grabbed my reel, and ran line into the tunnel. One hundred and twenty feet later, the passage terminated in a small room. It wasn't a long tunnel, but I was the first one in there, and it was about one third of the length of all of the lined passage in Devil's Hole. It was also my first virgin cave passage.

35

Giving the Devil its due

I had been bitten hard by the exploration bug. I became obsessed with finding virgin cave passage. I wanted to go back to Devil's Hole to look for more. I wanted to explore other caves. Unfortunately, obligations took priority, and it would be a while before I could do that. The day after finding my first virgin cave passage, I returned to Peacock Springs State Park to begin my full cave diving instructor internship. I was excited to be starting it, but the recent memory of Devil's Hole kept me distracted. It was all I could think about during my two-and-a-half-hour drive.

It was a slow summer for instruction, and no one had cave diving classes scheduled. I wanted to intern with different instructors than I had previously interned with, but my options were limited. I reached out to every instructor I knew, and while most had some classes scheduled, none were full cave diving classes, except Paul Heinerth. I had enjoyed my time with him, so I scheduled another internship. We spent the next four days diving Peacock I, Little River, Cow Downstream, and Orange Grove Sink. Jen tagged along during this internship. Paul only had two students, so the instructor to student ratio wasn't affected. Despite having interned with Paul previously, I continued to learn more about teaching cave diving. It was also a pleasure to dive with Paul again.

About a week and a half after the internship, I returned to Devil's Hole. I had been thinking about it non-stop. It was difficult spending twelve hours at the hospital when I could have been diving, but bills had to be paid. I pushed through each shift thinking about the dive I had planned during my first day off. I had seen another potential lead when I was exiting from the tunnel I found. I didn't have enough air to stop and check it out, though.

The day finally arrived when I could return to explore it. I descended below the surface and swam to the source. As I was pulling myself through the opening, I became enveloped in complete darkness. The dive light I held in my hand was no longer working. I shook my hand to no avail. I thought the power switch had possibly been knocked into the off position even with a protective cover around it to prevent that from happening. The cave opening was small, though, and I felt the battery canister rubbing against the top of it when I pulled myself through. Maybe it had somehow flipped off.

I was mostly inside the cave, so I grabbed a backup light from my shoulder strap and turned it on. I pulled myself the rest of the way into the cave and reached back to the power switch on the top of the battery canister. I flipped it one way and waited. I flipped it the other way. The light wasn't turning on. It was dead. My original HID canister light had a short cable connecting the battery canister and the light head that I held on the back of my hand. The short cable meant I had to mount the battery canister over the small of my back rather than over my thighs where I would have preferred it. When I pulled myself through the opening, I apparently squeezed the battery canister or the cable enough that it was damaged.

I exited the cave and once on the surface, I inspected the battery canister. There was no water inside and the battery wasn't leaking acid. The cable connection must have been pinched and shorted out. Fortunately, I had Jen's dive light in the van, so I grabbed it and headed back to the cave. I reentered the cave hoping nothing else went wrong. I was only one strike down. I returned to the area where I had seen the lead and it was smaller than I remembered. I tried to squeeze through, but it wasn't happening. It was too small for me to fit. I couldn't get in more than ten feet. I explored a small room to the right just before the bedding plane but found nothing there either. I had started the dive with less air in my tanks because of the light failure, so it was time to exit. I surfaced without leaving any line in the cave and with an expensive broken light in the van.

About a week later, I returned to Luraville to complete an internship with Jill Heinerth, Paul's ex-wife. She was also involved in many of the early underwater cave exploration projects in Florida, including a project at Wakulla Springs. She was a world-renowned underwater photographer who spent more time on assignment than teaching. I was fortunate that she happened to be teaching a class during that time.

It was an honor to be able to complete an internship with Jill. Her style was quite different than what I had witnessed so far. She spent a lot of time teaching and reviewing air management and dive planning. She was a stickler for the small details. It was refreshing to see this.

The internship with Jill finished in time for me to return to Marianna to teach my own cavern diving class. This was the day I met my future dive buddy, David. You can read about our adventures exploring the caves of Cozumel in the first book of my other true adventure series, *Beneath the Jungle of Cozumel: Connecting the Crowns*. David was diving a backmounted steel scuba tank during his cavern diver course. He was very protective of his scuba tanks. When I saw them, I thought they were brand new off of the showroom floor and I was a little concerned about David's level of experience. I soon learned that he had been diving with those tanks for ten years. At the end of the day, I found out how they had maintained their new appearance. David wrapped each tank in a beach towel, slid it into the bed of his truck, and strapped it down. They looked snug as a bug in a rug.

I convinced David to start diving sidemount before he continued with his cave diving training. He scheduled a sidemount diving class with me to begin his transition. The careful handling of the scuba tanks continued throughout his training. They maintained their pristine appearance during every class. When David and I began diving together as dive buddies, I introduced him to small passages and restrictions. It wasn't long before his tanks were scratched and marred. I knew David was fully converted when I saw him pushing his tanks into the bed of his truck with the towels nowhere to be found. I asked him about the towels, and he laughed and said he had given up on trying to keep them looking new after following me in the caves every month.

I continued to dive the caves in Merritt's Mill Pond and on the Chipola River. Sometimes I went diving with Jen. Sometimes I went with David. Most of the time, I was alone. I was learning the caves and searching for more virgin passages. I knew if I was going to be putting line in the caves, I would have to teach myself how to do underwater cave survey. One of the training agencies offered the class, but there weren't any instructors teaching it. I bought an old book about underwater cave survey and began learning. My approach to cave exploration was about to go through a big transformation.

Surveying underwater caves involves counting knots that are placed every ten feet on the lines we bring into the caves. We also obtain compass headings and take note of the depth. Whenever the line changes direction, a station is created and that's where we record depth and compass heading. We count knots between stations, estimating distance between a knot and a station when the station occurs between two knots. There are other methods of survey, but knotted line survey is the easiest and most reliable when doing it alone. I wanted to improve my technique and efficiency surveying caves, so I began to survey the caves around me. The gold line that was in Jackson Blue at the time had knots tied into it every ten feet, so I surveyed that first. Most of the white lines in the offshoot tunnels were also knotted. I surveyed the cave back to the Hall of the Mountain King including King's and Queen's Bypass. My survey skills were improving.

A couple of months after my second internship, I scheduled the final one. I would soon be eligible to receive my full cave instructor certification from one of the technical diving training organizations. I was starting to see the light at the end of the tunnel. I had to complete the instructor institute to get my instructor certification from the cave diving training organization just as I did for introductory cave diving instructor. I could have taken the easy road to being a cave instructor and only gotten certified with the technical training agencies, but I felt like I was a better instructor completing the process the way I did.

A month after my final internship, I headed to Ginnie Springs to participate in an International Underwater Cave Rescue and Recovery (IUCRR) course. This was a class created to teach cave divers how to safely recover the bodies of divers who had died inside of underwater caves. It was left to cave divers to recover the bodies and bring them out to law enforcement authorities. During the course, we were taught how to document the scene where we found the body and how to safely bring the body out of the cave with the least amount of risk to ourselves and the least amount of damage to the body. It wasn't a simple process.

The body must be maintained in a horizontal orientation to get it out of the cave with minimal resistance. It was a two-person task. One diver pulls the body while the second diver controls the legs to maintain the position. We assumed the roles of victims as well as recovery divers in the class. It was a sobering experience, but one that taught us much needed skills. Eight months later, I would be called upon to use the newly learned skills at Vortex Spring.

I wasn't quite done with my cave diving instructor internships. I had one additional internship to complete. I was working on a crossover to the other cave diving training organization and had to work with the training director before I could be issued a certification from that agency. I returned to Ginnie Springs where we spent four days diving Devil's Spring. Typically, three different caves must be used during the final four days of cave diving training. However, north Florida had received a lot of rain and most of the caves were not in adequate condition for diving. Peacock Springs State Park was flooded and the water inside the passages tannic. The county park where Little River was located was flooded and the parking lot was inaccessible. The only caves that still had good visibility were Devil's Spring and Manatee

269

Springs. Training standards allowed for a waiver when all caves within an hour's drive were flooded, so we remained at Devil's Spring.

It wasn't ideal for the students. They were only getting experience in a high flow cave and had to fight the current during every dive. Their buoyancy and trim couldn't be adequately evaluated because water current tends to hide issues with those skills. Nothing could be done about it short of rescheduling the class, but the students were from out of state. As it was, they were fortunate that Ginnie Springs wasn't flooded. There have been times when the Santa Fe River rose enough to flood the restrooms more than two hundred feet from its banks.

Once my internships were completed, Jen and I headed onto the Chipola River to look for a spring I had heard about. We easily found it and I turned the boat into the spring run. We cruised about three hundred feet to the spring. The spring run wasn't clear like the other spring runs we were used to seeing. The tannic river water had backed into it and turned the water a chocolate milk brown. The basin was brown as well, but it had a small boil visible at the surface over what I believed to be the entrance. Much like at Black Spring, Jen wasn't having it, but I wanted to take a look. I had ventured into worse conditions, not only at Black, but also Guy Revell and Devil's Hole. I geared up and got in the water hopeful the visibility would be clear inside. I took a few steps until I felt the bottom disappear. I had found the drop off to the opening.

I thought about the possibility of alligators waiting for me below. The water was cold, though, and they liked warm water. I stepped off the edge and floated above what I thought was the cave opening. I began a slow descent a bit fearful that I might find an alligator despite logic telling me it was unlikely. I pictured one nesting at the bottom of the basin in front of the opening, except I wouldn't see it until I was practically on top of it. The poor visibility didn't help matters. I also expected the boogeyman to jump out at me.

I didn't see any gators, or boogeymen, but I did find a low opening. I passed through it and found the beginning of the permanent guideline against the wall to the right. The visibility was five feet, seven at best, and it was cloudy. I felt better about being inside of the cave because the chance of encountering an alligator was much smaller than in the spring basin. Still… I slowly made my way through the cave hoping for the visibility to improve. It never did. After several minutes, I turned around and slowly headed out. All I could see was the wall to my left. The rest of the cave passage was lost in murkiness.

I learned that this cave is one that is only conducive to diving during drought conditions. The river level needs to be very low for visibility to be good. The river water needed to be clear. The low river level also meant I wouldn't be able to bring my boat up the spring run. Can't have it all. I was able to eventually see the cave. That didn't happen for a few years, but it was well worth the wait. It was one of my biggest exploration projects in Florida. I'll write about it in one of the subsequent books in this series.

I continued to explore the area caves. I made a decision about which DPV I wanted and purchased it. This was a top-of-the-line lithium battery scooter. It was fast and lasted more than two hours at low speed. At high speed, it could travel in excess of two hundred feet per minute. I took a demo model on my first dive in Jackson Blue and got to the traffic light located twenty-one hundred feet from the opening in only seventeen minutes. The current coming out of Jackson Blue was strong that day. This DPV was going to be a game changer.

I eventually returned to the Century Tunnel in Hole in the Wall. The visibility was restored, and I was finally able to see the passage. I've never seen it as bad as it was the first time Jen and I were there. I swam as far as the air in my scuba tanks allowed, leaving more than two-thirds for my exit. The distance to the end of that passage was a long way off. Waiting for me at the end of the passage was the champagne bottle placed by Sheck Exley.

* * *

I was fortunate enough to do a few more dives at Indian Springs during my Advanced Trimix class. My instructor used to be a groundskeeper at the campground and had the opportunity to do a lot of dives there. We did two dives for the class. I wasn't as nervous about diving where Parker Turner had died as I had been my first time. I thought about the collapse and entrapment, but I wasn't concerned about it happening again, at least not during our dives. This made the experience much more enjoyable. I knew what to expect and could focus on certain areas rather than looking around in awe of everything.

I returned to Jackson Blue a few days later for my second dive using the demo model of the DPV I ordered. Mine was being built. I scootered past the traffic light another eight hundred feet before parking the DPV on the line and heading to the left to explore Sweet Passage, a passage I had noted on the map and was curious about. I would eventually find virgin passages in this area, as well.

With a much faster DPV, I had more time to spend farther back in the cave. The shorter travel time meant I had more air to spend exploring because I was breathing less air during the scooter portion of the dive. The dives were planned based on the quantity of air needed to swim out from the farthest penetration rather than based on thirds or fourths. I hadn't even received my DPV yet, but I was seeing the benefits it would provide me.

A couple of weeks later, I attended my final instructor institute examination. The training director at that time was also a sidemount diver and allowed me to dive in sidemount configuration during the evaluation. We even went into a low passage that was considered a sidemount tunnel. Up until that point, I had been diving with backmounted scuba tanks during my internships. The other instructor evaluators weren't happy that I was diving sidemount. Sidemount diving was not widely accepted at the time. They had no say in the matter.

I not only received my instructor rating, but I also received a waiver to teach classes to students diving in sidemount configuration. At the time, the standards only allowed for it with a waiver. I continued to use backmounted tanks whenever I had students that were diving backmount, but the waiver allowed me to teach students in sidemount as long as they were also diving sidemount. I was one of the few cave diving instructors that was doing this back then. I was one of the first cave diving instructors for that organization that was issued that waiver. These days, sidemount diving is mainstream, and waivers are no longer required.

The day after my instructor institute I headed south to Hernando County, Florida to complete my Advanced Trimix class in one of the caves there. We were going to dive the Mount Everest of cave diving.

36

Diving Mount Everest

Eagles' Nest earned the reputation as the Mount Everest of cave diving due to a couple of factors. The first one was the depth of the cave. Divers can reach three hundred feet soon after the entrance. While Eagles' Nest isn't the only cave of such depth in Florida, it is the only one that is publicly accessible with no dive guide requirements. The other caves either limit diving with select guides or with a permit from the state. Another reason for the designation as the Mount Everest of cave diving is the number of fatalities that have occurred at Eagles' Nest over the years. The state went so far as to close the site to scuba divers from 1999 through 2003 because there had been six fatalities in the cave during the 1990s. The two Florida-based cave diving training organizations in existence at the time petitioned the state and managed to get it reopened to cave diving. Since regaining access, there have been five additional fatalities and more calls for diving to be restricted. The total number of deaths at Eagles' Nest is eleven. There are caves where more deaths have occurred, but none of them are as deep.

In the late 1980s and early 1990s, thirteen divers died in the cave at Vortex Spring. In response to this high fatality rate, the state threatened to close the site to diving. The owner had worked hard to build a scuba diving destination and came up with a solution that was acceptable to the state. In 1991, he installed a grate three hundred feet from the opening. Since that time, there have only been two additional deaths reported at Vortex. One of them was Ben McDaniel. The other was a diver who I was told went into the Vortex cave to search for McDaniel's body in hopes of receiving a reward that had been offered for information relating to the whereabouts of McDaniel or his remains.

While Eagles' Nest may not have the total highest body count, it likely has the highest percentage of fatalities to actual dives done at the location in large part due to the depth of the cave. Within a few minutes of entering the cave, divers can reach depths exceeding two hundred feet. Recreational scuba divers using only a single scuba tank can find themselves that deep. There isn't enough air in a single tank to sustain a diver at those depths for more than a minute or two. The pressure gauge needle moves with every breath. If they make it long enough, they will quickly reach depths exceeding three hundred feet.

Eagles' Nest is an advanced dive that requires additional training and planning. These aren't simple dives in which the diver can ascend to the surface, or swim out toward the opening and ascend immediately. Decompression stops must be done or certain death will result. Getting to the site requires divers to drive over dirt roads through the Chassahowitzka Wildlife Management Area for half an hour. Cellular service can be spotty. Emergency services have gate access located closer to the sinkhole than the access used by divers, but it's still a long response and egress time. There's nowhere to land a helicopter safely. Anyone who surfaces without making decompression stops will likely die before getting to a hyperbaric chamber.

The depth at this site has made it a popular dive site to conduct Advanced Trimix training dives for cave divers. However, it hasn't only been cave divers who have perished there. Four of the divers that died in Eagles' Nest after it was reopened to cave diving were not trained cave divers. Two of those were a father and his fifteen-year-old son who received new scuba equipment, including new sets of backmounted double scuba tanks for Christmas. According to news reports, the father had very little training as a scuba diver and the son had no formal training. After opening their gifts Christmas morning, they went to Eagles' Nest to try the new equipment. The sinkhole was the closest diving site and most convenient to their home. It was eventually revealed that they had been diving Eagles' Nest multiple times before their Christmas Day deaths.

The Christmas Day fatalities caused many people to call for the closure of Eagles' Nest to scuba diving. The family of the divers were especially vocal. Closure was avoided because representatives of the cave diving training organizations were able to convince the state that restricting cave divers from diving there wouldn't have kept the father and son from dying. The pair likely knew they weren't supposed to be diving there. They definitely knew that they weren't trained to be in an overhead environment and shouldn't have entered the cave. They were also not trained to be as deep as they had gone. They went anyway.

The floor of the Eagles' Nest spring basin is shaped like a bowl with the deepest section directly over the opening. It's similar to a sink and its drain. The drain is large enough for one diver to fit in comfortably. Two divers can squeeze in side by side, but it's very close quarters. Depending on the water level in the basin, the opening is thirty to forty feet deep. The father and son entered the basin and descended into the cave. The son continued deeper. His dive computer indicated he had reached a depth of two hundred and thirty-three feet. He was found with his tanks empty. It appeared his father died trying to reach him and donate one of his regulators. His scuba tanks were also empty. Much like many of the Mount Everest hikers, these two pushed the limits of their capabilities.

All of that aside, Eagles' Nest is a beautiful cave and one worth seeing if properly trained to cave dive to those depths. The visibility in the basin is usually hazy. There are guidelines in place leading from the entry point to a log that is conveniently located about ten feet deep where divers can rest during the longest part of their decompression stops. The line leads from the log directly to the opening in the center of the sinkhole. From there, it's a straight descent through a thirty-foot-tall shaft that opens into the Entrance Room, a large room with a debris mound at the bottom. The top of the mound is usually one hundred and twenty feet below the surface.

There are two lines at the top of the mound going in opposite directions. Upstream is the larger of the two passages and heads to the east and is the direction my Trimix instructor and I went for both dives. During the first dive, we reached a depth of two hundred and seventy-one feet before turning around based on the schedule we had planned. Deeper dives like these are not planned by turn pressure, but rather to the minute because of the length of time required for decompression before surfacing. The decompression portion of these dives always lasts significantly longer than the time spent at depth.

During this dive, we had twenty-five-minutes from the time we submerged until we reached the depth of our first decompression stop. Because our first decompression stop was at one hundred and forty feet of depth, we could swim into the cave for fifteen minutes before we had to turn around. Fifteen minutes. That was long enough for us to swim about seven hundred feet in from the opening.

It was enough to make it to the Super Room, a large room off to the side of the main tunnel. We hugged the ceiling to try to minimize our decompression obligation. The floor was about twenty feet below us. We turned around in the Super Room and swam back, reaching the bottom of the Entrance Room mound where we did our first decompression stop at one hundred and forty feet. We remained there for three minutes before we ascended to our next stop at one hundred and thirty feet of depth. We had to stop every ten feet with the stops getting longer as we got shallower. We had more than two hours of decompression before we could safely surface.

Two hours and thirty-three minutes after we descended into the cave, we finally surfaced and swam toward the steps. More than an hour of our decompression stops was done on the log at twenty and then ten feet of depth. It was a good experience. One I would be repeating the next day. I would return to Eagles' Nest on my own as well, but not very often. I much preferred to do two-hour long dives with twenty-five minutes of decompression stops. Having no decompression stops

277

was even better. Unfortunately, that isn't common in Florida caves.

I conquered the Mount Everest of cave diving. I completed two successful dives there. I had done my deepest dive, going to two hundred and seventy-one feet of depth. As much as I wasn't fond of long decompression stops, I would be going back to Eagles' Nest to do more dives. I wanted to see the downstream side of the cave. I wanted to dive there without an instructor watching over me.

37

Beyond the Grate

I began devoting more time to surveying the caves around me. The river levels were favorable for diving in Bozel, so I headed there. There were no known maps of that cave and I was determined to create one. Fortunately, the line in the cave was knotted. The only issue I faced was dealing with the current. Maintaining position to get the azimuth at each station was challenging, but I persevered and surveyed five hundred and eighty feet of line during my first dive. I hadn't quite made it to the line intersection located after the four-way intersection. It wasn't much, but it was a start.

The first three hundred feet of passage in Bozel is winding and has a lot of depth changes. The crack that allows us to enter this hidden river slopes down to forty-five feet of depth, begins to slope up to twenty feet, then back down to thirty-five feet, then back up to fifteen feet. Add to that several turns along the way. It almost feels like a roller coaster ride. There aren't very many straight shots for long distances. I encountered twenty-five survey stations in the first three hundred feet that required me to stop every five to twenty-five feet to record station data. There were only ten survey stations in the remaining two hundred and eighty feet.

Despite only surveying five hundred and eighty feet, I felt a sense of accomplishment. The first map of Bozel in more than ten years was beginning to form. I had contacted one of the previous explorers of the Florida panhandle caves and asked him if he knew of a map. He used to have one, but unfortunately, his house was destroyed during Hurricane Ivan and so were all of the maps of the area caves. He couldn't remember any details about the cave. He didn't know how far in the end of the line was. He didn't know how much line was in the cave. No one could remember how extensive Bozel was.

I hadn't gotten very far on my previous dives and what I did see was the main passage with a few short offshoot tunnels. I had been about a thousand feet down the main passage and explored the offshoot tunnels at the four-way intersection and the three additional line intersections after that, but I had not gotten any farther into the cave.

I didn't know if Bozel was fully explored or if there were virgin passages waiting to be found. A few years later, I would find a hidden section and we would end up doubling the length of lined passage in the cave. That story is for another book in this series.

Prior to beginning my survey of the cave, I had no idea how far I had swum because the current and rollercoaster passage slowed my pace. There were no distance markers on the guideline, so I had no way of determining the speed of my progression. The depth of the cave also made it difficult to get far. After the Stadium, the passage averaged depths from ninety-five to one hundred and twenty feet. These depths resulted in higher air consumption. I was going to have to bring a second stage tank with me if I wanted to penetrate farther into the cave.

* * *

Vortex Spring offered good conditions for teaching basic scuba diving classes, so I was often there with students. One such class I taught was introduction to technical diving, a class that teaches recreational divers the basic skills required for decompression diving. There's no decompression diving done during the class, nor cavern or cave diving. The class covers basic skills required as a foundation for the more advanced classes. Ben McDaniel was one of my introduction to technical diving students several weeks before his disappearance. I then ended up being one of the divers that was called to go into the cave to search for his body and bring it back out for the family. We never found his body.

Ben was a nice guy, and he was very enthusiastic about diving. Ben and I first met at Vortex Spring while I was teaching another class. He was at Vortex Spring almost every day and saw me there with my students a couple of times a month and approached me to ask about technical dive training.

Ben was certified as a Dive Con, a certification equivalent to divemaster, and had two hundred and seventy-one dives over a period of sixteen years. He became certified when he was a teenager but only resumed diving a few months before I met him. Ben expressed an interest in doing more advanced diving, such as cave and decompression diving, and I suggested he start with the introduction to technical diving class.

Ben was very motivated. However, when he expressed that he already knew how to do the dives and he just needed the certification cards, I emphasized the importance of going into the classes with an open mind and learning as much as he could. I told him he may have been very knowledgeable, but there was still a lot to learn. Like they say, you don't know what you don't know. Ben agreed with me.

There are a couple of metal caverns in the Vortex Spring basin that were placed there years ago by the Army Corps of Engineers. They aren't very realistic, but they give recreational divers something to explore in a relatively safe environment. Dive quarries in other states sink boats or busses for dive attractions. Vortex had manmade metal caverns constructed and sunk. During the first dive of the class, Ben turned his attention away from me and focused on the metal caverns. I redirected his attention to the skills we were doing and, after the first dive, stressed to him that he had to maintain focus on me. I also told him that he was not allowed to go into any kind of overhead environment during class. I stressed that he should not be going into any overhead environment until he was properly trained. Ben

281

acknowledged me and complied during the remaining three dives of the class.

Ben continued to talk about cave diving and asked me if I had any classes scheduled in the near future. I didn't have any cavern diving classes or available days to add a class in the coming months. I was scheduling classes three to four months out. Ben's dive equipment was not in the best shape or the most appropriate for a cavern diving class. It wasn't unsafe for recreational scuba diving, but it wasn't acceptable to use inside of a cave. He needed different length hoses, as well as DIN valves and DIN regulators, a type of regulator that screws into the valve rather than clamping onto it. I told Ben all of this and let him know that those changes would be required before he could take a cavern diving class. He took note and promised to purchase the equipment.

The next day, we returned to Vortex for three more dives. To Ben's credit, he continued to stay away from the metal caverns. However, when we descended down the chimney during the third dive of the class, Ben became distracted by the cave opening. Rather than focusing on the skills we were doing, he turned to look into the cave, requiring me to redirect his attention. Fortunately, we only spent a few minutes at the bottom of the chimney before beginning our ascent.

I talked to Ben after the dive to reinforce what we had discussed, stressing once again that he should not be going into the cave until he was properly trained. Ben asked about scheduling a cavern class with me again. I told him to contact me once his dive equipment was sorted. The last time I heard from Ben was at the end of that class. He never contacted me to tell me he had upgraded his dive equipment and was ready to continue his training. Seven weeks later, I received the call that he had not returned from a dive in Vortex Spring.

As I've mentioned, we never found Ben's body. The first team of divers went into the cave to search for it. They were supposed to locate it and secure it to the guideline with a safety spool. My team would then enter the cave, recover the body, and bring it to the surface. They didn't find Ben's body, so we became a search team rather than a recovery team. The other team had focused on the first eight hundred feet of passage. We would focus our search efforts on the remaining six hundred and fifty feet of the cave. My dive buddy and I were tasked with going to the very back of the cave beyond the fourth restriction. The other two divers on our team stopped at the third restriction and searched the offshoot tunnels in that area. There was a small room adjacent to the main passage near the third restriction as well as another short tunnel between the second and third restrictions.

My buddy and I passed the fourth restriction and continued toward the next one. We pulled ourselves into the restriction until it got too small. We got stuck and couldn't go any farther. There was no body back there. There was no body in the cave. Ben was slightly larger than me. He was shorter but huskier. He would not fit through a restriction that I couldn't fit through. He was not only not beyond the fourth restriction, but there was no sign that he had been that far back.

During the introduction to technical diving class, I have my students calculate their breathing rates. I remembered Ben's being average for a new diver. It wouldn't have improved much over seven weeks. He also had no training to dive in overhead environments. The only experience he had was what he had accumulated over the previous month when he was manipulating the grate to get beyond it. It was highly unlikely that Ben could have made it that far into the cave at those depths using the low pressure eighty-five cubic foot tanks he owned.

During the next two days, several more cave divers went into the cave at Vortex Spring to look for Ben's body. No signs of him were found. Searches continued for the next few weeks. Cadaver dogs were brought to Vortex Spring, and a remotely operated submersible was sent into the cave to try to squeeze into areas that a diver couldn't fit. That didn't work as well as they had hoped. The cable required to operate it kept getting caught whenever the tunnel changed directions. Ben still wasn't located.

Rumors began to surface. Some thought Ben was murdered. Others thought he died in the cave and his body was removed. There were also those who thought Ben had decided to throw away his old life and escape somewhere to Mexico or the Caribbean. With his brother's recent death and the failure of a business still on his mind, maybe Ben decided he wanted to get away from it all. I have my doubts about that. Ben left a dog in his condo, an hour south of Vortex Spring. and a wallet with several hundred dollars in his truck, according to the sheriff's office. Other findings didn't support Ben running away to start a new life.

We knew that Ben had been inside the cave at some point before this. He had been doing his own cave survey as evidenced by the drawings of the cave passages beyond the grate that were found in his truck by deputies. Ben had been manipulating the grate, getting beyond it, and drawing the cave to create his own map. The groundskeeper employed there at the time knew Ben was sneaking into the cave and began leaving the grate unlocked for him. He posted as much on Facebook, claiming that he knew Ben was going to go in there anyway, so he made it safer for him by leaving it open. He posted that he left it open for Ben the last day that Ben was seen.

I believe Ben died during that last dive. He pushed the limits and breathed his scuba tanks empty. He drowned. The following day, his body was found, removed, and disposed of. Maybe it was disposed of in the Gulf of Mexico. Maybe it was buried in the woods. All we know is that more than fifteen years later, we still don't know what happened to Ben McDaniel.

Ben's family hired a private investigator to look into the disappearance. She also theorized that he died in the cave and his body was removed and disposed of. The owner at the time had recently purchased Vortex Spring. Maybe he was concerned the state would try to ban diving at Vortex like they had in the early nineties. Ben's death was the first since the grate was installed. Maybe the owner didn't want bad publicity. The state didn't shut him down, but the publicity wasn't the greatest.

The park was closed the first weekend while we searched for Ben's body. Ben's disappearance happened in August right before what would have been a busy and profitable weekend. There was a lot of chatter on social media about the incident and some people expressed concerns about diving at a location where there was a dead body still unrecovered.

The owner at that time wasn't the most upstanding citizen. He faced charges of aggravated assault for allegedly attacking an employee with a baseball bat. It was rumored that he thought the employee was stealing from him and took him to look at some land. When they arrived, the owner allegedly removed a baseball bat from his truck and physically assaulted the employee. The owner never stood trial for that incident. He died before that could happen. A few months after Ben's disappearance, the owner passed away under suspicious circumstances. There was a large event at Vortex Spring, and he was found on the ground after having fallen down the steps of the Grandview Lodge. He was brought to his home in Ponce de Leon and the next morning, when someone went to check on him, he was found in his bathtub unconscious per news reports. The owner was rushed to the hospital, transferred to a higher level of care in Pensacola where he remained in the intensive care unit until he died a month later.

We may never know exactly what happened to Ben McDaniel. My book, *Beyond the Grate*, presents one possible explanation for his disappearance. It uses snippets of reality intertwined with fiction. The characters are fictional, but the story may have some truth to it. You be the judge. The saddest part is that the family never got closure on Ben's disappearance. They likely never will. What happened to Ben remains a secret in the hidden river of Vortex Spring.

Epilogue

I was very busy the months following Ben's disappearance. I was too busy. I had gained a lot of popularity as an instructor and was in high demand, not only for instruction but also for guided dives. Every free day I had was spent diving with students or clients. I also scheduled at least one day a week to go diving on my own. The caves became my workspace as well as my escape. I continued working as a nurse but had cut back on my shifts to pay more attention to the diving business.

David, the pristine tank student, finished his cave training. He was a very good diver, and he was the only student in that class. We did some great dives. I took him through Skiles' Passage and King's Back Door, places I didn't normally take my cave diving students. It was a pleasure to have such a skilled diver as a student and someone whose breathing rate was comparable to mine. With the exception of a few drills that had to be done during the dives, we were just out diving. This was one of the reasons I decided David would be a good candidate for the Cozumel trips about a year and a half later.

I returned to Guy Revell to see if conditions had improved. They hadn't. Visibility was even worse. I think the smell was, too. I continued into the passage I had found on my previous dive and kept swimming. The visibility remained bad. It wasn't worth the effort, but I wouldn't have known without trying. That's just the way things go sometimes.

The year came to a close. It had been a great year of diving with almost two hundred dives completed. I ended the year as a cave diving instructor and continued to deal my own version of crack to the diving community. I expanded my cave portfolio and saw many new caves, started to survey some of them, and even got to lay line in my first virgin passage. Jen and I decided to see the old year out and welcome the new year in a way only cave divers could. We headed to Jackson Blue to do a midnight dive. We entered the cave nine minutes after eleven and swam in for twenty-five minutes. We turned around at eleven thirty-five so we could be back in the cavern by midnight. The current helped us arrive a few minutes early, so we waited just inside the Rock Garden until midnight. I found some non-toxic, safe for kids and the environment glow sticks to celebrate bringing in the new year. We were about to see some underwater fireworks.

I can't claim originality for that idea. Another diver held a New Year's Eve dive every year at Ginnie Springs in which he entered the Ballroom and cracked open the glow sticks at midnight. The contents were then pushed out by the current. Shaking the sticks around allowed the glow to spread. I liked the idea and wanted to replicate it at Jackson Blue. A few minutes before midnight, we cracked the glow sticks and activated them. At the stroke of midnight, we pulled the caps off and waved the sticks around allowing the contents to make their way out through the Deco Room. Jen and I watched our own private fireworks display. We faced each other, removed our regulators from our mouths, and kissed. The new year had arrived. And this new year would bring with it new caves, new experiences, and the start of a major exploration project.

Thanks for reading *The Hidden Rivers of Florida: Discoveries* !

Please take a moment to leave a review or rating on Amazon. Reviews help provide more exposure to books. The more reviews a book has, the more likely Amazon will be to show it in search results. A simple star rating is all that's needed to help boost exposure. But if you're so inclined, a more thorough review is always appreciated. Rob does read the reviews and uses suggestions to help improve his writing. You can find a link to the Amazon listing on the List of Works page at RobNeto.com/list-of-works

If you liked this book and want to see more by Rob Neto, please visit RobNeto.com for a list of his other books. Make sure to subscribe to his newsletter while you're there. Email addresses are not sold or distributed, and you will only receive one email a month to update you on Rob's books and alert you to price specials as well as exclusive offers. You'll be the first to hear about new series, new books, and to see cover reveals.

Be sure to check out Rob's other award-winning adventure series, *Beneath the Jungle of Cozumel*. The first book, *Connecting the Crowns*, is already available for purchase in print, ebook, and audiobook. In this series, Rob gives a factual account of the cave exploration he has done in Cozumel. You might even recognize some of the scenes from *Beyond Hope* in it.

See you in the next book!

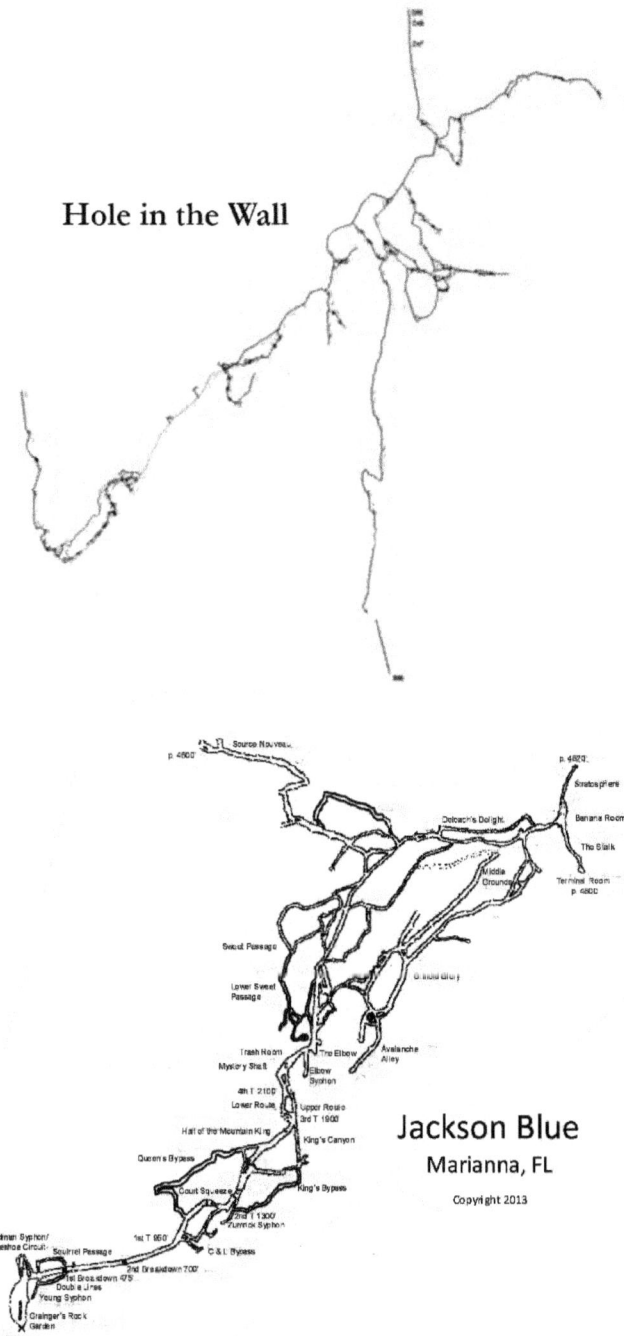

Hole in the Wall

Jackson Blue

Marianna, FL

Copyright 2013

Twin

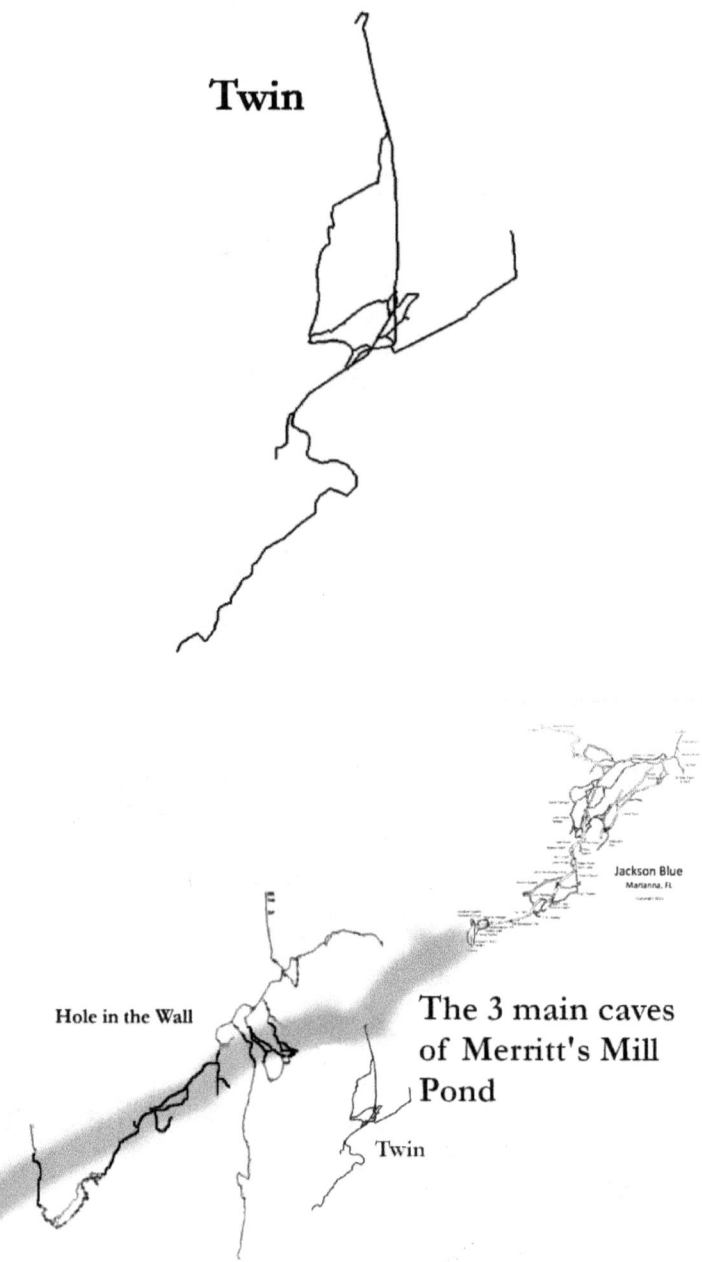

Jackson Blue
Marianna, FL

Hole in the Wall

The 3 main caves
of Merritt's Mill
Pond

Twin

ABOUT THE AUTHOR

Rob Neto is a cave diver who lives in the Florida panhandle just minutes away from some of his favorite caves. He is a cave explorer and retired cave and technical diving instructor. He spent more than ten years teaching scuba diving in Arizona and Florida. He is also the author of the international bestselling book, Sidemount Diving The *Almost* Comprehensive Guide, the first comprehensive book about sidemount diving. With almost three hundred pages of information and photos, Sidemount Diving is on its 3rd edition and has been translated into Dutch, German and Spanish, and is currently being translated into more languages. *Beyond the Grate*, the first novel in Rob's award-winning series was published in July 2023. *Beyond the Grate* was awarded a Silver Award in Suspense Thrillers by the Global Book Awards in September 2023 and has received numerous reviews on Amazon, GoodReads, and Facebook. Rob is already writing the fifth book in the Joey Simmons series, *Beyond the Shadows*. He is also writing the second book in his award-winning series, *Beneath the Jungle of Cozumel*. That book is titled *The Hidden Passages*. Visit his website at RobNeto.com to subscribe to his newsletter, keep up with his new releases, and receive exclusive offers.

Rob is married to his wonderful, supportive wife of more than twenty-two years and has a household of furry family members. At the time of this publication his family consists of four dogs, one inside cat, and several outside cats.

Coming Soon!

The Hidden Rivers of Florida:
The Journey Continues
Book 2

The Hidden Rivers Run Deeper…

The journey isn't over—it's just beginning.

In this thrilling sequel, I push deeper into the underwater labyrinths of Florida and beyond. From the secret rivers of the Sunshine State to submerged caves in Georgia and Missouri, I hunt the unseen, the untouched, the unmapped.

Nothing compares to the moment I found my first *virgin cave passage* in the legendary Jackson Blue. After countless dead ends and fading hopes, perseverance finally paid off—and the real adventure began.

Join me as I survey the depths of Jackson Blue, Hole in the Wall, Twin, and Bozel, uncovering hidden corridors and laying line through never-before-seen tunnels. This time, the cracks in the earth hold even more secrets.

If you thought the first book dove deep—this one plunges into the unknown.